Studies in Natural Language Processing
Sponsored by the Association for Computational Linguistics

Text generation

Studies in Natural Language Processing
Executive Editor: Aravind K. Joshi

This series publishes monographs, texts, and edited volumes within the interdisciplinary field of computational linguistics. Sponsored by the Association for Computational Linguistics, the series will represent the range of topics of concern to the scholars working in this increasingly important field, whether their background is in formal linguistics, psycholinguistics, cognitive psychology, or artificial intelligence.

Also in this series:

Natural language parsing, edited by David R. Dowty, Lauri Karttunen, and Arnold M. Zwicky

Text generation

**Using discourse strategies and focus constraints
to generate natural language text**

KATHLEEN R. McKEOWN
Department of Computer Science, Columbia University

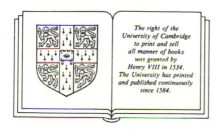

*The right of the
University of Cambridge
to print and sell
all manner of books
was granted by
Henry VIII in 1534.
The University has printed
and published continuously
since 1584.*

CAMBRIDGE UNIVERSITY PRESS

CAMBRIDGE

LONDON   NEW YORK   NEW ROCHELLE

MELBOURNE   SYDNEY

Published by the Press Syndicate of the University of Cambridge
The Pitt Building, Trumpington Street, Cambridge CB2 1RP
32 East 57th Street, New York, NY 10022, USA
10 Stamford Road, Oakleigh, Melbourne 3166, Australia

First published 1985
Reprinted 1986

Printed in the United States of America

Library of Congress Cataloging in Publication Data

McKeown, Kathleen R.

Text generation.

Bibliography: p.
Includes index.

1. Discourse analysis – Data processing.
2. Linguistics – Data processing. I. Title.
P302.M392   1985   410'.28'54   84–19889
ISBN 0 521 30116 5

P302
M392
1985

Contents

Preface	**ix**
1. Introduction	**1**
1.1 Problems in generating text	1
1.2 A processing model	5
1.3 A sketch of related work	6
1.4 A text generation theory and method	8
1.5 System overview	11
1.6 The database application	13
1.7 Other issues	16
1.8 Guide to remaining chapters	17
2. Discourse Structure	**19**
2.1 Rhetorical predicates	20
2.1.1 Linguistic background	20
2.1.2 Ordering communicative techniques	21
2.2 Analysis of texts	24
2.2.1 Predicate recursiveness	30
2.2.2 Summary of text analysis	37
2.3 Related research using rhetorical predicates	38
2.4 Use of schemata	38
2.4.1 Associating technique with purpose	40
2.5 Selecting a schema	42
2.6 Filling the schema	45
2.7 An example	47
2.8 Future work	52
2.9 Conclusions	53
3. Focusing in discourse	**55**
3.1 Computational theories and uses of focusing	56
3.1.1 Global focus	56
3.1.2 Immediate focus	57
3.2 Focusing and generation	58
3.2.1 Global focus and generation	59
3.2.2 Immediate focus and generation	60
3.2.3 Current focus versus potential focus list	63
3.2.4 Current focus versus focus stack	65
3.2.5 Other choices	67

3.2.6 A focus algorithm for generation	69
3.2.7 Selecting a default focus	69
3.2.8 Overriding the default focus	70
3.2.9 The focus algorithm	71
3.2.10 Use of focus sets	73
3.3 Focus and syntactic structures	75
3.3.1 Linguistic background	75
3.3.2 Passing focus information to the tactical component	77
3.4 Future work	79
3.5 Conclusions	80
4. TEXT system implementation	**83**
4.1 System components	84
4.2 Knowledge representation	87
4.2.1 Representation overview	87
4.2.2 Portability	90
4.2.3 Summary	91
4.2.4 The entity-relationship model	92
4.2.5 Use of generalization	93
4.2.6 The topic hierarchy	97
4.2.7 Relations	100
4.2.8 Distinguishing descriptive attributes	102
4.2.9 DDAs for database entity generalizations	103
4.2.10 Supporting database attributes	104
4.2.11 Based database attributes	106
4.2.12 DDAs for database entity subsets	109
4.2.13 Constant database attributes	111
4.3 Selection of relevant knowledge	113
4.3.1 Requests for information and definitions	113
4.3.2 Comparisons	114
4.3.3 Determining closeness	114
4.3.4 Relevancy on the basis of conceptual closeness	116
4.3.5 Conclusions	121
4.4 Schema implementation	122
4.4.1 Arc types	122
4.4.2 Arc actions	123
4.4.3 Registers	123
4.4.4 Graphs used	124
4.4.5 Traversing the graph	124
4.4.6 The compare and contrast schema	130
4.5 The tactical component	133
4.5.1 Overview of functional grammar	133
4.5.2 The grammar formalism	134
4.5.3 A functional grammar	138
4.5.4 The unifier	140
4.5.5 The TEXT system unifier	141

　　4.5.6　Unifying a sample input with a sample grammar　144
　　4.5.7　Grammar implementation　147
　　4.5.8　Morphology and linearization　151
　　4.5.9　Extensions　152
　　4.5.10　Disadvantages　152
　　4.5.11　Advantages　153
　4.6　The dictionary　155
　　4.6.1　Design　155
　　4.6.2　Structure of dictionary entries　156
　　4.6.3　General entries　157
　　4.6.4　An example　160
　　4.6.5　Creating the dictionary　164
　　4.6.6　Conclusions　167
　4.7　Practical considerations　168
　　4.7.1　User needs　168
　　4.7.2　Question coverage　169
　　4.7.3　Conclusions　169
5.　Discourse history　**171**
　5.1　Possible discourse history records　171
　5.2　Questions about the difference between entities　172
　5.3　Requests for definitions　178
　5.4　Requests for information　180
　5.5　Summary　183
6.　Related generation research　**185**
　6.1　Tactical components - early systems　186
　6.2　Tactical components - later works　187
　6.3　Generation in database systems　188
　6.4　Planning and generation　189
　6.5　Knowledge needed for generation　190
　6.6　Text generation　190
7.　Summary and conclusions　**195**
　7.1　Discourse structure　195
　7.2　Relevancy criterion　195
　7.3　Discourse coherency　196
　7.4　Generality of generation principles　196
　7.5　An evaluation of the generated text　197
　7.6　Limitations of the implemented system　199
　7.7　Future directions　200
　　7.7.1　Discourse structure　200
　　7.7.2　Relevancy　203
　　7.7.3　Coherency　203
　　7.7.4　User model　204
　　7.7.5　Conclusion　204
Appendix A. Sample output of the TEXT system　**205**
Appendix B. Introduction to *Working*　**223**

Appendix C. Resources used   225
Appendix D. Predicate Semantics   227
Bibliography   237
Index   244

Preface

There are two major aspects of computer-based text generation:
1) determining the content and textual shape of what is to be said; and
2) transforming that message into natural language. Emphasis in this
research has been on a computational solution to the questions of what to
say and how to organize it effectively. A generation method was developed
and implemented in a system called TEXT that uses principles of discourse
structure, discourse coherency, and relevancy criterion. In this book, the
theoretical basis of the generation method and the use of the theory within
the computer system TEXT are described.

The main theoretical results have been on the effect of discourse
structure and focus constraints on the generation process. A computational
treatment of rhetorical devices has been developed which is used to guide the
generation process. Previous work on focus of attention has been extended for
the task of generation to provide constraints on what to say next. The use
of these two interacting mechanisms constitutes a departure from earlier
generation systems. The approach taken here is that the generation process
should not simply trace the knowledge representation to produce text.
Instead, communicative strategies people are familiar with are used to
effectively convey information. This means that the same information may
be described in different ways on different occasions.

The main features of the generation method developed for the TEXT
strategic component include 1) selection of relevant information for the
answer, 2) the pairing of rhetorical techniques for communication (such as
analogy) with discourse purposes (for example, providing definitions) and 3) a
focusing mechanism. Rhetorical techniques, which encode aspects of discourse
structure, are used to guide the selection of propositions from a relevant
knowledge pool. The focusing mechanism aids in the organization of the
message by constraining the selection of information to be talked about next
to that which ties in with the previous discourse in an appropriate way.

This work on generation has been done within the framework of a
natural language interface to a database system. The implemented system
generates responses of paragraph length to questions about database structure.
Three classes of questions have been considered: questions about information
available in the database, requests for definitions, and questions about the
differences between database entities.

The work described in this book was done at the University of Pennsylvania and would not have been possible without the help of a number of people who deserve special mention. First and foremost, is the influence of my advisor, Aravind K. Joshi, who provided many of the insights and much appreciated guidance throughout all stages of the work. I am also grateful to Bonnie Webber for her many helpful suggestions, pointers to relevant papers, and editorial comments. The implementation of TEXT was greatly assisted by Kathleen McCoy and Steven Bossie who designed and implemented portions of the system. Kathy developed a system which automatically generated a portion of the knowledge base and implemented the knowledge base interface. Steve designed and partially implemented the tactical component used in TEXT.

Many people read and commented on various sections of the manuscript. Barbara Grosz's comments on the chapter on focusing were particularly valuable. Norman Badler, Peter Buneman, Richard Korf, Michael Lebowitz, Eric Mays, Kevin Matthews, Cecile Paris, and Ellen Prince also contributed in this area. Finally, the detailed and insightful comments of the unnamed reviewers must be mentioned as these were extremely helpful in improving the text.

Support for this work was provided in part by an IBM Research Fellowship, by National Science Foundation grant #MCS81-07290 awarded to the Department of Computer and Information Science of the University of Pennsylvania, by ONR grant N00014-82-K-0256 awarded to the Department of Computer Science of Columbia University, and by ARPA contract N00039-82-C-0427 awarded to the Department of Computer Science of Columbia University.

1
Introduction

In the process of producing discourse, speakers and writers must decide what it is that they want to say and how to present it effectively. They are capable of disregarding information in their large body of knowledge about the world which is not specific to the task at hand and they manage to integrate pertinent information into a coherent unit. They determine how to appropriately start the discourse, how to order its elements, and how to close it. These decisions are all part of the process of deciding what to say and when to say it. Speakers and writers must also determine what words to use and how to group them into sentences. In order for a system to generate text, it, too, must be able to make these kinds of decisions.

In this work, a computational solution is sought to the problems of deciding what to say and how to organize it effectively. What principles of discourse can be applied to this task? How can they be specified so that they can be used in a computational process? A computational perspective can aid our understanding of how discourse is produced by demanding a precise specification of the process. If we want to build a system that can perform these tasks, our theory of production must be detailed and accurate. Conversely, to build a system that can produce discourse effectively, determining content and textual shape, the development and application of principles of discourse structure, discourse coherency, and relevancy criterion are essential to its success.

1.1. Problems in generating text

To get a feeling for what a text generation theory must handle, consider an example of the kind of text the system should be able to generate (see (A) below). This text (taken from *The Hamlyn Pocket Dictionary of Wines* (Paterson 80)) was written for the explicit discourse goal of *defining* Flagey-Echezeaux. It presents information relevant to that goal in a comprehensible organizational framework. What must a generation system take into account to generate a text such as this one, given a specific discourse goal? To illustrate the problems inherent in language generation, I'll consider the following questions in light of example (A):

1

- How do problems in language generation differ from those of language interpretation?
- What are the range of choices a generation system must consider?
- How does generation of text differ from generation of single sentences?
- What is specific to written text as opposed to speech?

A) **Flagey-Echezeaux** *(France)* Important red wine township in the Cote de Nuits with two front-ranking vineyards, Echezeaux and Grands Echezeaux. The first produces a fine rich, round wine and the second, which is not a single vineyard but a group, is also capable of producing fine wines but, like other divided properties, the quality of its wine is variable. The lesser wines of Flagey-Echezeaux are entitled to the appellation Vosne-Romanee.

While researchers have investigated the problems involved in computer interpretation of natural language for some time now, interest in generating it has only recently begun to gain momentum. As a result, people are less familiar with the problems in language generation. Although there is research that suggests that the same information can be used both for interpretation and generation (e.g., Kay 79; Winograd 83; Wilensky 81), there are some important distinctions that can be made about the processes required for each task.

Interpretation of natural language requires examination of the evidence provided by a particular text in order to determine the meaning of the text and intentions of the writer who produced it. It necessitates using that evidence to examine the limited set of options the system knows to be available to the writer to determine the option actually taken. For example, in interpreting the second sentence of example (A), a system would use the evidence that "produce" occurs in the active form to determine that "a rich round wine" is the object being produced and Echezeaux (to which "the first" refers, one of many problems for interpretation that I don't discuss) is the agent that does the producing.

While interpretation involves specification of how a speaker's options are limited at any given point (for example, by writing grammars), it does not require a formulation of reasons for selecting between those options.[1] Thus, in interpreting sentence (2) of example (A), a system does not consider *why* the writer used the active form as opposed to any of the other options

---

[1]Note that as interpretation systems become more sophisticated, the analysis of reasoning behind the selection of a choice may be helpful in determining the goals of the speaker.

available at that point. In generation of natural language, however, this is exactly what is required. A generator must be able to construct the best utterance for a given situation by choosing between many possible options involving a wide range of knowledge sources. To produce the second sentence of the example, a generator must decide that although both the active and passive forms are possible (the passive would result in "a fine rich, round wine is produced by the first"), the active is better than the passive. Furthermore, the generator must have a principled reason for making that decision, which it can use in all similar cases. Where research on interpretation may describe limitations on options in order to more efficiently determine the option taken, research in generation must specify why one option is better than others in various situations.

The choices that a language generator must face include options regarding the content and textual shape of what is to be said and choices in the transformation of the message so determined into natural language. A language generation system must be able to decide *what* information to communicate, *when* to say what, and *which* words and syntactic structures best express its intent. In the last of these stages, local decisions such as syntactic and lexical choices are made, often using a grammar and dictionary to do so. It is in this stage that the active form would be selected for sentence (2) of the example. Until recently, this has been considered the extent of language generation research. But determining what to say and how to put it together above the sentence level also introduce language issues that must be addressed by any speaker or writer of extended discourse. These three classes of decisions constitute the full range of the language generation problem.

If connected text (and not simply single sentences) is to be generated, issues of discourse structure and discourse coherency are particularly important. Generation of text requires the ability to determine how to organize individual sentences. A writer does not randomly order the sentences in his text, but rather, plans an overall framework or outline, from which the individual sentences are produced. This is obvious in example (A). The author has chosen an organizational framework that is appropriate for providing definitions. Here, he first identifies Flagey-Echezeaux by describing its superordinate ("important red wine township in the Cote de Nuits") and then introduces two of its constituents (Echezeaux and Grands Echezeaux). Next, characteristic descriptive information about each of these vineyards is presented in turn, and finally, the author presents additional information about Flagey-Echezeaux (the item being defined) in the last sentence. To generate texts that are well organized, an analysis of the kinds of structures that are appropriate for achieving discourse goals such as *define* is needed as well as methods for formalizing the results so that they can be used by a computational process.

Discourse coherency is required if the generated text is to be a unit: the computational process must produce a text that "hangs together." This means that only information that is relevant to the discourse goal is included and that each sentence must be semantically related to the previous text. In example (A), only information supporting the definition of Flagey-Echezeaux is included in the text. This is due partly to the fact that the author only considers information that is related to Flagey-Echezeaux, but it is also due to the organizational strategy he has chosen. It dictates that information about each of the two constituents be included and not information about the Cote de Nuit, for example. Furthermore, each sentence relates to the previous sentences. Having introduced Echezeaux and Grands Echezeaux in the first sentence, the author continues talking about them in the second sentence. If a system is to produce coherent text, a formalization of the factors that contribute to coherency is necessary so that the computational process can make use of it.

These issues suggest a contrast between the generation of text and the generation of single sentences. Generation of text differs from generation of single sentences within dialogue in that a text is more or less a linguistically complete structure. Because a text has an organizational framework and is coherent, it constitutes a *unit* that in and of itself has a meaningful interpretation. This is in contrast to a dialogue sentence which may only be comprehensible in the context of the preceding discourse.

Considerations of context are also important for the generation of text however. Generation of a single sentence within a text must take into account the preceding and succeeding text. Even if the overall organization of the text provides an appropriate framework for the single sentence, the sentence must nonetheless be semantically linked in some way to the preceding and succeeding sentences if the resulting text is to be coherent. If the text is generated within an interactive environment, preceding discourse may also affect its generation.

Although speakers do produce discourse consisting of more than one sentence, the concern here is with text that more closely resembles written than spoken text. This means that some of the phenomena which normally occur in speech, such as self-correction, incomplete or ungrammatical sentences, informal styles or phrases (e.g., "yeah ...", "well"), interruption, and circularity, are not of importance. It also means that an investigation of the process of planning text is important, since writers typically spend more time planning the organization and content of what is to be said than do speakers. For practical reasons, the use of written text is more appropriate since natural language systems produce their output in written form on a terminal screen and reading transcribed spoken text is difficult.

The problem dealt with here can now be stated more concisely: How can a computer system determine what to say in service of a given discourse goal such that a coherent, well organized text is generated? The system's choices across all phases of the language generation process must not be arbitrary; rather, they must be well founded on linguistic principles which clearly justify the choice the system has made.

1.2. A processing model

In the preceding section, I have delineated the orientation and themes of this work: generation of multi-sentential text as opposed to single sentences, determination of textual content and organization as opposed to the surface text, and generation of written as opposed to spoken text. In order to focus on just these problems, a model of language production has been adopted that divides processing into two phases. In the first phase, the content and structure of the discourse is determined. The component embodying this phase is termed the "strategic" component, following Thompson (77). The second, the "tactical" component, uses a grammar to translate the message into English. This distinction allows focus on the problems and processes of the strategic component.

The output of the strategic component is an ordered message; all decisions about what to include in the text and when to include it have been made.[2] The strategic component, furthermore, must be capable of providing information needed by the tactical component to make decisions about lexical and syntactic choices. Although the discourse planning process need not know how to express its message in natural language, it must provide the information on which choices about expression can be made.

The strategic component embodies both *semantic* and *structural* processes. Semantic processes determine relevancy: of all that could be said, the component must be capable of selecting that information that is relevant to a given discourse goal. The strategic component must also be capable of determining an organizational strategy that is appropriate for the given discourse goal. Communicative techniques, comprising the strategy, must be selected and integrated to form the text. Such strategies determine the structure of the text. In the formation of the text, semantics are also necessary, in part to ensure that each sentence is related to previous text.

Although some of the decisions that must be made are basically semantic

---

[2]Although processing in this research was based on a division of the two stages such that the results of the strategic component were completely determined and then passed to the tactical component, a control structure which allowed for backtracking between the tactical and strategic component such as Appelt suggests (Appelt 81) would also be possible. The approach I have taken clearly specifies how processes in the planning of the text influence the realization of a message in natural language. Backtracking would allow for processes that produce the surface expression to influence the planning of the discourse. See Chapter Six for further discussion of this issue.

in nature, while others are structural, the mechanisms that handle these decisions need not each use only semantic or structural information. In fact, I claim that each of these decisions is determined by an interaction between structural and semantic processes. The organizational strategies used in the text will affect its content and the information that is determined to be relevant will influence the chosen organization of the text.

For example, suppose the generation system was to generate a definition of Flagey-Echezeaux as in example (A). A diagram illustrating the different mechanisms involved is shown in Figure 1-1. The strategic component would receive as input the discourse goal *define (Flagey-Echezeaux)*. It has access to a knowledge base containing information about the world, including many townships. From this knowledge base, the semantic processes select just information pertaining to Flagey-Echezeaux. Structural processes, also part of the strategic component, select an organizational strategy for the text. The double arrow between these two components in the diagram indicates interaction between the two processes. I have yet to define this interaction exactly. A message, represented in internal form, is produced by the strategic component and passed to the tactical component which generates the final English text.

1.3. A sketch of related work

What is known about language generation? Is there a previous body of work from which this work can draw? The majority of work done to date[3] on computer generation of language has focused on problems in the tactical component. This has ranged from work on direct translation of an underlying formal representation (e.g., Simmons and Slocum 72; Chester 76), the development of grammars and mechanisms for using those grammars to produce language (e.g., McDonald 80; Kay 79), and the development and representation of criteria for making decisions about vocabulary as part of a dictionary (e.g., Goldman 75; McDonald 80). While such work has little to say about determining the content and organization of the text, it does offer well tried mechanisms and procedures for translating a message into language and much of the tactical component implemented here draws off this knowledge. It should be noted that most of this previous work deals with the generation of single sentences and thus, questions about how the surface text must link in with the previous text have gone largely unanswered. This is a place where the development of a well founded strategic component can provide answers.

------

[3]This section outlines previous work in generation and orients it in the strategic/tactical division. Only work which is directly related is outlined. For a full discussion of previous work in natural language generation, see Chapter Six.

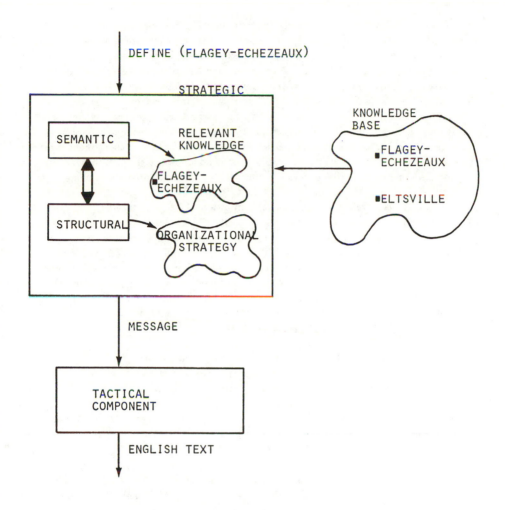

DEFINE (FLAGEY-ECHEZEAUX)

STRATEGIC

KNOWLEDGE BASE

SEMANTIC

RELEVANT KNOWLEDGE

FLAGEY-ECHEZEAUX

STRUCTURAL

ORGANIZATIONAL STRATEGY

■FLAGEY-ECHEZEAUX

■ELTSVILLE

MESSAGE

TACTICAL COMPONENT

ENGLISH TEXT

Figure 1-1:   Strategic and Tactical Components

Relatively little work has been done on problems in the strategic component. The work that has been done can be characterized as addressing one of three main issues: knowledge needed for generation (e.g., Swartout 81; Meehan 77), planning to determine an appropriate speech act (e.g., Cohen 81a), and textual organization (e.g., Mann and Moore 81; Weiner 80). Of these, the works of Mann and Weiner address issues most similar to the ones I am concerned with. They are both concerned with achieving the best ordering of information in a given knowledge base, but assume that all information pertains to the discourse task and thereby avoid the problem of determining textual content. The approach I take to textual organization is significantly different from both of their approaches. These differences are explored in more detail in Chapter Six.

Linguistic research also bears on the questions I am considering. There are two main classes of work that are related. These involve research on textual and discourse organization and research on discourse coherency. The work on textual organization (e.g., Williams 1893; Shipherd 26; Grimes 75) provides an analysis of the structure of text, identifying the basic structural units of which text is composed. This is useful for generating text, since the same basic units can be used, but it leaves open questions about how units can be combined and fails to be very precise. These analyses are significantly extended in this work so that they can be applied in a generation system.

Linguistic work on discourse coherency (e.g., Halliday 67; Prince 79; Firbas 74) identifies how coherency is expressed in a text (e.g., how certain syntactic constructions and coreferentiality can be used to increase the coherency of the text), but does not address how coherency of content and structure can be achieved *before* the surface text is generated. Their results can be used by the tactical component in generating the surface text, but do not apply to the problems of the strategic component. There has been a significant amount of work on discourse coherency in the computer science field for interpretation of natural language (e.g., Grosz 77; Sidner 79) which uses a formulation of the speaker's focus of attention. As I shall show, this work is applicable to the problem of generating coherent textual content.

1.4. A text generation theory and method

The main theoretical emphasis of this work has been on the effect of discourse structure and focus constraints on the generation process. This has involved a formulation of discourse structure that is commonly used in naturally occurring texts. I present a representation of discourse structure that specifies a computational model of rhetorical devices that can be used for generation, an approach that has not previously been taken. This means that the generation process is able to use the same strategies that people commonly use to produce effective text.

One of the strategies formalized for the generation process is the *constituency* strategy that was used in the example text for defining Flagey-Echezeaux. This strategy is used in many naturally occurring texts and thus is a common one for producing effective texts. It is characterized by three main steps:

1. Present the constituents of the item to be defined.

2. Present characteristic information about each constituent in turn.

3. Present additional characteristic information about the item to be defined.

By representing the strategy formally, the system can use it to determine the ordering and, in part, the content of the text it generates. Other strategies developed are presented in Chapter Two along with the formal representation.

Strategies for effective communication are used in combination with a treatment of focus constraints on language generation. A model of focus of attention, which represents the focus of the text constructed so far, is used to constrain what can be said next at any point when a choice exists. The model extends the use of focus constraints for interpretation (Sidner 79) for generation through the development of a preference ordering. The use of ordered focus constraints ensures that the resulting text will be coherent.

Not only does focus of attention provide a basis for deciding what to say next when the discourse strategy allows for a choice, but it also provides information needed by the tactical component to decide how to express the text. This is evident in the Flagey-Echezeaux definition. In the first sentence, the author focuses on Flagey-Echezeaux, but introduces its two constituents, Echezeaux and Grands-Echezeaux. In the first part of the second sentence, he shifts focus to Echezeaux and this determines his choice of the active form as it allows him to signal his focus to the readers.

The result is a formal theory of discourse strategy and focus of attention, as well as a specification of their interaction. These formulations have been embodied in the semantic and structural processes of the strategic component. That these processes interact with each other results in a greater variety of possible texts. A single plan for generation used in different situations does not always produce the same text because of the focus constraints (and different underlying knowledge). Similarly, although the same information may be produced by semantic processes for satisfying two different discourse goals, the texts generated may be different since different strategies are associated with the discourse goals.

These analyses have been implemented as part of the strategic component of a generation system called TEXT. The main features of the

generation method developed for the TEXT strategic component include
1) the pairing of rhetorical techniques for communication (such as analogy)
with discourse purposes (for example, providing definitions), 2) selection of
relevant information for the current discourse goal, and 3) a focusing
mechanism. *Rhetorical techniques*, which encode aspects of discourse
structure, are used to guide the selection of propositions from a *relevant
knowledge pool*: a subset of the knowledge base which serves as the source
for all information which can be included in the text. The *focusing
mechanism* helps maintain discourse coherency. It aids in the organization of
the message by constraining the selection of information to be talked about
next to that which ties in with the previous discourse in an appropriate way.
These processes operate in a cooperative fashion to produce the textual
message.

The relevant knowledge pool is constructed by semantic processes after
receiving a discourse goal. It contains information determined by the system
to be relevant to the given goal. Use of a relevant knowledge pool provides
a limit on the information that needs to be considered when constructing a
text for a given goal, thus increasing the efficiency of the program while at
the same time providing a model of a speaker's narrowing of attention when
producing a text.

Rhetorical techniques are the means which a speaker has available for
description. In the TEXT system, these techniques have been encoded as
schemata which represent patterns of discourse structure. Use of schemata
reflects the fact that people have preconceived ideas about how to provide
different kinds of descriptions. The choice of a particular schema to use for
an answer is affected by a characterization of the information available and
by the discourse purpose of the current answer. The schema is effectively a
plan for the text and is used to guide the generation process in its decisions
about what to say next.

Focusing constraints, which define how focus can shift from one sentence
to the next, are used to ensure that the generated text is coherent. Since
text is about something, what is said at any given point must be
appropriately related to what has already been said. The focusing
mechanism tracks focus of attention as a text is created and, where there are
choices for what to say next, it eliminates options that violate its knowledge
about valid shifts in focusing. The focus constraints monitor the use of the
schemata in the TEXT system.

1.5. System overview

The TEXT system was developed to generate text in response to a limited class of questions about the structure of a military database. The system consists of four basic modules: the semantic processor which produces the relevant knowledge pool, the schema selector, the schema filler, which uses both the selected schema and focus constraints to do its job, and the tactical component. A diagram providing a simple overview of the generation process is shown in Figure 1-2.

To answer an incoming question, TEXT first selects a set of possible schemata to be used for the answer. These are the strategies associated with the discourse purpose of the current answer (for example, to provide a definition). On the basis of the input question, semantic processes produce a pool of relevant knowledge. The type of information available in this pool is used to select a single schema from the set of possible schemata. This marks the beginning of interaction between the structural and semantic processes in the system; here semantics influences the structure selected for the answer.

The answer is constructed by "filling" the schema: propositions are selected from the relevant knowledge pool which match the rhetorical techniques in the schema. Each rhetorical technique has associated semantics that indicate which types of propositions in the knowledge base it matches. These semantics are dependent on system type (such as database versus computer aided instruction system), but are not dependent on the domain of the system. A focusing mechanism monitors the matching process; where there are choices for what to say next (i.e., where the rhetorical technique matches several propositions in the knowledge pool), the focusing mechanism selects that proposition which ties in most closely with the previous discourse. When a proposition has been selected, focus information about the proposition is recorded.

When the schema has been filled, the system passes the constructed, ordered message to the tactical component. The tactical component uses a functional grammar, based on a formalism defined by Kay (79), to translate the message into English. The main theoretical emphasis at this level is on the use of information derived by the strategic component to determine surface choices. The grammar was designed so that it can use the focus information provided in the message to select appropriate syntactic constructions.

A sample text produced by the system in response to a request to *define* a guided projectile is shown below in (B). The system used the constituency strategy to produce this text.

11

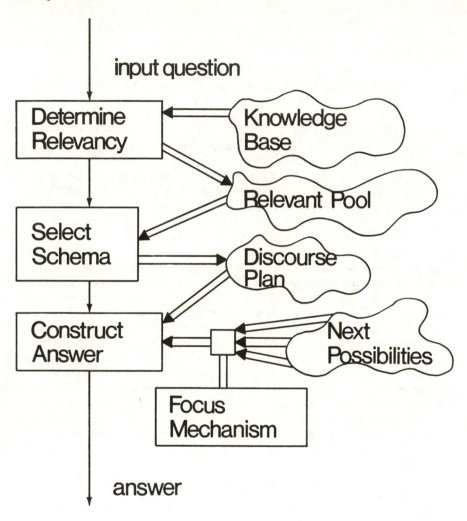

Figure 1-2: System Overview

B) A guided projectile is a projectile that is self-propelled. There are 2 types of guided projectiles in the ONR database: torpedoes and missiles. The missile has a target location in the air or on the earth's surface. The torpedo has an underwater target location. The missile's target location is indicated by the DB attribute DESCRIPTION and the missile's flight capabilities are provided by the DB attribute ALTITUDE. The torpedo's underwater capabilities are provided by the DB attributes under DEPTH (for example, MAXIMUM OPERATING DEPTH). The guided projectile has DB attributes TIME TO TARGET & UNITS, HORZ RANGE & UNITS and NAME.

1.6. The database application

In order to test principles about natural language generation, an application was selected that could provide a motivation for generation as well as a restricted yet interesting domain. A system was developed, therefore, within the framework of a natural language interface to a database system that addressed the specific problem of generating answers to questions about the database structure. To date, natural language database systems have concentrated on answering factual questions, providing answers in the form of lists or tables of objects in the database.[4] These questions query the existence or identity of restricted classes of objects in the database. An answer is provided by searching the database for objects which meet the given restrictions.

To ask such questions, the user must already know what information is stored in the database and how it is structured. (Note that even if the user already knows what type of information is available, its structure in the database is not always intuitive.) A user who is not aware of the nature of information stored and its structure can neither request the system to supply this information (since current systems do not possess this capability) nor phrase appropriate questions about the database contents.

The task of the TEXT system is to generate responses to such meta-level questions. Three classes of questions have been considered: questions about information available in the database, requests for definitions, and questions about the differences between database entities. In this context, input questions provide the initial motivation for generating text.

Although the specific application of answering questions about database

---

[4]Note that in some systems, the list (especially in cases where it consists of only one object) may be embedded in a sentence, or a table may be introduced by a sentence which has been generated by the system (Grishman 79). In a few systems (e.g., Malhotra 75; Codd 78), a one or two sentence reply about the information in the database may be generated, but this reply is usually stored as a whole in the knowledge structure.

structure was used primarily for testing principles about text generation, it is a feature that many users would like. Several experiments (Malhotra 75; Tennant 79) have shown that users need to ask questions to familiarize themselves with the database structure before proceeding to make requests about the database contents.

Malhotra's experiment involved a simulated management decision support system in which users typed in questions at a terminal. These questions were intercepted by a person familiar with the system, who rephrased the questions using syntax acceptable to the system. When questions were asked which the system could not answer, the interceptor would either answer the question himself or construct a series of questions necessary to answer the one asked. Subjects were given a problem to solve which required using information stored in the database. Transcripts of the user sessions indicate that people often begin by asking questions to familiarize themselves with the material available before asking questions particular to the given problem. Typical of the questions that were asked are the following:

- What kind of data do you have?
- What do you know about unit cost?
- What is the difference between material cost and production cost?
- What is production cost?

Tennant's experiments were done on two natural language database systems: the PLANES system, which accesses a large database containing information about naval aircraft, and the Automatic Advisor, which accesses a smaller database containing course information. University students were asked to solve database problems after reading introductory information about the database. Tennant found that systems tended to be lacking in conceptual coverage. Like Malhotra, he found that users often asked questions which were not interpretable as database queries. These included questions about the database (e.g., "What do you know?") and questions about vocabulary (e.g., "What is a buser?").

Responding to questions such as these requires more than a simple search of the database. These types of questions do not provide as clear restrictions on what information is sufficient to answer them as do specific questions about the database content. In fact, there is often no single correct way to answer such questions. Since answers to questions about the structure of the database will usually require more than a single sentence, the application provides an appropriate testbed for generation principles. The system will be required to determine how to select the appropriate information to be included in the answer and how to organize it into a multi-sentential text.

Implementation of the TEXT system for natural language generation used a portion of the Office of Naval Research (ONR) database that contains information about vehicles and destructive devices. Some examples of questions that can be asked of TEXT include:

- What is a frigate?
- What do you know about submarines?
- What is the difference between an ocean escort and a cruiser?

Examples of questions and responses from this domain will be used throughout the book. The kind of generation of which the system is capable is illustrated by the response it generates to question (C) below.

C) What kind of data do you have?
   All entities in the ONR database have DB attributes REMARKS. There are 2 types of entities in the ONR database: destructive devices and vehicles. The vehicle has DB attributes that provide information on SPEED INDICES and TRAVEL MEANS. The destructive device has DB attributes that provide information on LETHAL INDICES.

The type of response generated by the TEXT system could be used not only for specific questions about the database structure, but also as supportive explanations for yes/no questions[5] or as explanations for structural presumption failures (Mays 80).[6]

As an example, consider the question "What is the draft and displacement of the whisky?". A plausible response is given in (D) below. This is very similar to some of the responses currently generated by the TEXT system.

D) The database contains no information on DRAFT and DISPLACEMENT for the whisky. Ships have DB attributes DRAFT and DISPLACEMENT. The whisky is an underwater submarine with a PROPULSION TYPE of DIESEL and a FLAG of RDOR. The submarine's underwater capabilities are provided by the DB attributes under DEPTH (for example, OPERATING DEPTH) and MAXIMUM SUBMERGED SPEED. Other DB attributes of the submarine include OFFICIAL NAME, FUEL (FUEL TYPE and FUEL CAPACITY), and PROPULSION TYPE.

A system for generating textual responses to questions requiring

---

[5]Kaplan (79) also discusses the use of supportive explanations for yes/no questions.

[6]The system developed is not capable of detecting an intensional failure. Assuming that such a failure has been found, the system could be extended to generate a response that explains the failure.

descriptions or explanations could be useful in other application areas in addition to the database query system. Computer assisted instruction systems (Collins, Warnock and Passafiume 74) and expert systems (Grosz 77) are examples of areas where the provision of descriptions and explanations would be useful. The methods for generation developed for the TEXT system are not specific to the database application and could be adapted for systems where generation of descriptions of static information is required. That is, the schemata capture discourse strategies in terms of text structure, and their representation does not rely on domain (or system) dependent concepts. Similarly, the focus constraints describe general preferences for what should be appropriately said next and apply to all situations in which coherent text must be produced.

1.7. Other issues

In order to develop a system that can generate text in response to questions about database structure, problem areas outside the realm of text generation per se had to be considered. These include the knowledge representation which contains the information to be described, interpretation of the user's question and user modelling.

Knowledge representation and content is important since it limits what the generation component is able to talk about unless an extensive inferencing component is available. A knowledge representation was implemented (McCoy 82) which draws heavily on features used in other database models. It is based on the Chen entity-relationship model (Chen 76) and also includes a generalization hierarchy on entities, a hierarchy on attributes, and distinguishing characteristics of entities in the generalization hierarchy. This combination of features incorporates both information about the actual database and its structure as well as a real world view of the data.

No facility for interpreting a user's questions is provided in the TEXT system implementation since this work is on the generation of language and not interpretation. Questions must be phrased using a simple functional notation which corresponds to the types of questions that can be asked. The TEXT system provides a canned explanation of this notation when it is invoked and it is fairly easy to use.

For a user model, the system assumes a casual and naive user and gears its responses to a level appropriate for this characterization. An extensive user modelling facility, which can represent and infer information about different types of users, was not implemented as part of the TEXT system. An analysis was done, however, on the effect of previous discourse on the generation of responses. This analysis indicates how a generation system can make use of the previous dialogue to tailor its responses to the current user and is described in Chapter Five.

The research described here focuses on issues concerning the content and organization of the generated text. These two problems have not, for the most part, been addressed in the past and they represent areas about which little is known. In order to handle them appropriately, a comprehensive treatment of discourse structure and focusing constraints and their relation to the generation of natural language was necessary.

1.8. Guide to remaining chapters

A discussion of discourse structure, its effect on generation, and the implementation of the schemata is provided in Chapter Two. The focus constraints, both as they affect discourse coherency and as they restrict attention to relevant information, are discussed in Chapter Three. These two chapters describe the major part of the text generation theory and are essential to the remaining chapters. The implementation of the TEXT system is described in Chapter Four. This includes the knowledge base used, the method used to determine relevancy, the dictionary and the tactical component. Chapter Four closes with a discussion of practical considerations, discussing how close the system comes to meeting the needs of real users. Chapter Four will be of interest to those who want to get a real feel for how the system works. It will be of less interest to those who lack a computer science background, although the section on the tactical component is recommended for those with a linguistic background. Chapter Five gives an analysis of how the previous discourse could be used to improve the quality of the responses generated. A comparison of this work to other research in natural language generation is provided in Chapter Six and the final chapter presents some conclusions, along with suggestions for future work. Appendix A provides examples of the TEXT system in operation.

2
Discourse structure

The approach I have taken towards text generation is based on two fundamental hypotheses about the production of text: 1) that how information is stored in memory and how a person describes that information need not be the same and 2) that people have preconceived notions about the ways in which descriptions can be achieved.

I assume that information is not described in exactly the same way it is organized in memory. Rather, such descriptions reflect one or more principles of *text* organization.[7] It is not uncommon for a person to repeat himself and talk about the same thing on different occasions. Rarely, however, will he repeat himself exactly. He may describe aspects of the subject which he omitted on first telling or he may, on the other hand, describe things from a different perspective, giving the text a new emphasis. Chafe (79) has performed a series of experiments which he claims support the notion that the speaker decides as he is talking what material should go into a sentence. These experiments show that the distribution of semantic constituents among sentences often varies significantly from one version of a narrative to another.

The second hypothesis central to this research is that people have preconceived ideas about the means with which particular communicative tasks can be achieved as well as the ways in which these means can be integrated to form a text. In other words, people generally follow standard patterns of discourse structure. For example, they commonly begin a narrative by describing the setting (the scene, the characters, or the time-frame).

In the TEXT system, these types of standard patterns of discourse structure have been exploited through the use of *schemata*. A schema is a

---

[7] I make no claims about the nature of stored knowledge in this research. For the purposes of text generation, any representation of knowledge could have been used. In practice, however, a particular representation for the given application had to be selected. Questions about how a representation can restrict the generation process, either in terms of content or ease of inferencing, are discussed in Section 4.2.

representation of a standard pattern of discourse structure which efficiently encodes the set of communicative techniques that a speaker can use for a particular discourse purpose. It defines a particular organizing principle for text and is used to structure the information that will be included in the answer. It is used to *guide* the generation process, controlling decisions about what to say when in a text. This mechanism embodies a computational treatment of rhetorical devices, which have not previously been formalized in such a way.

2.1. Rhetorical predicates

Rhetorical predicates are the *means* which a speaker has for describing information. They characterize the different types of predicating acts he may use and they delineate the structural relations between propositions in a text. Some examples are *analogy* (the making of an analogy), *constituency* (description of sub-parts or sub-types), and *attributive* (providing detail about an entity or event). Linguistic discussion of such predicates (e.g., Williams 1893; Shipherd 26; Grimes 75) indicates that some combinations are preferable to others. The following sections give the linguistic background of rhetorical predicates.

2.1.1. Linguistic background

The notion of the *means* available to a speaker or writer goes back to Aristotle, who describes the means which a speaker can use for persuasive argument (McKeon 41). He distinguished between *enthymemes* (or *syllogisms*) and *examples*, where syllogisms are argument types and examples provide evidence for different arguments.

Both Williams (1893) and Shipherd (1926), old-style grammarians, categorize sentences by their function in order to illustrate to the beginning writer how to construct paragraphs. The functions Williams identifies include: *topic, general illustration, particular illustration, comparison, amplification, contrasting sentences*, and *conclusions*. Although Williams enumerates many of the "do's" and "don'ts" of writing, he says nothing about combining sentence functions to form paragraphs. He merely cites examples of prose that he considers well done and identifies the function of each sentence in the examples.

In more recent years, Grimes describes rhetorical predicates as explicit organizing relations used in discourse (Grimes 75). Grimes distinguishes three functions that predicates can serve in discourse:

1. supporting or supplementary (which add detail, explain, or substantiate what has come before. The three examples of predicates given above fall into this category.)

2. setting (which locate an object or event in space or time)

3. identification (which establish or maintain reference to an object)

Grimes claims that the predicates are recursive and can be used to identify the organization of text at any level (i.e. proposition, sentence, paragraph, or longer sequence of text), but does not show how this is done.

Rhetorical predicates have also been called *coherence relations* (e.g, Hirst 81) and have been used as an aid in anaphora resolution (Hobbs 78; Lockman 78). Hirst (81) proposed a set of relations extracted from a variety of sources including *elaboration, contrast, effect, cause, syllogism, parallel,* and *exemplification*. Works using coherence relations concentrate on their aid in interpretation for the specific task of anaphora resolution.

2.1.2. *Ordering communicative techniques*

Although the use of rhetorical predicates in text as structuring devices has been considered, most researchers have not discussed the ways in which they may be combined to form larger units of text. Both Grimes and Williams imply this use however. Grimes claims that the predicates are recursive, and Williams cites examples of well-written prose, identifying the predicates used.

My own examination of texts and transcripts has shown that not only are certain combinations of rhetorical techniques more likely than others, but certain ones are more appropriate in some discourse situations than others. For example, I found that *identification* of objects was frequently achieved by employing some combination of the following means: (1) identification of an item as a member of some generic class, (2) description of an object's function, attributes, and constituency (either physical or class), (3) analogies made to familiar objects, and (4) examples. These techniques were rarely used in random order; for instance it was common to identify an item as a member of some generic class before providing examples.

For this analysis of rhetorical predicates, a variety of texts were examined - ten different authors, in varying styles, from very literate written to transcribed spoken texts formed the basis of the study. Short samples of *expository writing* were used since these are most relevant to the system being developed. This also avoided problems involved in narrative writing (e.g., scene, temporal description, personality). The data were drawn from the following texts: *Working* (the introduction plus two transcriptions) (Terkel 72), *Dictionary of Weapons and Military Terms* (Quick 73), *Encyclopedia Americana* (Encyclopedia 76), *The Hamlyn Pocket Dictionary of Wines* (Paterson 80), *The Poorperson's Guide to Great Cheap Wines*

Williams' predicates are illustrated by providing an example paragraph from his text in which each sentence is classified as one of his predicates. The classifying predicate follows the sentence.

Comparison   Topic
General illustration   Particular illustration
Amplification   Contrasting
Conclusion

"What, then, are the proper encouragements of genius? (**topic**) I answer, subsistence and respect, for these are rewards congenial to nature. (**amplification**) Every animal has an aliment suited to its constitution. (**general illustration**) The heavy ox seeks nourishment from earth; the light chameleon has been supposed to exist on air. (**particular illustration**) A sparer diet than even this satisfies the man of true genius, for he makes a luxurious banquet upon empty applause. (**comparison**) It is this alone which has inspired all that ever was truly great and noble among us. It is as Cicero finely calls it, the echo of virtue. (**amplification**) Avarice is the pain of inferior natures; money the pay of the common herd. (**contrasting sentences**) The author who draws his quill merely to take a purse no more deserves success than he who presents a pistol. (**conclusion**) "

Figure 2-2:   Williams' Predicates

2.2. Analysis of texts

My analysis has shown that, with slight variations, similar patterns of predicate usage occur across various expository texts. These patterns have been represented as schemata. The schemata are recursive descriptions and may be embedded in other schemata to form paragraphs. In addition, in the texts, a paragraph was sometimes introduced by the *positing* predicate. Allowing for schema embedding and positing initial sequences, each paragraph that was examined (a total of 56) could be described by one of the schemata developed. Four schemata were found to capture the structure of the 56

1. Identification
     ELTVILLE (Germany) An important wine village of the Rheingau region.

2. Renaming
     Also known as the Red Baron.

3. Positing
     Just think of Marcus Welby.

Figure 2-3:   Additional Predicates Needed For The Analysis

paragraphs.[10]   These schemata are not intended to capture the structure of all written text. Additional analysis is necessary to capture common strategies used for discourse goals other than those considered here.

The schemata identified are shown in Figures 2-4 - 2-7. "{}" indicates optional constituents, "/" indicates alternatives, "+" indicates that the item may appear 1 to n times, and "*" indicates that the item is optional and may appear 0 to n times. Each schema is followed by a sample paragraph taken from the data and a classification of the propositions contained in the paragraph. ";" is used to represent classification of ambiguous propositions in the paragraph. These were translated into the schemata as alternatives.

The attributive schema (Figure 2-4) can be used to illustrate a particular point about a concept or object. The sample paragraph, taken from the Introduction to *Working*, *attributes* the topic (working and violence) to the book, *amplifies* on that ("spiritual as well as physical") in proposition (2), and provides a series of *illustrations* in the third sentence. Note that the third proposition could either be classified as many *illustrations* or as a single *illustration*, both of which are covered by the schema. The fourth

---

[10]Note that, in order to make such an analysis, the function of each proposition had to be determined and a predicate assigned to it. Since there are no hard and fast rules for predicate assignment, the analysis is subjective and could have had somewhat different results if done by someone else. This affects both the form of the resulting schemata and the number of schemata necessary to cover all 56 paragraphs. If rules for predicate assignment could be developed, then the schemata could be used for interpretation as well: if an input textual sequence were captured by a schema, its discourse purpose would be discernible. See Section 2.8 for further discussion.

proposition presents a single example as *representative* of the problem and the fifth *amplifies* on that instance. The fifth proposition illustrates an ambiguous classification, since it could conceivably function as either *amplification* or *explanation*.

The identification schema (Figure 2-5) is used to identify entities or events. The characteristic techniques it uses to do so include *identification, particular illustration, evidence, analogy, renaming*, and various descriptive predicating acts. It should be noted that the identification schema was only found in texts whose primary function was to provide definitions (i.e., dictionaries and encyclopedias). The other texts simply did not have occasion to provide definitions. Moreover, the schema represents the types of definitions provided in the particular examples analyzed but does not dictate what every definition must look like. For example, some definitions may be provided by describing process information associated with the term.

The constituency schema (Figure 2-6) describes an entity or event in terms of its sub-parts or sub-types. After identifying its sub-types, the focus can either switch to each of its sub-types in turn (following the depth-identification or *depth-attributive* path) or can continue on the entity itself, describing either its attributes (*attributive* path) or its functions (*cause-effect* path). Note that there are three possible predicates that can be used for each sub-type if the *depth-identification* or *depth-attributive* path is taken (this is indicated by indentation of the entire set in the figure). Two of these are optional and need not occur (i.e., *particular-illustration/evidence* and *comparison/analogy*), but if they do, this portion of the schema will expand into three propositions for each subtype. The schema may end by optionally returning to discussion of the original by using the *amplification, explanation, attributive,* or *analogy* predicate.

In the sample paragraph, taken from the *American Encyclopedia*, part of the entry under torpedo includes a description of its classification. In the section title and first sentence, the two types of torpedoes are introduced. First, the steam-propelled model is identified by citing facts about it, and then the electric-powered model is compared against it, with the most significant difference cited.

The contrastive schema (Figure 2-7) is used to describe something by contrasting it against something else. The speaker may contrast his major point against a negative point (something he wishes to show isn't true). The lesser item (to be contrasted against) is introduced first. The major concept is then described in more detail using one or more of the predicates shown in the second option of the schema. The closing sequence makes a direct comparison between the two. This schema dictates the structural relation between the two concepts -- the use of A and ~A (not A) in the schema represent the major and lesser concepts -- but is less restrictive about which predicates are used.

Attributive Schema

Attributive
{Amplification; restriction}
Particular illustration*
{Representative}
{Question; problem
Answer} /
{Comparison;contrast
Adversative}
Amplification/Explanation/Inference/
    Comparison

Example

"1) This book, being about work, is, by its very nature, about violence
- 2) to the spirit as well as to the body. 3) It is about ulcers as well as
accidents, about shouting matches as well as fistfights, about nervous
breakdowns as well as kicking the dog around. 4) It is, above all (or beneath
all), about daily humiliations. 5) To survive the day is triumph enough for
the walking wounded among the great many of us." (Terkel 72)

Example Classification

1. Attributive
2. Amplification
3. Particular illustration
4. Representative
5. Amplification; explanation

Figure 2-4: The Attributive Schema

Identification Schema

Identification (class & attribute/function)
{Analogy/Constituency/Attributive/Renaming/Amplification}*
Particular-illustration/Evidence+
{Amplification/Analogy/Attributive}
{Particular illustration/Evidence}

Example
"**Eltville** (Germany) 1) An important wine village of the Rheingau region. 2) The vineyards make wines that are emphatically of the Rheingau style, 3) with a considerable weight for a white wine. 4) Taubenberg, Sonnenberg and Langenstuck are among vineyards of note." (Paterson 80)

Example Classification

1. Identification (class & attribute)
2. Attributive
3. Amplification
4. Particular illustration

Figure 2-5: The Identification Schema

Constituency Schema

Constituency
Cause-effect*/Attributive*/
   { Depth-identification/Depth-attributive
      {Particular-illustration/evidence}
      {Comparison/analogy} } +
{Amplification/Explanation/Attributive/
   Analogy}

Example
"Steam and electric torpedoes. 1) Modern torpedoes are of 2 general
types. 2) Steam-propelled models have speeds of 27 to 45 knots and ranges
of 4000 to 25,000 yds. (4,367 - 27,350 meters).   3) The electric powered
models are similar 4) but do not leave the telltale wake created by the
exhaust of a steam torpedo." (Encyclopedia 76)

Example Classification

1. Constituency
2. Depth-identification; (depth-attributive)
3. Comparison
4. Depth-identification; (depth-attributive)

Figure 2-6:   The Constituency Schema

In the sample paragraph, the contrastive schema is used to show how people form a bad self-image by comparing themselves against those in the movies. In the first sentence, the movie standard is introduced (the negative point or ∼A). In the second and third sentences, real-life occupations and the feelings associated with them are described (the major point or A). Finally, a direct comparison is made between the two situations and an inference drawn: "people form a low self-image of themselves."

2.2.1. Predicate recursiveness

Although the examples above only show how the schemata work at the paragraph level, there is evidence that such organization also occurs at higher levels of text. The schemata were found to apply to a sequence of paragraphs, with each predicate in the schema matching an entire paragraph, instead of a single proposition. The Introduction to *Working*, for example, covers three major topics, each of which is introduced and closed within four or five paragraphs. The first topic group follows the attributive schema (the text for this topic group is reproduced in Appendix B); each paragraph in the group matches a single rhetorical predicate.[11] Figure 2-8 shows a tree representing the first topic group of the Introduction. Paragraphs are numbered nodes in the tree. The tree is described by the predicates listed at the bottom of the figure which is an instantiation of the attributive schema.

Thus, the predicates do indeed seem to function recursively as Grimes suggests. Schemata, since they consist of predicates, also function recursively; that is, each predicate in a schema can expand to another schema. The structure of a text when described by the schemata is, therefore, hierarchical. Each node in the hierarchical structure corresponds to a predicate. The predicate can either be interpreted as a single predicate or can be expanded to another set of predicates representing the schema named.

Recursion functions to describe the structure of text at all levels. For example, a single sentence may be used to attribute information to an entity or a longer sequence of text may be used for the same purpose. The analysis of texts was made in order to discover just how predicates are combined to form a longer sequence of text having a specific function. Thus, the resulting schemata describe combinations of predicates which serve the function of a single predicate. For this reason, each schema is associated with a single predicate and is given its name.

Schema recursion is achieved by allowing each predicate in a schema to expand to either a single proposition (e.g., a sentence) or to a schema (e.g., a text sequence). The structure for a text generated from this application of schemata will be a tree structure, with a sub-tree occurring at each point

---

[11]Note that this analysis is somewhat subjective.

Compare and Contrast Schema

Positing/Attributive (∼A)
{Attributive (A) /
    Particular illustration/Evidence (A) /
    Amplification (A) /
    Inference (A)/
    Explanation (A) } +
{Comparison (A and ∼A) /
    Explanation (A and ∼A) /
    Generalization (A and ∼A) /
    Inference (A and ∼A) } +

"1) Movies set up these glamorized occupations. 2) When people find they are waitresses, they feel degraded. 3) No kid says I want to be a waiter, I want to run a cleaning establishment. 4) There is a tendency in movies to degrade people if they don't have white-collar professions. 5) So, people form a low self-image of themselves, 6) because their lives can never match the way Americans live -- on the screen." (Terkel 72)

Example Classification

1. Positing (∼A)
2. Attributive (A)
3. Evidence (A)
4. Comparison;explanation (A and ∼A)
5. Inference (A and ∼A)
6. Comparison;explanation (A and ∼A)

Figure 2-7:   The Compare and Contrast Schema

Introduction to *Working*

Topic Group 1

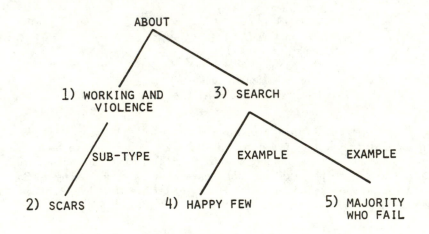

1) Attributive
2) Restriction
3) Attributive
4) Particular-illustration
5) Particular-illustration

Figure 2-8: Introduction to *Working*

----

where a predicate has been expanded into a schema. Propositions occur at the leaves of the tree.

Schemata, therefore, are similar in concept to hierarchical plans (Sacerdoti 77). Each predicate in the schema is a generation goal which can be achieved either by fulfilling a number of sub-goals (the predicate expands to a schema) or producing a single utterance (the predicate expands to a proposition).

Figure 2-9 illustrates how schema recursion works through the use of a constructed example. The identification schema is used in response to the question "What is a Hobie Cat?". The first step the hypothetical speaker takes is to identify the Hobie Cat as a class of catamarans (1). To do so, however, he also provides a definition of a catamaran, assuming that his listener knows little about sailing and simply identifying the Hobie Cat as a catamaran is not adequate for him. The identification predicate expands to the identification schema, where the speaker identifies the catamaran as a sailboat (2) and provides an analogy between the two, which consists of their similarities (3) and differences (4). Note that these two steps are dictated by an analogy schema. After pointing out a catamaran to the listener (5), he pops back to the original identification schema to provide additional information about the Hobie Cat (6) and finally, cites two types of Hobie Cats, the 16-ft. and the 14-ft. (7).

ID Schema

identification ->

attributive
particular-illustration

ID Schema

identification
analogy   ->

particular-illustration

Analogy Schema

similarities
differences

1) A Hobie Cat is a brand of catamaran, 2) which is a kind of sailboat. 3) Catamarans have sails and a mast like other sailboats, 4) but they have two hulls instead of one. 5) That thing over there is a catamaran. 6) Hobie Cats have a canvas cockpit connecting the two pontoons and one or two sails. 7) The 16 ft. Hobie Cat has a main and a jib and the 14 ft. Hobie Cat has only a main.

Figure 2-9:   Schema Recursion

Full recursion, such as is illustrated in the above example, is not currently implemented in the TEXT system. In order for the system to be fully recursive, a schema must be written for each rhetorical predicate. Right now, schemata for only four of the predicates (out of a total of ten predicates) are written. (In the above example, the analogy schema shown is assumed to correspond to the compare and contrast schema, but this would require more analysis to verify.)

Another, perhaps more interesting side to the recursive use of schemata is the question of when recursion is necessary. Clearly, there are situations where a simple sentence is sufficient for fulfilling a communicative goal, while in others, it may be necessary to provide a more detailed explanation. One test for recursion hinges on an assessment of the listener's knowledge. In the above example, the speaker provided a detailed identification of the Hobie Cat, because he assumed that the listener knew very little about sailing. In order to achieve comprehensive treatment for providing more detailed information a full user model (Moore 80; Rich 79; Allen 80) would have to be developed to determine how much detail is needed for each user at different times.

Another test for recursion hinges on the amount of information available about a given concept in the knowledge pool. No matter how much detail a user needs to understand a concept, it cannot be supplied if nothing more is known about the concept. On the other hand, if a speaker knows a great deal about a concept he is discussing, he will probably want to say it unless he's sure the listener already knows about it. Neither user modelling nor assessments of the amount of information which can be talked about have been implemented in the TEXT system. The machinery for actually performing the recursive push to an associated schema (i.e., entering a new schema and saving the states associated with the old on a stack) has been implemented, so that once the extra schemata are written and sufficient tests for providing detailed information developed, full recursion would be possible.

There are situations where a full-blown user model is not necessary to determine that recursion is necessary. One such case has been implemented in the TEXT system, where recursion is used in answering a question about the difference between two very different items. In this case, simply asking the question signifies to the system that the user has no idea what these two items are. Since the most appropriate information to include in the answer is about generic classes (see Section 4.3), it is the only information provided in the relevant knowledge pool. Therefore, double identification of the two questioned objects is necessary (as was the case in identifying a Hobie Cat). When a question is asked about two very different items, it triggers the tagging of the super-ordinates of the questioned objects as unknown to the user.

For example, in asking about the difference between a destroyer and a bomb, the questioner indicates that he doesn't understand that one is a vehicle and the other a destructive device, two objects with totally different functions.[12]   During schema filling, the presence of an unknown tag indicates that the user needs more detailed information and a recursive push is performed.   In (A) below the answer to the question "What's the difference between a destroyer and a bomb?" is shown.   Two recursive schema invocations were made, both from one identification predicate to the next (proposition 1 to 2 and proposition 3 to 4), resulting in a double identification. Note that since no information other than identificational information is available in the relevant knowledge pool, an early exit from the embedded schema is taken.

---

[12]Note that the system does not address itself to the question of why the user thinks they are similar, another possible way of answering the question.

(difference DESTROYER BOMB)

Schema selected: compare&contrast-identification

proposition selected:
1) (identification DESTROYER SHIP (restrictive ((DRAFT)) (((DRAFT (15 222))))) (non-restrictive TRAVEL-MODE SURFACE))

focus: DESTROYER

Schema selected: identification

proposition selected:
2) (identification SHIP VEHICLE (non-restrictive FUNCTION TRANSPORTATION))

focus: SHIP

Schema exited

proposition selected:
3) (identification BOMB FREE-FALLING (restrictive TARGET-LOCATION SURFACE) (non-restrictive TRAVEL-MEANS GRAVITY-PULL))

focus: BOMB

Schema selected: identification

proposition selected:
4) (identification FREE-FALLING DESTRUCTIVE-DEVICE (non-restrictive FUNCTION LETHAL-KILL))

focus: FREE-FALLING

Schema exited

proposition selected:
5) (inference DESTROYER BOMB very-different-entities)

focus: (DESTROYER BOMB)

Message through dictionary. Entering tactical component
    A destroyer is a surface ship with a DRAFT between 15 and 222. A ship is a vehicle. A bomb is a free falling projectile that has a surface target location. A free falling projectile is a lethal destructive device. The bomb and the destroyer, therefore, are very different kinds of entities.

EXAMPLE A

2.2.2. Summary of text analysis

The analysis of texts and transcripts shows that patterns do occur across a variety of text styles. It appears, however, that the patterns are very loose. Each schema contains a number of alternatives, indicating that a speaker has a wide variety of options within each type of structure. Moreover, since it is difficult to precisely define a predicate, the interpretation of each predicate in the schema allows for additional speaker variation.

Encoding this extent of variability in schemata is intentional. It reflects the observation that at the text level speakers have more options in constructing English than at the sentence level: there is less agreement on what constitutes a bad paragraph than a bad sentence. Moreover, these choice points allow other factors to influence textual structure. In the current system, focus of attention is the sole influence (see Chapter Three), but influences such as a user model could also be incorporated.

Despite variability, the schemata do provide definite constraints on the ordering of paragraph constituents. A higher level view of the identification schema, the least constrained of the schemata, illustrates this. The schema consists of an *identification*, a *description*[13], and an *example*[14], in that order, with the option of an additional *descriptive* statement or *example* following, a reasonably constrained organization.

It should be noted that the schemata are descriptive and not prescriptive. Any discourse norm developed over a period of time will eventually be broken in order to achieve a desired literary effect. Poetic license, in fact, is based on the breaking of norms. It may be that norms at the discourse level are broken to create implicatures similarly to the creation of implicatures at the sentence level (Grice 75). All this points to the fact that the schemata do *not* function as grammars of text.

The schemata do, however, identify common means for effectively achieving certain discourse goals. They capture patterns of textual structure that are frequently used by a variety of people. Thus, they describe the norm for achieving given discourse goals, although they do not capture all the means for achieving these goals. Since they formally capture means that are used for achieving a discourse goal, they can be used by a generation system to produce effective text.

---

[13]where *description* --> *analogy/constituency/attributive/amplification*

[14]where *example* --> *particular-illustration/evidence*

2.3. Related research using rhetorical predicates

One computational use of rhetorical predicates is for the interpretation of arguments (Cohen 81b). Cohen's goal is to determine argument structure. She uses linguistic clues in the text to aid in determining the rhetorical function of a proposition and, thereby, the supporting relations between propositions in the text. Some of the predicate types which Cohen uses include *claim*, *evidence*, and *inference*. It should be noted that Cohen assumes an "oracle" which does the classification of propositions as predicates. In Cohen's work, predicates are used for the interpretation of language, as opposed to its generation.

Another proposed use of rhetorical predicates is in the generation of paragraphs (Jensen et al. 81). Jensen assumes that the content of the paragraph has already been determined. Her system then determines the function of each proposition and uses it to aid in the development of paragraph style. By identifying the underlying structure between propositions, they can be combined appropriately in text. This is in contrast to the use of predicates here to guide the determination of content as well as to determine ordering.

As mentioned earlier, Hobbs (78) and Lockman (78) both used predicates (or coherence relations) as an aid in the interpretation of anaphora. These works use formal definitions of coherence relations to identify the relations between juxtaposed sentences. These relations then help to predict what kind of anaphora can occur. This work has application to natural language interpretation, but has little to say about the use of coherence relations in generation.

Rumelhart's story grammars (Rumelhart 75) are similar to schemata as they describe textual structure for stories. He uses the grammars to recognize the underlying structure of a story, as opposed to generating it, and to summarize the important events of a story. Rumelhart's grammars differ from schemata in that they include both a structural and a semantic component, the non-terminals of the grammar (e.g., setting, episode, event) do not correspond to the rhetorical predicates used for TEXT, and he captures the structure of narratives, while I am more interested in the structure of descriptions.

2.4. Use of schemata

In the TEXT system, schemata describing discourse structure are used to guide the generation process. They are used to decide what is said first, what next, and so forth. The four schemata shown in Figures 2-4 - 2-7 above (*identification, attributive, constituency,* and *compare and contrast*) are used in the TEXT system with minor variations.

The identification, constituency, and attributive schemata were modified by eliminating several predicates for which no corresponding information exists in the specific application. Specifically, the *renaming* predicate was eliminated from the identification schema since synonyms are not represented or used in the TEXT system, and the *cause-effect* predicate was eliminated from the constituency schema since no process information is represented. TEXT's attributive schema is even more constrained than the original. The *analogy* predicate is used in place of the *comparison* predicate and the *classification* predicate is used instead of *restriction*, as neither the *classification* nor the *restriction* predicate have a translation in the database domain. In addition, several alternatives and options were deleted from the attributive schema, notably *question-answer*, *adversative*, and all alternatives of the last line except *explanation*. The modified schemata are each a subset of their corresponding originals; that is, the structures the modified schemata generate are generated by the originals, but they do not generate all structures generated by the originals.

The compare and contrast schema was modified to allow for equal discussion of the two items in question. Recall that the contrastive schema which emerged from the text analysis called for contrasting a major concept against a minor one. The minor concept, had, in most cases, either been discussed in the preceding text, or was assumed by the writer to be familiar to the reader. Thus, more discussion of the major concept was provided. Since no history of discourse is currently maintained in the TEXT implementation (see Chapter Five for suggestions for future work) and no user model, other than a static one, is constructed, the system does not know whether the user has more knowledge about one concept than another and the comparison, therefore, must be equally balanced between the two. An example of an equally balanced comparison taken from the texts analyzed is shown below in (B) (the basic outline of the compare and contrast schema used in TEXT is shown).

(B) "Made by" vs. "Produced by" (Nelson 77)

Similarities

Each listing also states that the wine was "produced and bottled by," or "made and bottled by," or "cellared and bottled by" a particular vintner. In the case of California wines, this is a very rough guide to how much of the wine in the bottle was actually fermented and finished by the company that put it into the bottle.

Differences
      If the label states "produced and bottled by," then at least 75 percent of the wine was fermented and finished by that winery. If the label says "made and bottled by," then only 10 percent of the wine need have been produced by the winery, and the other 90 percent or some portion of it may have been bought from another source and blended into the final product. If the label says anything else -- "cellared," "vinted," "bottled," "perfected," or any long and glorious combination of these words, then none of the wine in the bottle need have been produced by that winery.

Inference
      The fact that the label says simply "Bottled by Jones Brothers Winery" doesn't mean the wine is no good, however. It may be excellent. Its goodness will simply depend on the ability of the Jones Brothers to *buy* good wine, rather than on their ability to make it.

2.4.1. *Associating technique with purpose*

In the texts I analyzed, different rhetorical techniques were found to be used for different discourse purposes. In the TEXT system, this association of technique with discourse purpose is achieved by associating the different schemata with different question-types. For example, if a question involves defining a term, a different set of schemata (and therefore rhetorical techniques) is chosen than if the question involves describing the type of information available in the knowledge base. The discourse purposes under consideration correspond to the three response types handled by TEXT:

1. define: provide a definition
2. describe: describe available information
3. compare: compare differences

The identification schema was found to be used for definitions. (In fact, in TEXT it is only used in response to a request for a definition.) On the other hand, the purpose of the attributive schema is to provide detailed information about one particular aspect of any concept and it can therefore be used in response to a request to describe available information. In situations where an object or concept can be described in terms of its sub-parts or sub-classes, the constituency schema is used. It may be selected in response to requests for either definitions or information. The compare and contrast schema is used in response to a question about the difference between objects. It makes use of each of the three other schemata (see Section 4.4.6). A summary of the assignment of schemata to question-types is shown in Figure 2-10.

---

requests for definitions

> identification
> constituency

requests for available information

> attributive
> constituency

requests about the difference between objects

> compare and contrast

Figure 2-10:   Schemata used for TEXT

It should be noted that the compare and contrast schema actually has many uses and is an expository device frequently used in many of the texts analyzed. This schema is appropriate as the response structure for any question type when an object similar to the questioned object has been discussed in the immediately preceding discourse or is assumed to be familiar to the reader. In such situations, it serves two purposes: 1) it can point out the ways in which the questioned object differs from a concept familiar to the user; and 2) it can be used to parallel the structure of an earlier answer. This type of response would require using the one-sided compare and contrast schema that most of the analyzed texts used. In order for TEXT to use the compare and contrast for questions other than "What's the difference ..." questions a discourse history record would have to be implemented and maintained throughout a session.

2.5. Selecting a schema

Textual organization is influenced both by a speaker's goal and by what he has to say. Thus, the selection of a textual strategy is dictated by the discourse purpose and by knowledge that is relevant to that purpose. Each discourse purpose has a set of schemata associated with it that restricts the choice of which textual strategy to use to a small number of possibilities. A characterization of the information relevant to that purpose can then be used to select a single schema from the small set of possible schemata. Basically, this characterization specifies how much information is potentially relevant to the discourse purpose.

In TEXT, processing for schema selection models this view. Once a question has been posed to the system, a schema is first selected for the response structure. It will later be used to control the decisions involved in deciding what to say when. On the basis of the given question, which defines the discourse purpose, a small set of schemata is selected as possible structures for the response. This set includes those schemata associated with the given question-type (see Figure 2-10, above). A single schema is selected out of this set on the basis of the information available to answer the question.

In response to requests for definitions and information, the constituency schema is selected when the relevant knowledge pool contains a "rich" description of the questioned object's sub-classes and less information about the object itself. When this is not the case, the identification schema is used for definition questions and the attributive schema is used for information questions. The test for what kind of information is available is a relatively simple one. If the questioned object occurs at a higher level in the knowledge base hierarchy than a pre-determined level, the constituency schema is used. Note that the higher an entity occurs in the hierarchy, the less descriptive information is available to describe the set of instances it represents since the larger the class, the less common features occur across it. Thus, above this level the constituency schema will be used and below it the attributive or identification schema will be used. This process assumes a hierarchically structured knowledge base and could not be done on an unstructured one (see Section 4.2 for a description of the knowledge base used in the TEXT system).

(C) and (D) below show two examples of a request for a definition. For the question "What is a guided projectile?" (C) the constituency schema is selected since the guided projectile occurs above the determined level in the hierarchy and thus more information is available about the guided projectile's sub-classes than about the guided projectile itself, while the identification schema is selected for the question "What is an aircraft-carrier?" (D).

(definition GUIDED)

Schema selected: constituency

identification
constituency
attributive
attributive
evidence
evidence
attributive

Message through dictionary.   Entering tactical component
A guided projectile is a projectile that is self-propelled.   There are 2 types of guided projectiles in the ONR database: torpedoes and missiles.   The missile has a target location in the air or on the earth's surface.   The torpedo has an underwater target location.   The missile's target location is indicated by the DB attribute DESCRIPTION and the missile's flight capabilities are provided by the DB attribute ALTITUDE.   The torpedo's underwater capabilities are provided by the DB attributes under DEPTH (for example, MAXIMUM OPERATING DEPTH).   The guided projectile has DB attributes TIME TO TARGET & UNITS, HORZ RANGE & UNITS and NAME.

EXAMPLE C

-- -- -- -- -- -- -- -- -- -- -- -- -- -- -- -- -- -- --

(definition AIRCRAFT-CARRIER)

Schema selected: identification

identification
analogy
particular-illustration
amplification
evidence

Message through dictionary. Entering tactical component
  An aircraft carrier is a surface ship with a DISPLACEMENT between 78000 and 80800 and a LENGTH between 1039 and 1063. Aircraft carriers have a greater LENGTH than all other ships and a greater DISPLACEMENT than most other ships. Mine warfare ships, for example, have a DISPLACEMENT of 320 and a LENGTH of 144. All aircraft carriers in the ONR database have REMARKS of 0, FUEL TYPE of BNKR, FLAG of BLBL, BEAM of 252, ENDURANCE RANGE of 4000, ECONOMIC SPEED of 12, ENDURANCE SPEED of 30 and PROPULSION of STMTURGRD. A ship is classified as an aircraft carrier if the characters 1 through 2 of its HULL NO are CV.

EXAMPLE D

-- -- -- -- -- -- -- -- -- -- -- -- -- -- -- -- -- --

  The compare and contrast schema, as intimated above, is significantly different in format from the other schemata. It dictates a contrastive structure without specifying which predicates are to be used. Use of predicates varies, depending upon what is being talked about. To achieve this variation, while allowing the schema the same guiding role as the other schemata, the compare and contrast schema makes use of one of the three other schemata as part of the response depending on the semantic information available about the two entities.
  The type of information included in the relevant knowledge pool for this

kind of question is dependent on the conceptual similarity[15] of the two entities. In building the relevant knowledge pool, the semantic processor categorizes the entities as **very close** in concept, **very different** in concept, or in between these two extremes (see Section 4.3 for a description of how this is done). This classification is available for deciding which schema to use. If the two entities are very close in concept, the attributive schema is used since detailed information about each of the entities is available in the knowledge pool. If the entities are very different in concept, the identification schema is used since the only information available in the knowledge pool is hierarchical classification. For entities in between these two classifications, the constituency schema is used since the class difference in the hierarchy can be discussed as well as some of the entities' attributes.

2.6. Filling the schema

Once a schema has been selected, it is filled by matching the predicates it contains against the relevant knowledge pool (Section 4.3). Semantics associated with each predicate define the type of information that it can match in the knowledge pool. These are semantics in the sense that they define what a predicate **means** in the database system; that is, what it can refer to in the database. The semantics defined for TEXT are particular to database systems and would have to be redefined if the schemata were to be used in another type of system (such as a tutorial system, for example). The semantics are not particular, however, to the **domain** of the database. When transferring the system from one database to another, the predicate semantics would not have to be altered.

Before describing predicate semantics in more detail, it is important to note the difference between a rhetorical predicate and a proposition. A rhetorical predicate specifies a generic type of speech act (Searle 75). Each predicate is essentially a type of an **inform** act. Associated with each predicate are arguments which can take any value of a given type. The number and types of arguments associated with a predicate are defined by its semantics. A proposition is an instantiation of a predicate; the predicate arguments have been filled with values from the knowledge base. Furthermore, although predicates, loosely speaking, match propositions in the knowledge base, propositions are not stored as wholes in the knowledge base (see Section 4.2 for a description of the knowledge base representation). Instead, pieces of the knowledge base are selected as values for the predicate arguments to construct a proposition.

The semantics for each predicate indicate the data-types of information

_____

[15]For another approach to determining similarities, or drawing analogies, see (Winston 79).

in the knowledge base that can satisfy its arguments. A single predicate may have more than one way in which its arguments can be satisfied. The semantics for the attributive predicate, for example, indicate that the following two English sentences both attribute information to the missile:

1. The missile has database attributes TIME TO TARGET & UNITS, LETHAL RADIUS & UNITS, ALTITUDE, SPEED, and PROBABILITY OF KILL. (database attributes)

2. The missile has a target location in the air or on the earth's surface. (distinguishing descriptive attribute)

The constituency predicate, on the other hand, has only one interpretation. It matches the sub-classes of an entity in the generalization hierarchy and would translate to an English sentence like: "There are two types of water-going vehicles in the ONR database: ships and submarines."

The semantics of the predicates are represented as functions. Associated with each predicate is a function that accesses the relevant knowledge pool and retrieves values for the predicate arguments. Each predicate has the effect of providing information about something. The attributive propositions in the two examples given above attribute information to the missile. Likewise, the constituency example above presents the sub-classes of water-going vehicles. This specialized entity is the *given* argument of the predicate. It is passed as input to the predicate function. The function searches for the remaining predicate arguments that are associated with the given argument in the relevant knowledge pool.

The values for the arguments which are passed to the predicate functions are supplied by the previous discourse or the input questions before any discourse has been constructed. Where possible, they are supplied by the focus of the discourse. In other cases, the function extracts an instance of the data type it is looking for from the most recent proposition which contains it.

The predicate arguments and their ordering, specified by the predicate semantics, are called the *message formalism* in the TEXT system. Each predicate has its associated formalism. When a predicate is evaluated, one or more of its arguments are given and the others are filled by values in the database to form a proposition. This proposition is the actual output of the predicate function. A complete specification of the predicates and their formalism, along with examples, is given in Appendix D.

A schema is filled by stepping through it, using the predicate semantics to select propositions that match the predicates. At any choice point in the schema, the focus constraints (described in Chapter Three) are used to decide which proposition should be selected. This is a place where additional information, such as a user model, could be incorporated as an influence on the generated text. For cases where a single predicate has several types and matches more than one proposition in the knowledge base, information about how focus of attention can shift is used to select the most appropriate proposition (see Chapter Three). In places where alternative predicates occur in the schema, all alternatives are matched against the relevant knowledge pool, producing a set of propositions (if more than one predicate succeeds). Again, focus of attention dictates how to select the most appropriate proposition. When an optional predicate occurs in the schema, both the optional predicate and the predicate which would succeed it are matched against the knowledge pool. If the optional predicate has no match, the successor's match is selected. If both predicates match, focus of attention is used to select the most appropriate proposition.

After a proposition has been selected, it is marked in order to prevent repetition in a single answer. Since a proposition may be composed of pieces of information in the knowledge pool, each piece of information is marked by adding the property "used" to it. When selecting propositions, this property is checked to determine whether it has already been said. Since no tracking of discourse is done right now, the "used" property is removed after the generation of each answer.

2.7. An example

To see exactly how a schema is filled, consider the process of answering the question "What is a ship?" (in functional notation, "(definition SHIP)"). Two schemata are associated with definitions: *constituency* and *identification*. A test on the generalization hierarchy indicates that the ship occurs at a level where a large amount of information is available about the entity itself. The identification schema is therefore selected and the process of schema filling begins.

The first predicate in the TEXT identification schema (shown in Figure 2-11) is *identification*. The relevant knowledge pool constructed for this question is shown in Figure 2-12 (see Section 4.3 for the determination of relevant information). Since this is the first statement of the answer and no preceding discourse exists to provide a context for the predicate to use, the questioned object (all that has been mentioned) is passed as argument to the identification function. In this case, the questioned equals SHIP. The identification predicate is matched against the relevant knowledge pool and the ship's super-ordinate in the hierarchy, plus certain descriptive information as dictated by the semantics of the predicate, are selected. Note that the identification predicate has only one type and therefore, only one proposition matches it:

(identification SHIP WATER-VEHICLE (restrictive TRAVEL-MODE SURFACE) (non-restrictive TRAVEL-MEDIUM WATER))[16]

Identification (class & attribute / function)
{Analogy/Constituency/Attributive}*
Particular-illustration/Evidence+
{Amplification/Analogy/Attributive}
{Particular-illustration/Evidence}

Figure 2-11:   The TEXT Identification Schema

The second step in the schema specifies an optional alternative. The alternative includes the descriptive predicates *analogy*, *constituency*, and *attributive*. Each of these predicates is matched against the relevant knowledge pool. Since each of these predicates takes an entity as its given argument, both SHIP and WATER-VEHICLE are passed to the various predicate functions (SHIP and WATER-VEHICLE are the only entities mentioned so far). Since quite a bit of information remains about the SHIP in the relevant knowledge pool, each of these predicates matches and three propositions are produced. Since the only remaining information about the WATER-VEHICLE is its sub-classes, only the *constituency* predicate matches for the WATER-VEHICLE. The 4 matched propositions are:

---

[16]Here, the arguments of the identification predicate are filled by the entity SHIP (what is being identified), the entity WATER-VEHICLE (its superordinate), and two distinguishing descriptive attributes, one of which distinguishes SHIPS from all other WATER-VEHICLES (labelled "restrictive"), and the other which describes all WATER-VEHICLES (and therefore is labeled as "non-restrictive").

1. (analogy rels SHIP ON GUIDED GUNS)

2. (constituency SHIP (AIRCRAFT-CARRIER FRIGATE ...))

3. (attributive db SHIP (name OFFICIAL_NAME) (topics
   SPEED_DEPENDENT_RANGE DIMENSIONS) (duplicates
   (FUEL FUEL_TYPE FUEL_CAPACITY)) (attrs PROPULSION
   MAXIMUM_SPEED))

4. (constituency WATER-VEHICLE (SHIP SUBMARINE))

Since the alternative is optional, its succeeding step (an alternative
between *particular-illustration* and *evidence*) is also matched against the
relevant knowledge pool. The same entities are passed as given arguments to
the predicate functions. Since the second argument required by the
particular illustration predicate does not exist in the discourse so far, there
is nothing to illustrate and the particular-illustration predicate fails. The
evidence function succeeds for the entity SHIP since there are several
database attributes which indicate that it travels on the surface. It does not
succeed for the WATER-VEHICLE, however, so this step matches one
proposition:

1. (evidence based-db SHIP (TRAVEL-MODE SURFACE) (HAVE
   DRAFT) (HAVE DISPLACEMENT))

One proposition is then selected from this set of five by applying
constraints based on how focus of attention can shift. In this case, the
proposition matching the *evidence* predicate is selected, although the reasoning
behind the choice is not discussed here since it depends on the focus
constraints (see Section 3.2.9 for the focus algorithm). The answer created so
far and the updated relevant knowledge pool (information occurring in the
answer is marked as used) are shown in Figures 2-13 and 2-14. This process
is then repeated for the next step in the schema to complete the answer, but
is not shown here. It should be noted that the identification schema encodes
more alternatives than the other schemata and is therefore less efficient in
deciding what to say next. Less restrictive schemata necessarily entail more
inefficiency than others as more processing must be done to explore the
additional choices.

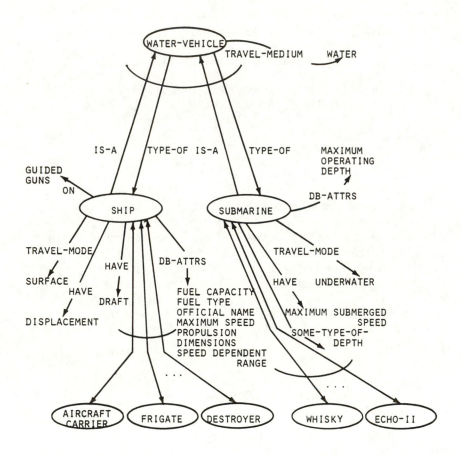

Figure 2-12: Sample Relevant Knowledge Pool

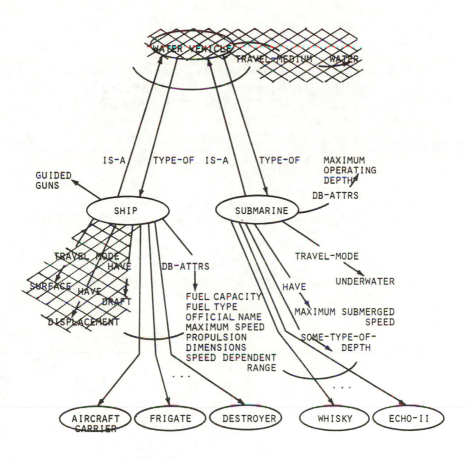

Figure 2-13: Updated Relevant Knowledge Pool

Selected Propositions

(identification SHIP WATER-VEHICLE (restrictive TRAVEL-MODE SURFACE) (non-restrictive TRAVEL-MEDIUM WATER))
(evidence based-db SHIP (TRAVEL-MODE SURFACE) (HAVE DRAFT) (HAVE DISPLACEMENT))

Eventual Translation

The ship is a water-going vehicle that travels on the surface. Its surface going capabilities are provided by the DB attributes DRAFT and DISPLACEMENT.

Figure 2-14:   Selected Information

2.8. Future work

There are several directions of research which this work suggests. Currently, the model of generation allows for several influences on the structure of generated text, including rhetorical strategies (encoded as schemata), potentially relevant information, discourse goal, and focus of attention (Chapter Three). One influence not taken into account is knowledge about the user's beliefs and goals. This information could be taken into account both in the initial selection of a schema and in deciding between alternatives within a schema. Which of several alternatives at a schema choice point should be taken is currently determined by the focus constraints alone, which select the proposition that ties in most closely with the previous discourse. When filling the schema, conditions on focus are tested to determine which alternative to take. These conditions are essentially preconditions to taking a particular action (predicate) in the text plan (schema). They provide the hooks for using tests based on the system's beliefs about the user to select a predicate most satisfactory for the user, given what he already knows.

The development of full recursion is related to the incorporation of a user model. The use of full recursion would mean the system would have the ability to provide different responses to the same question which vary by level of detail. In order to develop such a capability, it will be necessary to investigate the influences on level of detail, some of which will be part of a user model, and incorporate these as conditions on recursion. This is a direction that I have already begun to pursue.

Another direction, hinted at earlier, is the use of schemata to aid in the interpretation of natural language. Schemata could be used to determine the discourse goals of the user when interacting with the system. If a schema matches a sequence of input questions from the user, then the goal he is pursuing over that sequence of dialogue will be a goal associated with the matched schema (e.g., definition if the identification schema matches). This information will be useful both in responding to individual questions and anticipating follow-up questions.

2.9. Conclusions

Schemata have been used in the TEXT system to model common patterns of text structure. The schemata embody a number of alternatives, thereby allowing for a good deal of structural variety in text. Moreover, it was shown that schemata are not *grammars* of text; many experienced and talented writers purposely break norms in order to achieve a striking literary effect. Rather, the schemata describe common patterns of description that are used to effectively achieve the discourse purposes considered. They capture, in a computationally useful formalism, techniques that are frequently used. Although not a complete grammar of text in general, they serve as a grammar for TEXT (i.e., they delineate the extent of text structures it can generate).

Schemata are used in the TEXT system to guide the generation process. They initiate the process of what to say next; their decisions are monitored by the focusing mechanism which selects between alternatives. Since the schemata were shown to be recursive, describing text structure at many levels, they are much like a hierarchical plan for text.

The schemata developed for the TEXT system encode structures suitable for description of static information. Other text types will require different kinds of schemata and probably different kinds of predicates as well. Descriptions of processes involving cause and effect, reasoning involved in explanation, and narrative are all examples of different text types that will require additional examination of text to determine commonly used means of description and explanation, but were not relevant to the application.

3
Focusing in discourse

Focusing is a prevalent phenomenon in all types of naturally occurring discourse. Everyone, consciously or unconsciously, centers their attention on various concepts or objects throughout the process of reading, writing, speaking, or listening. In all these modalities, the focusing phenomena occur at many levels of discourse. For example, we expect a book to concern itself with a single theme or subject; chapters are given headings, indicating that the material included within is related to the given heading; paragraphs are organized around topics; and sentences are related in some way to preceding and succeeding sentences. In conversation, comments such as "Stick to the subject ...", "Going back to what you were saying before ..", or "Let's change the subject ..." all indicate that people are aware that the conversation centers on specific ideas and that there are conventions for changing the focus of attention.

The use of focusing makes for ease of processing on the part of participants in a conversation. When interpreting utterances, knowledge that the discourse is about a particular topic eliminates certain possible interpretations from consideration. Grosz (77) discusses this in light of the interpretation of definite referring expressions. She notes that although a word may have multiple meanings, its use in an appropriate context will rarely bring to mind any meaning but the relevant one. Focusing also facilitates the interpretation of anaphoric, and in particular, pronominal, references (see Sidner 79). When the coherence provided by focusing is missing from discourse, readers and hearers may have difficulty in determining what a pronoun refers to. When speaking or writing, the process of focusing constrains the set of possibilities for what to say next. Having decided that he wants to talk about the weather, for example, a speaker need not consider what he could say about yesterday's movie. When a speaker or writer has not decided ahead of time on the specific themes he wants to convey, he will experience difficulty in proceeding. Incoherent text or conversation is often the result of such a situation.

Focusing also influences *how* something is said. Changing what is focused may involve marking the move for the hearer by using a different syntactic form. Continuing discussion of the same topic may require pronominalization[17]. The use of marked syntactic structures can highlight new information about a previously mentioned item.

This use of focusing is what makes a sequence of sentences a whole. The fact that a sequence of sentences is *about* something makes that sequence connected, coherent, and in some sense, a unit. Intuitively then, a text is a connected, coherent sequence of sentences. In order to generate texts, some account of the use of focusing must be given.

3.1. Computational theories and uses of focusing

Focusing has been used effectively as a computational tool in the interpretation of discourse by several researchers in artificial intelligence. Although theories about the process of focusing were developed specifically for use in the *interpretation* of discourse, some of the ideas developed are applicable to the generation of natural language. Some background on previous work in this area is presented before discussing the use of focusing in this research.

3.1.1. Global focus

Grosz (77) identified the role of focusing in the interpretation of referring expressions in dialogue. In particular, she was concerned with the distinction between two types of focus: *global* and *immediate*. Immediate focus refers to how a speaker's center of attention shifts or remains constant over two consecutive sentences. Both the ordering of sentence constituents and the interpretation of sentence fragments are affected by the immediate focus. Global focus, on the other hand, describes the effect of a speaker's center of attention throughout a set of discourse utterances on succeeding utterances. A speaker's global focus encompasses a more general set of objects than his immediate focus. In her work, Grosz concentrated on defining the representation and use of global focus. She did not address the problem of defining and using immediate focus.

Grosz represented global focus by partitioning a subset of the entire knowledge base containing focused items from the remaining knowledge base. Determining what is focused on throughout discourse was part of the theory she developed. She distinguished between items that were explicitly focused on, as a result of having been mentioned, and those that were implicitly in focus by virtue of their association with mentioned items. Knowing which items are focused makes further interpretation of discourse easier.

---

[17]The use of a pronoun to refer to a person, place, or thing (e.g., "he" or "it").

Considering only a subset of the knowledge base at a given time limits the search for referents of definite noun phrases occurring in the discourse and makes it more likely that the correct referent will be found.

Grosz's representation of focus is, in fact, slightly more complicated than this. In the implementation of a focusing mechanism Grosz termed the subset of the knowledge base that contains items in focus a *focus space*. A focus space is "open" (i.e., its contents are currently in focus) if items within it have been recently mentioned. By not bringing items into the focus space until mentioned, the efficiency of the search for referents is increased. Items are "implicitly" in focus if they are related to items in an open focus space, but have not yet been mentioned. Mention of one of these items opens the implicit focus space. The old open focus space remains open but is stacked. An open focus space is closed only when conversation returns to a stacked open focus space. In this case, conversation returns to an earlier topic thereby closing recent discussion. The highly structured task domain in which this work was done was used to guide changes in focus.

3.1.2. Immediate focus

Sidner (79) extended Grosz's work with an extensive analysis of immediate focus. She used focus for the disambiguation of definite anaphora and thus for aiding in the interpretation of discourse. She was able to explain types of anaphora which Grosz did not consider, particularly the use of pronouns. A major result of her work was the specification of detailed algorithms for maintaining and shifting immediate focus.

Tracking immediate focus involves maintaining three pieces of information: the immediate focus of a sentence (represented by the *current focus*), the elements of a sentence which are potential candidates for a change in focus (represented by a *potential focus list*), and past immediate foci (represented by a *focus stack*[18]). Current focus indicates the constituent of a sentence being focused on. The potential focus list records

---

[18]By *focus stack* I mean specifically a data structure classically known as a *stack*. Briefly, a stack is a list to which one can only add and delete items from one end of the list, called the *top* of the stack. Stacks are also known as *last-in first-out* lists. The stack operations that are referred to here are:

- *pop*: remove and return the top element off the stack. If a specific item on the stack is popped, then all elements above that item are deleted from the stack and the item is deleted and returned.

- *push*: add a new element to the top of the stack. The verb *stack* is also used to mean push.

constituents within the sentence that are candidates for a shift in focus. The potential focus list is partially ordered. The focus stack is updated every time a change in focus occurs. When conversation shifts to a member of the previous potential focus list, the old focus is pushed on the stack and the current focus becomes the new focus. When conversation returns to an item previously discussed, the stack is popped to yield that item.

Because the concept of focusing is meaningful only in the context of at least two sentences, Sidner's algorithms specify rules for maintaining and shifting focus from one sentence to the next. Briefly, she claims that the speaker has four options:

1. continue talking about the same thing
   (current focus remains the same)

2. switch to talk about an item just introduced
   (current focus becomes a member of the previous potential focus list)

3. return to a topic of previous discussion
   (current focus becomes the popped member of the focus stack)

4. talk about an item implicitly related to the current focus
   (general world knowledge is needed to determine that such a switch has been made)

These rules are only part of an algorithm which is used to determine the referent of an anaphoric expression in the incoming sentence. Tracking the focus of the current sentence is part of the process of determining the referent of an anaphoric expression.

3.2. Focusing and generation

In previous research in computational linguistics, the use of focusing has been considered as a factor in the comprehension of discourse and in particular, definite anaphora in discourse. In this research, I show how it can be used as a tool for the generation of discourse. The use of a focusing mechanism provides constraints on the possibilities for what can be said. Global focus constrains the entire knowledge base, producing a subset containing items which can be talked about. Immediate focus further constrains the subset since after any given utterance a smaller set of choices will be possible. Furthermore, the use of focusing provides a computationally tractable method of producing coherent and cohesive discourse. Use of a focusing mechanism ensures discourse connectivity by ensuring that each proposition[19] of the discourse is related through its focused argument to the previous discourse.

The following sections describe how to make use of the focusing mechanisms and guidelines developed by both Grosz and Sidner in the generation process. Several problems arise in adapting this work to generation. Since it considers *interpretation*, there is no need to discriminate between members of the set of legal foci; when more than one possibility for global or immediate focus exists after a given sentence, the next incoming sentence determines which of the choices is taken. The kinds of choices that must be made in generation, as well as the extensions which must be included in the focusing mechanism to accommodate these decisions, are described in the following sections.

3.2.1. Global focus and generation

In the TEXT system, a relevant knowledge pool which contains information determined by the system to be relevant to the input question is constructed for each answer. It is equivalent to Grosz's concept of an open focus space. The relevant knowledge pool contains those items which are in focus over the course of an answer. It contains all that can be talked about further. Since it is a subset of the entire knowledge base, it contains a limited amount of information.

I claim that, in generating discourse, one way that global focus may shift is when a recursive push on a schema is taken (see Section 2.2.1). That is, when it is necessary to provide a more detailed description of a particular concept (in identifying it, attributing information to it, providing an analogy about it, etc.), it is necessary to describe information related to the concept in question and therefore implicitly in focus. Such information is not part of the open focus space since it has not been mentioned previously, but it is related to the information explicitly in focus. When the push is taken, the focus shifts to this information and it remains in focus for the duration of the new schema. Thus, a new open focus space has been created. Note that the old focus space remains open; due to the nature of recursive pushes on schemata, the text will continue where it left off when the task of providing more detailed information (the push) is completed. When the pop from the sub-schema occurs, the new open focus space is closed and the old open focus space again becomes the active one.

As an example, consider the problem (described in Section 2.2.1) of defining a Hobie Cat to someone who knows nothing about sailing. The text for identifying the Hobie Cat is reproduced below. Remember that in identifying a Hobie Cat as a type of catamaran, it was also necessary to

---

[19]A proposition corresponds to a single sentence in the generated text.

define a catamaran for the listener. In this case, the features of a catamaran are implicitly in focus when talking about the Hobie Cat. When the push is made to identify the catamaran, the features of the catamaran are focused. They remain in focus throughout the definition of the catamaran (the Hobie Cat is not discussed now) and when the discussion is finished, mention of the Hobie Cat brings the old open space back into focus and closes the space containing catamaran features (see Figure 3-1).

1. A Hobie Cat is a brand of catamaran,
2. which is a kind of sailboat.
3. Catamarans have sails and a mast like other sailboats,
4. but they have two hulls instead of one.
5. That's a catamaran there.
6. Hobie Cats have a canvas cockpit connecting the two pontoons and one or two sails.
7. The 16 ft. Hobie Cat has a main and a jib and the 14 ft. Hobie Cat has only a main.

It should be noted that this feature of shifting global focus is not currently implemented in the TEXT system, although the design has been worked out. Its implementation is dependent upon the implementation of full recursion (see Chapter 2, Section 2.2.1) which requires the development of a user-model, a major research effort.

3.2.2. Immediate focus and generation

The previous sections have shown that the speaker is limited in many ways to what he will say at any given point. He is limited by the goal he is trying to achieve in his current speech act, which in the TEXT system is to answer the user's current question. To achieve that goal, he has limited his scope of attention to a set of objects relevant to this goal, as represented by global focus or the relevant knowledge pool. The speaker is also limited by his higher-level plan of how to achieve the goal (the schema). Within these constraints, however, a speaker may still run into the problem of deciding what to say next.

In the TEXT system an immediate focusing mechanism is used to select between these remaining options. It constrains the process of filling the selected schema with propositions from the relevant knowledge pool. Recall that the schemata describe normal patterns of discourse structure and encode a number of alternatives. Hence, they only partially constrain the choice of what to say. During the process of schema filling, more than one proposition may match the next predicate in the schema. This can occur either because 1) alternative predicates appear in the schema and propositions in the relevant knowledge pool match more than one alternative, or 2) more than one proposition matches a single predicate. The decision as to which

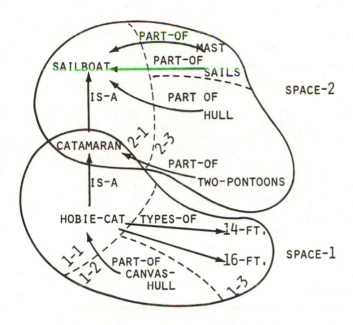

For sentence 1: Space 1-1 open
Space 2-1, 1-2, 1-3 implicit
For sentence 2: Space 1-1 open but stacked,
Space 2-1 open
Space 2-2, 2-3 implicit
For sentence 3: Space 1-1 open but stacked
Space 2-1, 2-2 open
Space 2-3 implicit
For sentence 4: Space 1-1 open but stacked
Space 2-1, 2-2, 2-3 open
For sentence 5: same
For sentence 6: Space 1-1, 1-2 open and active
Space-2 closed
For sentence 7: Space 1-1, 1-2, 1-3 open
Space 2 closed

Figure 3-1:   Global Focus Shifts

proposition is most appropriate is made by the focusing mechanism. It eliminates any propositions whose current focus does not meet the legal restrictions specified by Sidner. That is, the focus of the next proposition must be the same as the current focus of the last proposition, a member of the potential focus list of the last proposition, or a member of the focus stack.

The representation of immediate focus and guidelines for shifting and maintaining focus used in the **TEXT** system follow Sidner. As each proposition is added to an answer,[20] its focus (termed current focus) and its potential focus list (a partially ordered list of items within the proposition that are potential candidates for a shift in focus) are recorded. Thus, focus is maintained and may shift or remain constant across each proposition. A focus stack is maintained throughout the course of an answer and it is updated every time the current focus changes. When the current focus shifts to a member of the potential focus list, the old current focus is stacked. When the current focus shifts to a member of the focus stack (conversation returns to a topic of previous discussion) the focus stack is popped to return to a previous focus.

Although this information suffices for interpretation, additional mechanisms are needed for generation which can decide among focus alternatives. In the interpretation of discourse, this is not necessary because the choice is dictated by the incoming sentence. For generation, however, the speaker may have to decide between any of the valid foci at any given point. Figure 3-2 shows the choices that a speaker may have to make. The following sections describe how the **TEXT** system selects between these alternatives.

3.2.3. Current focus versus potential focus list

The choice between current focus and items on the potential focus list corresponds to choosing between continuing to talk about the same thing or starting to talk about something introduced in the last sentence.

As an example, consider the following situation. Suppose I want to tell you that John is a new graduate student. Suppose I also want to tell you that new graduate students typically have a rough first semester and I want to tell you a lot of other things about John: what courses he's taking, what he's interested in, where he lives. If I decide to tell you all the other things about John first, when I finally get around to telling you about the first semester of new graduate students, I will somehow have to re-introduce it into the conversation, either by reminding you that John is a new graduate student, by relating it to rough times, etc. If, on the other hand, I first told

---

[20]Each proposition will translate to a sentence.

$$\text{Choice} := \text{CF (new sentence)} = \text{CF (last sentence)}$$
$$\text{vs.}$$
$$\text{CF (new sentence)} \; \xi \; \text{PFL (last sentence)}$$

$$\text{Choice} := \text{CF (new sentence)} = \text{CF (last sentence)}$$
$$\text{vs.}$$
$$\text{CF (new sentence)} \; \xi \; \text{focus-stack}$$

Figure 3-2:   Choices between valid foci

you that new graduate students typically have a rough first semester, I would have no trouble in continuing to tell you the other facts about John. In fact, in continuing talking about John, I will be returning to a topic of previous discussion, a legal focus move. In other words, the current focus of the next sentence will be a member of the focus stack. Note that discussing new graduate students after an ensuing conversation about John is not a legal focus move, since "new graduate students" never became the focus of conversation, but was only a potential focus list member.[21]

Thus, for reasons of efficiency, when one has the choice of remaining on the same topic or switching to one just introduced, I claim the preference is to switch. If the speaker has something to say about an item just introduced and he does not present it next, he will have to go to the trouble of reintroducing the topic at a later point. In summary,

---

[21]In this example, I am ignoring the effect of discourse structure and planning on the choice of what to say next for purposes of illustration only. Normally, the schema or discourse plan would also constrain what a person could say next.

Choice := CF (next sentence) = CF (last sentence)
vs.
CF (next sentence) ξ PFL (last sentence)

Preference := CF (next sentence) ξ PFL (last sentence)

Reason := if preference is not taken, speaker will have
to re-introduce PFL-member (last sentence)
at a later point.

If this rule is followed, it will have the effect of producing "topic clusters", each spinning off of and clustered around an item just introduced, rather than producing an extended discourse about a single topic. This causes the formation of sub-topics which results in a more interesting text than if a single topic were consistently maintained over a sequence of sentences. In the imagined conversation about John, one instantiation would produce the discourse shown below in Figure 3-3. Two topic clusters are *John as a new graduate student* and *the courses John is taking*.

John is a new graduate student.

New graduate students typically have a rough first semester.

John is taking four courses: intro to programming, graphics, analysis of algorithms, and hardware.

Graphics is the most interesting one.

John lives at Graduate Towers.

Figure 3-3:   Topic Clusters

Several consecutive moves to potential focus list members are not a problem. In fact, they occur frequently in written text. In the following example, taken from "Pseudo-silk" in *Future Facts* (Rosen 76), focus shifts in every case but one.

1. Finally in November 1973, two Japanese scientists, Seigo Oya and Juzo Takahashi, announced that they had synthesized a fiber which "very much resembles silk."

2. The base for their pseudo-silk is glutamic acid,
   focus = their pseudo-silk (a fiber which "very much resembles silk")

3. one of the 20 amino acids that make up all proteins
   focus = one (glutamic acid)

4. and a chemical long used in the production of monosodium glutamate,
   focus = a chemical (glutamic acid)

5. the controversial seasoning found in many meals,
   focus = the controversial seasoning (monosodium glutamate)

6. ranging from baby food to egg rolls.
   focus = <gap> (meals)

If this rule were applied indefinitely, however, it would result in a never-ending side-tracking onto different topics of conversations. The discourse would be disconcerting and perhaps incoherent. However, TEXT is operating under an assumption that information is being presented in order to achieve a particular goal (i.e., answer a question). Only a limited amount of information is within the speaker's scope of attention because of its relevance to that goal. Hence only a limited amount of sidetracking can occur. The rule is viable because global focus constrains consecutive shifts, illustrating the necessity for the interaction between global and immediate focus.

3.2.4. Current focus versus focus stack

The choice between current focus and returning to an item on the focus stack corresponds to the choice between continuing talking about the same thing or returning to a topic[22] of previous discussion.

Consider an extension of the discourse about John. Suppose I have

---

[22]Topic is used here loosely to refer to the subject or theme of a discourse. It does not refer to the linguistic notion of topic.

already told you that John is a new graduate student and that new graduate students have a rough first semester (the first two sentences of Figure 3-3). Suppose that in addition to telling you the other facts about John (about his courses and where he lives), I also want to tell you that new graduate students are required to maintain a B or above average or they will not be allowed to continue their studies (a fact not mentioned in the last discourse). I have the choice of telling you this immediately after sentence 2 of Figure 3-3 (in which case CF (new sentence) = CF (last sentence) = new graduate students) or of telling you the other facts about John first (in which case CF (new sentence) = focus-stack member = John).

If I should decide to tell you the other facts about John first, I would not run into the same problem of re-introducing a topic since "new graduate students" had been focused on. There is, however, something odd about this choice. Here, the issue of global focus is more important than that of local focus. Having switched the local focus to "new graduate students", I opened a new focus space for discussion. If I switch back to John, I close that focus space (see (Grosz 77) for a detailed discussion of opening and closing focus spaces), thereby implying that I have finished that topic of conversation. I am implying, therefore, that I have nothing more to say about the topic, when in fact I do. The preference I claim in this case is to continue talking about the same thing rather than returning to a topic of previous discussion. Having introduced a topic, which may entail the introduction of other topics, one should say all that needs to be said on that topic before returning to an earlier one.

Choice :== CF (new sentence) = CF (last sentence)
$$\text{vs.}$$
CF (new sentence) ξ focus-stack

Preference :== CF (new sentence) = CF (last sentence)

Reason :== to avoid false implication of a finished topic

These two guidelines for changing and maintaining focus during the process of generating language provide an ordering on the three basic legal focus moves that Sidner specifies:

1. change focus to member of previous potential focus list if possible
   CF (new sentence) ξ PFL (last sentence)

2. maintain focus if possible
   CF (new sentence) = CF (last sentence)

3. return to topic of previous discussion
   CF (new sentence) ξ focus-stack

I have not investigated the problem of incorporating focus moves to items implicitly related to current foci, potential focus list members, or previous foci into this scheme. This remains a topic for future research.

3.2.5. Other choices

Even the addition of constraints induced by immediate focusing, however, is not sufficient for ensuring a coherent discourse. Although a speaker may decide to focus on a specific entity, he may want to convey information about several properties of the entity. The guidelines developed so far prescribe no set of actions for this situation. Rather than arbitrarily listing properties of the entity in any order, I claim that a speaker will group together in his discussion properties that are in some way related to each other.

Thus, strands of semantic connectivity will occur at more than one level of discourse. An example of this phenomenon is given in discourses (1) and (2) below. In both, the discourse is focusing on a single entity (the balloon), but in (1), properties that must be talked about are presented randomly. In (2), a related set of properties (color) is discussed before the next set (size). As a result, (2) is more connected than (1).

1. The balloon was red and white striped. Because this balloon was designed to carry men, it had to be large. It had a silver circle at the top to reflect heat. In fact, it was larger than any balloon John had ever seen.

2. The balloon was red and white striped. It had a silver circle at the top to reflect heat. Because this balloon was designed to carry men, it had to be large. In fact, it was larger than any balloon John had ever seen.

This type of phenomenon is very common in literary texts. Consider the following example, taken from the introduction to *Working* (Terkel 72).[23] Except for the last sentence, where the current focus changes to "daily humiliations", the focus remains unchanged throughout the paragraph (current focus = this book). An undercurrent of related themes occur from one sentence to the next. Violence, physical violence, spiritual violence, and examples of violence are all related properties of the book that are described.

---

[23]Other literary techniques, which I am ignoring here, such as syntactic parallelism, also serve to make the text a cohesive unit. Again, it is difficult to single out any one of these devices as the main mechanism for achieving cohesiveness.

This book, being about work, is, by its very nature, about violence - to the spirit as well as to the body. It is about ulcers as well as accidents, about shouting matches as well as kicking the dog around. It is, above all (or beneath all), about daily humiliations. To survive the day is triumph enough for the walking wounded among the great many of us.

(p. xiii)

This phenomenon manifests itself as links between the potential focus lists of consecutive propositions in discourse. Consider the focus records for the first two sentences of the *Working* paragraph:

1. CF = this book
   PFL = violence
         {spirit; body}
         being about work
         is about

2. CF = this book
   PFL = {ulcers; accidents,
         shouting matches; fist fights,
         nervous breakdowns; kicking the dog around}
         is about

In this example the first item of the potential focus list (PFL) of sentence (2) (a list) provides instances of violence and is thus related to the first item in sentence (1)'s PFL. The elements of the list also exemplify the spiritual/physical dichotomy of violence and are thus related to the second item in sentence (1)'s PFL. Note furthermore that the PFL links are implicit links; ulcers and accidents are sub-types of violence, spiritual and physical. Although the current focus of a sentence is often a definite reference (pronominal or otherwise) to a previously mentioned item, definite reference across potential focus lists rarely occurs.

These potential focus links result in a layering of foci that corresponds to the speaker's global focus. More than one thing is focused on at a time (global focus) and one of them is distinguished as immediate focus. In the generation process, this phenomenon is accounted for by further constraining the choice of what to talk about next to the proposition with the greatest

number of links to the previous potential focus list. This constraint ensures
that the text will maintain the global focus of the speaker when possible. If
application of the guidelines discussed above does not constrain the
possibilities to a single proposition, links between potential focus lists are
examined to select the single proposition with the most links to the previous
discourse (i.e., that proposition containing the greatest number of links to
elements already mentioned). When this constraint is included, the ordering of
focus maintaining and shifting rules becomes:

1. shift focus to member of previous PFL
   CF (new sentence) ξ PFL (last sentence)

2. maintain focus
   CF (new sentence) = CF (last sentence)

3. return to topic of previous discussion
   CF (new sentence) ξ focus-stack

4. select proposition with greatest number of implicit
   links to previous potential focus list
   PFL (new sentence) related-to PFL (last sentence)

3.2.6. A focus algorithm for generation

Before describing exactly how these guidelines for maintaining and
shifting focus are incorporated into an algorithm that can determine what to
say next, the assignment of focus and potential focus list to a proposition
must be discussed. In TEXT, the assignment of focus involves a process of
give and take between what the focus could be and what the guidelines
about focus maintenance claim as preference. Initially, a default focus is
assigned to a proposition. This focus can be overridden, however, if another
item within the proposition allows for the application of one of the higher
rules on the ordered list of guidelines.

3.2.7. Selecting a default focus

Selecting a default focus is a simple look-up procedure. A single
argument of each predicate is singled out as the one most likely to be
focused on. This information is stored in a table and the entry for the given
predicate accessed when needed. Use of a default focus implies that a
predicating act has a marked and unmarked syntax associated with it, the
unmarked dictated by the default focus. This does not seem unlikely.
Consider the attributive predicate, which is exemplified in sentences (1) and
(2) below. In its usual use, it attributes features to an entity or event. The
unmarked use assumes an entity has been focused on: the entity is being

talked about and some of its features are being described (see Sentence (1) below). The opposite case, of associating talked-about features with a different entity, is less usual (see Sentence (2) below).

1. The chimpanzee has fine control over finger use.
2. Fine control over finger use is also common to the chimpanzee.

Use of a default focus also assumes that a particular class of words will be used to verbalize the predicate: those that allow the default focus to appear in surface subject position. For the attributive predicate, the default focus would allow verbs such as "have" and "possess" as a translation, both of which are possible in Sentence 1, but not "is common to" or "belongs", which are possible in Sentence 2. Use of a default focus here is different than Sidner's default focus. She associates the default focus with the theme of verb rather than surface subject, but she uses default focus to predict what the focus of the next sentence might be, while I use it to establish the focus of the current sentence.

3.2.8. Overriding the default focus

The default focus of a proposition is overridden if taking a different predicate argument as focus will allow the application of a more preferable guideline for focus movement. For example, if the default focus of a proposition is the same as the current focus of the last proposition, guideline (2) would apply (CF (new sentence) = CF (last sentence)). If, however, another predicate argument of the proposition is a member of the previous proposition's potential focus list, that argument is selected as the proposition's focus, since it allows for the application of guideline (1) (CF (new sentence) ξ PFL (last sentence)). The assignment of focus to propositions is made when a proposition is selected which ties in most closely with the preceding discourse according to the focus constraint guidelines.

Although the default focus can be overridden, it is useful since it provides some indication of the usual way of presenting information. It is needed to determine which argument to focus on in discourse initial propositions where no information exists to override it. In addition, since it indicates the most likely case, it can result in savings in processing time within each guideline application. If, for example, one proposition of a set of possible next propositions has an argument that is a member of the previous potential focus list, it will be selected by application of guideline (1). If that argument is the proposition's default focus, the proposition will be selected after the default focus of each proposition is checked for membership in the previous potential focus list, requiring one test per proposition. If default focus is not represented, the proposition will only be selected after each argument of each proposition is checked for membership in the previous potential focus list, requiring many tests per proposition.

Moreover, if following a single guideline of the focus constraints would allow more than one proposition argument to qualify for focus, the default focus indicates which of these to use. If, for instance, a proposition has several arguments which occur in the previous potential focus list, the default focus is selected as the argument to be focused on.

3.2.9. The focus algorithm

The algorithm for using focus constraints in the selection of propositions is given below. This algorithm does not specify exactly how a schema is selected or filled and, as such, is not a complete algorithm for the strategic component (see Chapter Two for details on these processes).

I. Select schema

II. Initialization of focus records
GF (global focus) = argument of goal
(e.g., for (definition AIRCRAFT-CARRIER),
GF = AIRCRAFT-CARRIER
for (difference OCEAN-ESCORT CRUISER),
GF = {OCEAN-ESCORT CRUISER} (the set))
CF (current focus) = GF
PFL (potential focus list) = nil

III. For each entry in schema:

1. Select all propositions in relevant knowledge pool that match the predicate (see Appendix D for a description of predicate semantics)

   If schema allows for a choice of predicates, select all possible propositions for each predicate

2. If options exist (i.e., more than one proposition matched), use immediate focus constraints:
   a. Select proposition(s) with default-focus ξ PFL.
      Set proposition-focus = default-focus
   b. If none exist, select proposition(s) having some other argument-entry ξ PFL.
      Set proposition-focus = other argument-entry
   c. If none exist, select proposition(s) with default-focus = CF.
      Set proposition-focus = CF
   d. If none exist, select proposition(s) having some other argument-entry = CF.
      Set proposition-focus = other argument entry

    e. If none exist, select proposition(s) with default-focus ξ focus-stack.
       Set proposition-focus = default-focus
    f. If none exist, select proposition(s) with other argument-entry ξ focus-stack.
       Set proposition-focus = other argument entry
    g. If none exist, set proposition-focus of each
       with proposition = default-focus

3. If options exist (i.e., more than one proposition remains after application of immediate focus constraints), use potential focus list links
    a. Select that proposition with greatest number of links to PFL

4. Record predicate, proposition pair
    a. Add to message
       i. Add CF, PFL, focus-stack for last proposition to message
       ii. Add new proposition to message
    b. Update focus records
       i. If proposition-focus ξ focus-stack.
       Pop focus-stack.
       CF = proposition-focus.
       ii. If proposition-focus $\sim=$ CF.
       Stack CF on focus-stack.
       CF = proposition-focus.
       iii. Else no change to CF and focus-stack.
       iv. Set PFL:
          1. member 1 = default-theme[24] of proposition if proposition-focus $\sim=$ default-theme.
          Else = default-focus
          2. last-member = predicate (corresponding to sentence verb)
          3. Other PFL members = arbitrary listing of other predicate argument in proposition

Note that if no suitable focus for the next proposition is found (step 2g), the proposition's default focus is used and the proposition added to the message.

---

[24]As is the case for focus, a table of proposition arguments that function as unmarked theme (that item that is most likely of all introduced items to be focused on next) is maintained. Note that theme is a vaguely defined concept (see, for example, Sidner 79) and for that reason, is minimally used.

This type of conversational move is the equivalent of a total shift in focus. Since the strategic component maintains a focus record, the tactical component could use this information to select an appropriate syntactic cue to signal this kind of abrupt shift.

Note also that the potential focus list of each proposition is only partially ordered. Its first member is the default theme and its last member is the predicate, or what will eventually be the verb of the sentence. Other entries are set in arbitrary order.

The focus algorithm makes a breadth-first search of all possible next propositions. In other words, each possible proposition is retrieved and then the focus constraints are applied. Another approach would be a depth-first search of the possibilities, retrieving only propositions that have an argument which meets the first focus preference and if that fails, retrieving propositions which meet the second focus preference, etc. To determine which propositions meet a focus preference, however, it is necessary to retrieve all propositions and examine their arguments, making the depth-first search a more expensive alternative.

3.2.10. Use of focus sets

Sidner notes that a discourse need not always focus on a single central concept. A speaker may decide to talk about several concepts at once and yet the resulting discourse is still coherent. She terms this type of phenomenon "co-present foci". She gives the following discourse as an example of the use of co-present foci:

1. I have 2 dogs.
2. The one is a poodle;
3. the other is a cocker spaniel.
4. The poodle has some weird habits.
5. He eats plastic flowers and likes to sleep in a paper bag.
6. It's a real problem keeping him away from the flowers.
7. My cocker is pretty normal,
8. and he's a good watchdog.
9. I like having them as pets.

In this discourse, a set of two elements is introduced as focus in sentence (1). Each element of the set is specified in (2) and (3) by "the one .... the other" construction (Sidner, in fact, relies heavily on this type of construction to identify the use of co-present foci). The discourse then proceeds to focus on each element of the set in turn.

Sidner notes that the use of co-present foci in discourse is a highly regulated phenomenon. For this reason, focusing on more than one central concept does not result in an incoherent discourse. She says:

Co-present foci reflect a special kind of structure that occurs in discourse. Several elements are introduced. When continuing discussion of one of the elements extends the discourse, the focus moves to that element. When that discussion is complete, the focus cannot simply move onto any other thing the speaker wants to mention. The discussion should return to the other elements, and those elements discussed. However, the discussion of one element for an extended part of the discourse may involve introduction and consideration of other elements. The real constraint in the foregoing analysis is that discussion should eventually *return* to the other elements via co-present foci. When it does not, the hearer is left to wonder why co-presence was used in the first place.

(Sidner 79), p. 195.

Although Sidner describes the restrictions on how co-present foci can occur, she does not describe the reasons for its use or for the focus moves to elements of the focused set. Again, for interpretation of discourse, the use of co-present foci is given by the incoming discourse, and there is no need to decide when its use is appropriate. Generation of discourse, however, requires that these kinds of decisions be made.

Decisions to use co-present foci rest in part on the rhetorical techniques used in discourse and thus the discourse structure (e.g., the decision to define an object in terms of its sub-classes). They also depend on the discourse goal (e.g., the decision to answer a question about the difference between two objects). In the first case, definition of a concept in terms of its sub-classes suggests the use of the constituency schema, a particular structure for discourse. Use of the constituency schema implies focusing on the questioned object, followed by the introduction of its sub-classes and extended discussion of each of these in turn. In this case, the structure of the discourse forces the use of co-present foci and the changes in focus to set members. In the second case, the discourse purpose is to provide a description of the differences between the two objects. Associated with this discourse purpose are the rhetorical techniques encoded in the compare and contrast schema. Although the exact structure dictated by this schema varies depending on the type of information available in the relevant knowledge pool (see Section 2.3), its basic outline is a discussion of the similarities between the two objects, followed by a discussion of their differences. Thus, the discourse will first center on the two objects and their common attributes; focus will then switch to the questioned objects in turn. Again, the structure of the discourse forces the use of co-present foci and the changes in focus to set members.

In the TEXT system, schemata control the introduction of focus sets and changes in focus to their elements. Arc actions on the schemata (see Section 4.4 for a discussion of the ATN nature of schemata) can force selection of a set as focus and dictate moves to their elements. The focus algorithm continues as usual, with the exception that it allows decisions involving that focus set to override its own. Once discussion involving the focus set is over, the focus algorithm proceeds normally.

3.3. Focus and syntactic structures

3.3.1. Linguistic background

Phenomena similar to what is called "immediate focus" have been studied by a number of linguists. Terminology and definitions for these vary widely; some of the names which have emerged include topic/comment, presupposition and focus, theme/rheme, and given/new. It should be noted that a major difference between these concepts and focus, as discussed in this chapter, is that focusing describes an active process on the part of speaker and listener. The item in focus is that item on which the speaker is currently centering his attention. These linguistic concepts describe a distinction between functional roles elements play in a sentence. A brief description of each of these linguistic concepts follows.

Topic/comment articulation is often used to describe the distinction between what the speaker is talking about (topic) and what he has to say about that topic (comment). Definitions of topic/comment for a sentence usually do not depend upon previous context, although some linguists (in particular, Sgall, Hajicova and Benesova 73) provide different definitions of the distinction for sentences that contain a link to previous discourse and for those that do not. Others who have discussed topic/comment articulation include Lyons (68) and Reinhart (81).

Presupposition has been used to describe information which a sentence structure indicates is assumed as true by the speaker. Presupposition has a very precise definition for formulations which consider meaning the equivalent of truth and has been analyzed by many (e.g., Weischedel 75; Keenan 71). It refers to all that must hold in order for a sentence to be true.

Focus, as defined by linguistic precedents, labels information in the sentence which carries the import of the message. Note that this term does not refer to the same concept as used in this work. Linguistic focus refers to the focus of the *sentence*, while AI researchers use focus to refer to the focus of the *speaker*. The linguistic focus of a sentence is usually determined by the position where phonological stress occurs (see Chomsky 71; Quirk and Greenbaum 73; Halliday 67).

The given/new distinction identifies information that is assumed by the speaker to be derivable from context (given) -- where context may mean either the preceding discourse or shared world knowledge -- and information that cannot be (new). The given/new distinction has been discussed by Halliday (67), Prince (79), and Chafe (76).

Theme/rheme is a distinction used in work by the Prague School of linguists (see Firbas 66; Firbas 74). They postulate that a sentence is divided into a theme -- elements providing common ground for the conversants -- and a rheme -- elements which function in conveying the information to be imparted. In sentences containing elements that are contextually dependent, the contextually dependent elements always function as theme. Thus, the Prague School version is close to the given/new distinction with the exception that a sentence always contains a theme, while it need not always contain given information. Halliday also discusses theme (Halliday 67), but he defines theme as that which the speaker is talking about now, as opposed to given, that which the speaker *was* talking about. Thus, his notion of theme is closer to the concept of topic/comment articulation. Furthermore, Halliday always ascribes the term theme to the element occurring first in the sentence.

Focus of attention is like topic (and Halliday's theme) in that it specifies what the speaker is focusing on (i.e., talking about) now. But it is also like given information in that immediate focus is linked to something that has been mentioned in the previous utterance and thus is already present in the reader's consciousness. It combines these two concepts. The potential focus list is akin to new information in that it has not previously been referred to and it specifies the items to which focus of attention is likely to shift.

These paragraphs provide only a brief overview of these various distinctions. Fuller discussions are provided in (Prince 79) and (Chafe 76) which also give overviews of the conflicting descriptions and definitions of these concepts. What is important to this work is that each of these concepts, at one time or another, has been associated with the selection of various syntactic structures. For example, it has been suggested that focus, new information, and rheme usually occur toward the end of a sentence (e.g., Halliday 67; Lyons 68; Sgall et al. 73; Firbas 74). In order to place this information in its proper position in the sentence, structures other than the unmarked active sentence may be required (for example, the passive). Structures such as *it-extraposition, there-insertion, left-dislocation*, and *topicalization*[25] have been shown to function in the introduction of new information into discourse (Sidner 79; Prince 79), often with the assumption

---

[25]Some examples of these constructions are:

1. It was Sam who left the door open. (it-extraposition)
2. There are 3 blocks on the table. (there-insertion)
3. Sam, I like him. (left-dislocation)
4. Sam I like. (topicalization)

that it will be talked about for a period of time. Pronominalization is another linguistic device associated with these distinctions (see Akmajian 73; Sidner 79). In the following sections, I describe how these observations have been implemented in the TEXT system.

3.3.2. Passing focus information to the tactical component

Since focus information has been used to constrain the selection of propositions, a record containing each proposition's focus and its potential focus list is available for the tactical component to use when determining the specific syntactic structures and linguistic devices that should be used in the answer. The tactical component can examine this information to determine how a proposition is related to previous discourse: whether the focus has shifted to a new topic, whether a return to a previous topic was made, or whether, in extreme cases, a total shift in topic has been made and the proposition is totally unrelated to what came before. Some of the uses that can be made of this information and the linguistic effects that can be achieved are described in this section.

Pronominalization is a linguistic device that has long been linked with concepts such as focus of attention (Akmajian 73; Sidner 79; McDonald 80). Sidner uses it to aid in determining focus. If an entity remains in focus over a sequence of sentences, references to it can be pronominalized.[26] The following two sentences illustrate this:

John was late coming home.
He got caught in a traffic jam.

In the TEXT system, focus information is used in some limited situations to test whether pronominalization can be used. Part of an answer where pronominalization was selected is shown in (A) below. In the first sentence of the answer, the ship is being focused on and reference to it in the following sentence can therefore be pronominalized. Note that definite reference such as "the ship" would also be appropriate, but in the TEXT system, pronominalization is selected wherever it is determined possible.

---

[26]McDonald shows that some additional tests for pronominalization must be made before a pronoun can be used. See (McDonald 80) for a discussion of subsequent reference.

A)   (definition SHIP)
A ship is a water-going vehicle that travels on the surface.   *Its*
surface-going capabilities are provided by the DB attributes
DISPLACEMENT and DRAFT. ...

Focus information has also been shown to affect the use of different
syntactic structures, as discussed in Section 3.3.1. Depending upon which
constituent of the sentence is in focus, the passive construction might be
selected over the active construction.   There-insertion and it-extraposition can
be used to introduce items as the focus of continued discussion.

These constructions provide a mechanism for reordering the constituents
of a sentence based on thematic information.   The passive construction is
used when the logical subject of the sentence is not in focus.   Passivizing the
sentence moves the focused constituent (logical object or beneficiary) to the
surface subject position, thus allowing the focused information to appear as
sentential subject.   Passivization does not apply when the logical subject of
the sentence is focused.   Sentences with the verb "to be" cannot be
passivized.   In such cases, there-insertion must be used to achieve thematic
reordering of constituents.

Currently, in the TEXT system, focus information is used to discriminate
between the use of passive and active constructions.   Relations in the ONR
database used for TEXT are binary and can be described from the point of
view of either entity.   In the ONR database, weapons are associated through
the relation "carry" with different vehicles.   When answering a question
about a missile, a weapon, the passive construction is used to describe the
relation that holds between the missile and various vehicles, since the missile
is in focus.   When answering a question about the ECHO II, a type of
submarine, the active construction is used in order to attribute information to
the "ECHO II" and not to the weapons.   These examples are shown in (B)
and (C) below.

B)   (differense MISSILE TORPEDOE)
The missile's target location is indicated by the DB attribute
DESCRIPTION and its flight capabilities are provided by the DB
attribute ALTITUDE.   Other DB attributes of the missile include
PROBABILITY OF KILL, SPEED, ALTITUDE, LETHAL RADIUS
& UNITS and TIME TO TARGET & UNITS.   *Missiles are carried*
by water-going vehicles and aircraft. ...

C) (information ECHO-II-SUBMARINE)
All Echo IIs in the ONR database have REMARKS of 0, FUEL
TYPE of NUCL, IRCS of 0, MAXIMUM OPERATING DEPTH of
700 and NORMAL OPERATING DEPTH of 100. There are no
sub-classes of Echo II in the ONR database. *Echo IIs carry 16*
torpedoes, between 16 and 99 missiles and 0 guns. ...

The use of there-insertion by the TEXT system is shown below in (D) as
part of the answer generated to the question "What is a guided projectile?".
Although the construction is associated with the constituency predicate in the
constituency schema (i.e., a decision to use this construction is not based on
a test of focus information), the constituency schema is used to introduce a
set as the focus and then forces a shift in focus to each of the set members.
  Since the constituency schema is theoretically tied to a shift in focus to a
set of objects (see Section 3.2.10), it can similarly be used to control the
choice of a surface structure to mark this shift for the reader. Use of there-
insertion in this situation is one way to introduce the set of sub-classes as
focus into the discourse.

D) (definition GUIDED)
A guided projectile is a projectile that is self-propelled. *There are 2*
types of guided projectiles in the ONR database: torpedoes and
missiles. The missile has a target location in the air or on the
earth's surface. The torpedo has an underwater target location. ...

3.4. Future work

The TEXT system can be viewed as an implementation of the linguistic
relation between focus of attention and ordering of sentence constituents for
the selection of three specific syntactic constructions (active, passive and
there-insertion) as well as for the selection of pronominalization. Other
syntactic constructs which have been shown to be related to the given/new
distinction include it-extraposition, topicalization, and left-dislocation.
Developing the means for selecting these constructions on the basis of the
given/new distinction would be a significant next step in language generation.
  Several other linguistic effects, which were neither implemented in the
TEXT system nor related previously to these distinctions, can be achieved
through the use of focus information. In an examination of texts and
transcripts (see Chapter 2 for a discussion of this analysis), I found that
parallel sentence structure was often used when focus remained the same
from one sentence to the next. Parallel structure can be used to increase the

cohesiveness of the text through syntactic devices when the semantic cohesiveness is not as rich. The first paragraph of the Introduction to *Working* (Terkel 72) illustrates the use of parallel sentence structure for consecutive sentences with the same focus (also see (Hobbs 78) on parallel structure):

> This book ... is about violence - to the spirit as well as to the body. It is about ulcers, as well as accidents, ...

When focus shifts in a proposition to an item just introduced into conversation in the last proposition, subordinate sentence structure can be used to combine the two propositions into a single complex sentence. A sample use of subordinate sentence structure for this purpose is shown below. In the main sentence, "the happy few" are introduced as focus using there-insertion. In the subordinate sentence, focus is shifted to elements of the happy few (the Indiana stonemason and the Chicago piano tuner).

> There are, of course, the happy few who find a savor in their daily job: the Indiana stonemason, who looks upon his work and sees that it is good; the Chicago piano tuner, who seeks and finds the sound that delights; ...

Focus information can also signal the use of textual connectives or semantic markers. When there are no referential links from one sentence to the next (i.e., a proposition was selected which did not meet the legal criteria specified by Sidner), a textual connective can be used to provide the needed link from one sentence to the next.

3.5. Conclusions

In the TEXT system, focus of attention has been used to constrain the choice of what to say next. The choices are constrained in two ways: 1) by global focus and 2) by immediate focus. When deciding what to say next, the system need only consider information that is relevant to the question currently being asked, as opposed to all information in the knowledge base. This information is contained in the "relevant knowledge pool" and determines the system's global focus. After every generated utterance, the system is further limited by a set of immediate focus constraints on what it can say next.

The specification of legal focus moves extends work on immediate focus for interpretation (Sidner 79) to the generation process. In particular, guidelines for ordered application of these moves were developed for those situations where the constraints did not limit the set of choices to a single possibility. The use of focusing was also extended to allow for strands of semantic connectivity to occur at more than one level of the discourse. Using global and immediate focus proves to provide a computationally tractable approach to the problem of deciding what to say next. Furthermore, it guarantees the production of a semantically cohesive text.

Since focus information was used in producing the text message, it is available for the tactical component to use in making decisions about relatively sophisticated linguistic devices. In the TEXT system, tests for pronominalization and varying syntactic structures (active, passive, and there-insertion) on the basis of focus information have been implemented. Other linguistic devices, such as parallel sentence structure, subordinate sentence structure, and semantic markers were shown to be related to focusing, but were not actually implemented in the TEXT tactical component.

4
TEXT system implementation

A portion of an Office of Naval Research (ONR) database was used to test the TEXT system. The portion used contains information about military vehicles and weapons. The ONR database was selected for TEXT in part because of its availability (it had been in use previously in a research project jointly with the Wharton School of the University of Pennsylvania) and in part because of its complex structure. Even using only a portion of the database provided a domain complex enough to allow for an interesting set of questions and answers.

As discussed in Chapter One, TEXT accepts three kinds of questions as input. These are:

- What is a <e>?
- What do you know about <e>?
- What is the difference between <e1> and <e2>?

where <e>, <e1>, and <e2> represent any entity in the database. Since the TEXT system does not include a facility for interpreting English questions, the user must phrase his questions in the functional notation shown below which corresponds to the three classes of questions.

- (definition <e>))
- (information <e>)
- (differense <e1> <e2>)[27]

Note that the system only handles questions about objects in the database. Although the system can include information about relations when relevant to a question about a particular object, it can not answer questions about relations themselves.

---

[27] The function "differense" is spelled with an "s" because of the existence of the Lisp function "difference".

4.1. System components

The TEXT system consists of six major components: a schema selector, a relevant knowledge selector, the schema filler, the focusing mechanism, a dictionary interface, and a tactical component. A brief outline of the flow of control and interaction between these components is given below before going into more detail on the implementation of each component. It will be helpful to refer to Figure 4-1 during this discussion.

The strategic component consists of processes that handle the construction of the relevant knowledge pool, selection of an appropriate schema for the answer, filling of the schema with propositions from the relevant knowledge pool, and monitoring of schema filling through the use of focus constraints. On receiving a question (arrow 1, Figure 4-1), the TEXT system selects a set of possible schemata to use for the answer. A digression is then taken from the schema selector to the relevant knowledge selector (arrow 2). At this point, semantic processes construct the relevant knowledge pool on the basis of the input question. A characterization of the information available in this pool is then used to select a single schema from the set of schemata (arrow 3). Control passes to the schema filler (arrow 4) where predicate semantics are used to select propositions from the relevant knowledge pool which match the predicates in the schema. The focusing mechanism monitors the matching process (arrow 5). Where there are alternative predicates in the schema or where a predicate matches more than one proposition in the knowledge pool, the focusing mechanism selects the most appropriate proposition for the answer.

The output of the strategic component is passed to a dictionary interface between the strategic and tactical component (arrow 7). The dictionary translates each proposition in the message into a deep structure representation of the sentence to be generated. This involves translating the predicate into the sentence verb and mapping the instantiated predicate arguments into the case roles of the verb. This process entails the selection of lexical items for the instantiated arguments.

Dictionary output is fed to the tactical component (arrow 8), which uses a functional grammar to translate the message into English. It is at this point that the actual surface structure of the answer is determined.

The remainder of this chapter describes the implementation methods used for the TEXT system components in some detail. Since the discussion of many of the system components depends on the knowledge representation, its contents and structure are described in detail (Section 4.2) before setting out the processing components. Following this, Section 4.3 describes how relevant knowledge is selected, 4.4 describes the implementation of the schemata, 4.5 the tactical component, and 4.6 the dictionary interface. The focusing mechanism is not discussed in any more detail here (see Chapter Three). The chapter concludes with a discussion of the practical aspects of the system and what could be done to improve those aspects. Examples of TEXT system output are provided in Appendix A.

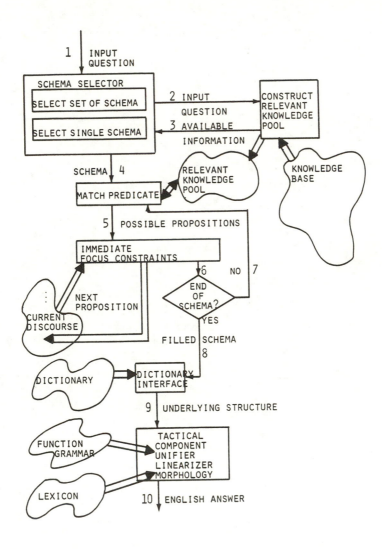

Figure 4-1:   System Components and Flow of Control

4.2. Knowledge representation

Answering questions about the structure of the database requires access to a high level description of the classes of objects in the database and the relationships between the classes. Knowledge representation is an important aspect of a generation system. The information that is, and can be, represented in the knowledge base limits the overall expressive power of the generation system. Unless the generation system includes a powerful inferencing mechanism, information that is not contained in the knowledge base cannot be expressed.

In order to develop a practical system compatible with existing database systems, a decision was made to do very little development of new representation features. Instead, features used in data models of previous natural language database systems were selected for use in the TEXT system knowledge base. By restricting the representation to include features found in other database models, questions about how useful such a representation is for generation can be answered. In addition, it is clear how the generation system can be used as a module for other database systems.

The main features of the TEXT knowledge base are entities, attributes, and relationships (Chen 76). A generalization hierarchy on entities (Smith and Smith 77; Hendrix 79) was developed and characteristic features of each sub-type in the hierarchy were represented, indicating the basis for the splits in the hierarchy. A topic hierarchy on attributes (Schubert, Goebel and Cercone 79) was also developed. While the main portion of the knowledge base was hand encoded, sub-types of entities which exist as physical records in the database were generated automatically and added to the generalization hierarchy before the knowledge base was used in order to avoid extensive inferencing (McCoy 82).

Since TEXT does not include an extensive inferencing facility, it is basically limited in content to describing information that is part of the knowledge base. In evaluating its generated text, it is important to take into account the information it has to start with. The following sections delineate the extent of the TEXT knowledge base.

4.2.1. Representation overview

The knowledge base used for the TEXT system consists of the following data types:

1. **Entities:**
   A generic class consisting of instances which occur in the actual database. Entities have both generalizations and sub-types, which are also entities.

Relations:
Database relations between entities in the hierarchy. These include both instances (relations that actually occur in the database) and generics (representing features common to a set of instances).

2. **Database attributes:**
Either attributes for which values exist in the database or generalizations of those attributes in the topic hierarchy. Attributes are associated with both entities and relations.

3. **Distinguishing descriptive attributes (DDA), names and values:**
These provide characteristic descriptive information on the distinguishing features of an entity sub-type. They are attached at each split in the generalization hierarchy. This is the one piece of information, along with supporting database attributes, that is not normally present in a database model.

4. **Based database attributes:**
Uniquely identifying attribute-value pairs which indicate the basis for a breakdown on entities. These are used in place of distinguishing descriptive attributes whenever such unique values exist.

5. **Supporting database attributes:**
A subset of database attributes which support the choice of a distinguishing descriptive attribute.

These data-types provide the required information about what is represented in the actual database as well as descriptive information linking that information to real-world concepts. The knowledge base thus provides a meta-level description of the database. While this brief description of the data-types is sufficient for understanding later chapters on system implementation, a more detailed definition of the form and content of each of these data types is given in later sections for those interested.

The knowledge base is implemented by maintaining a set of nodes which correspond to entities. Each node has a name (entity name) and a set of links which point to associated node information. Each link is labeled by the data type of the associated information, with the exception of links in the generalization hierarchy. These links are either labeled as "is-a" links or "type-of" links (the hierarchy is double-threaded: "is-a" points to a superordinate of an entity and "type-of" points to a sub-type). A pictorial representation of a portion of the knowledge base used in TEXT (Figure 4-2) shows entities as circles and relations as diamonds. Link names can be any of the following: is-a, type-of, DDA-name, DDA-value, db-attr, have, some-type-of, based-db, <role-name> (e.g., carrier), or mutual-exclusion.

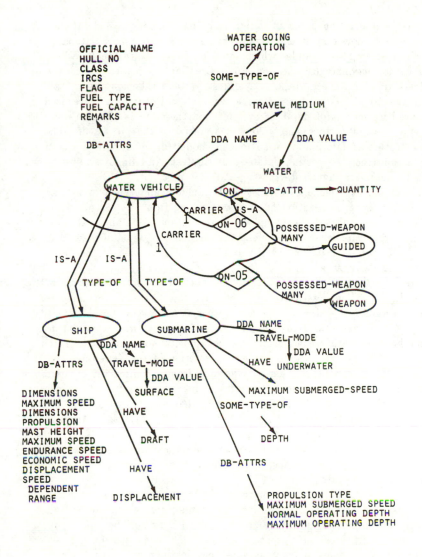

Figure 4-2: Knowledge Base Sample

4.2.2. Portability

A frequent question asked of designers of natural language database systems regards how easy it is to transfer the system to a new database. In the TEXT system, the modules which must be changed are the knowledge base and the dictionary (see Section 4.6). Creating a knowledge base for a new domain is not an easy task. Several steps were taken, however, to simplify the process. The first of these was to use features that are used in many database models of database systems and therefore familiar to database managers. Secondly, steps were taken to systematize the process of adding the new feature of information used in this model (distinguishing descriptive attributes and their supporting database attributes). And finally, a system was written to automatically create sub-types of database entity classes.

Part of the knowledge base must be formulated and typed in by hand. This includes the generalization hierarchy (working from the set of entities taken from the database schema upward), association of database attributes with the appropriate level in the hierarchy, association of database relations with the appropriate level in the hierarchy, and the creation of the distinguishing descriptive attributes (both name and value) and their supporting database attributes. Creation of both the generalization hierarchy and the distinguishing descriptive attributes is subjective to a certain extent. Names and values of distinguishing descriptive attributes for database entity classes and their generalizations should be developed by first examining the different kinds of database attributes associated with nodes in the hierarchy. This information can be used to guide the selection of the dimension across which sub-classes of an entity vary. Choosing from a limited set of attribute names (standard functional terms, or cases of higher level attribute names or values) aids this process. Steps for specifying the supporting database attributes are given in Section 4.2.10. Note that only database attributes that support the distinguishing descriptive attribute are chosen. Thus, although all vehicles have the database attribute REMARKS, it does not indicate that its function is transportation and it is therefore not used as a supporting database attribute.

Running McCoy's system to automatically generate entity sub-types on a new database requires: 1) completion of the hand-generated hierarchy and associated information, 2) specification of a set of very specific axioms, if desired, and 3) specification of specific axioms. The very specific axioms are tables of sub-type names and unique sub-type identifier value (this is a value or partial field of a database attribute). They allow the user to specify apriori breakdowns. This step can be omitted if the user has no such breakdowns in mind. The specific axioms are a list of attributes considered important for the particular domain. The system attempts to form breakdowns based on the attributes specified. The system also generates all associated information for each sub-type specified in the breakdown. Both the very specific and specific axioms can be altered and the system rerun until an acceptable sub-typing is obtained.

4.2.3. Summary

The knowledge base used in the TEXT system includes features standard to many database models. It draws primarily on work done by Chen (76) and the Smiths (77) in data modeling. The reason for doing this was twofold: 1) the emphasis in this work was on generation of language and not on knowledge representation, and 2) to see how far generation could be pushed when using a relatively standard data model. Using a standard data model also makes the TEXT system more practical for actual use in a database system.

Since extended inferencing is not practical in the generation system, it was decided that a simple data model, such as the Chen entity-relationship model, does not contain sufficient information for the task at hand. Such models represent only the types of values that are stored in the database for a particular entity. Features such as the generalization hierarchy and the topic hierarchy were adopted in order to encode additional knowledge about the database concepts into the knowledge base. Distinguishing descriptive attributes, which provide real-world characteristics about sub-class distinctions, and sub-typing of entities based on world-knowledge axioms (McCoy 82) were also added to the knowledge base for this reason.

Many issues in knowledge representation were not addressed by this work and are left for future research. The content of the knowledge base clearly limits the semantic power of any generation system. The formalism chosen for the representation also, although less clearly, limits its expressive power. Although form can always be manipulated to produce the specific form necessary for the task at hand, there are situations where the manipulations required to do so are prohibitively expensive. This kind of situation is illustrated by the use of a system to automatically enhance the generalization hierarchy (McCoy 82) before the generation system is used. Although the information produced by the system could be deduced only when needed, the time required to do so makes that option impractical. Researchers in artificial intelligence have been experimenting with the effectiveness of various formalisms including KL-ONE (Brachman 79), semantic networks (Hendrix 79), and first-order predicate calculus based formalisms (e.g., Schubert et al. 79; Moore 81). Further development of research on issues of both content and formalism are extremely important to work done in natural language generation.

The remaining sections of this chapter on knowledge representation define each of the data-types of the knowledge base in some detail. These sections will be of interest to those considering a meta-level generation facility for their own database and to those interested in implementation details of the knowledge base. Those who are not interested in the fine details of the representation can skip the following sections.

4.2.4. The entity-relationship model

The knowledge representation used in the TEXT system is based on the Chen entity-relationship model (Chen 76). Such a model is standard in database modeling and is the minimum required to represent the contents of the database. This model consists of entities, relations between entities, and attributes of entities. An entity represents a class of instances in the database (each instance is composed of a list of values). In other words, an entity is an object-type occurring in the database. In this work, a class of objects in the database is termed an *entity* and an object in the database an *instance*.

Each entity has a set of attributes associated with it. An attribute is a function (given a name) from an entity into a value set. Restrictions on that value set are noted. The attribute LENGTH, for example, may map from the entity SHIP into the set of non-negative integers less than 1000. An instance is actually a tuple of values corresponding to the attributes associated with the entity. Each entity has a *primary key* which is one or more attributes whose value uniquely identifies an instance in the database.

Definition 4.2.1
Entity: A class of instances in the database with common database attributes and relations.

Definition 4.2.2
Attribute: A function from an entity into a restricted value set.

Definition 4.2.3
Primary key: One or more attributes whose value uniquely identifies an instance of an entity in the database.

Relations occur between two or more entities. In the database used for the TEXT system, only binary relations occurred. The cardinality of the relation (whether it is one-to-one, one-to-many, many-to-one, or many-to-many) is indicated as well as the roles the entities play in the relation. This information is particularly useful for relations between more than two entities. Although the ONR database only contains binary relations, a change in database would not require a change in knowledge representation formalism. Relations also may have attributes associated with them. The SHIP, for example, *CARRIES* GUIDED PROJECTILES. The attribute QUANTITY indicates how many GUIDED PROJECTILES the SHIP carries. The CARRY relation is one-to-many, from SHIPs to GUIDED PROJECTILEs; the SHIP is the carrier and the GUIDED PROJECTILE is the possessed weapon.

Definition 4.2.4
Relation: A named tuple of entities with the following features:

- A named role is assigned to each entity in the tuple.

- A cardinality (either *one* or *many*) is assigned to each entity in the tuple. Cardinality specifies the number of instances of an entity which may participate in the given relation.

- The tuple possesses attributes.

A simple example of the Chen entity-relationship model is shown in Figure 4-3. A circle represents an entity and a diamond represents a relation. Lines from relations to entities are labeled by the role the entity plays and its cardinality in the relation. Attributes are illustrated by labeled arrows into value sets (hatched circles). In the example, two entities, SHIP and AIRCRAFT, are shown to be related through the CARRY relation. The SHIP is the carrier and the AIRCRAFT is the carried object. A single SHIP may carry more than one AIRCRAFT. A SHIP is shown to have four attributes: OFFICIAL NAME, MAXIMUM SPEED, DISPLACEMENT, and LENGTH; and AIRCRAFT has three: NAME, ALTITUDE, and FUEL TYPE. (Both entities actually have more attributes in the ONR database. These were not shown for reasons of clarity.)

Note that the Chen entity-relationship model portrays a limited view of the data and does not contain a rich enough description for the type of generation required here. For example, ships can only be described in terms of types of values contained in the database, although other features of the ship may be important in describing it to a user.

4.2.5. Use of generalization

Features that have been used in a number of database models for natural language database systems, but are not present in the Chen entity-relationship model, were also adopted for use in the TEXT system. One of these is the concept of generalization (Smith and Smith 77), a technique in modeling also used in semantic networks (Hendrix 79). A generalization hierarchy is an important feature for generation both because it allows the generation system to compare entities via their relationship in the hierarchy and because it allows the system to make connections between real-world

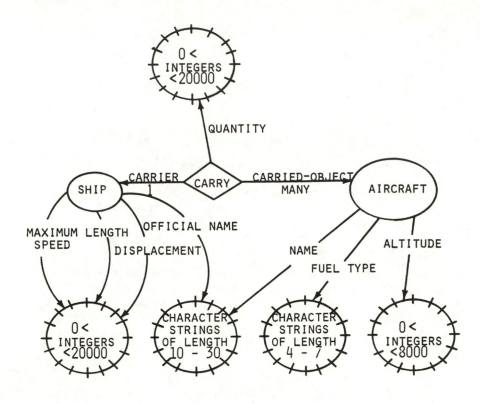

Figure 4-3: The Entity-Relationship Model

concepts which may not actually be referred to in the database (i.e., the generalizations) and entities which occur in the database. It also allows the system to refer concisely to groups of entities which have common features. In the TEXT system, a generalization hierarchy (Lee and Gerritsen 78) on entities is used. A superordinate of a set of entities is formed if they have common features and can be grouped together as a class. In the ONR database, for example, the SHIP and the SUBMARINE are generalized to WATER-VEHICLE and AIRCRAFT is generalized as AIR-VEHICLE. Both the WATER-VEHICLE and the AIR-VEHICLE are generalized as VEHICLE. Part of the generalization hierarchy used in the TEXT system is shown in Figure 4-4.

The generalization hierarchy extends in depth to include sub-types of records in the physical database. For example, sub-types of the entity SHIP,

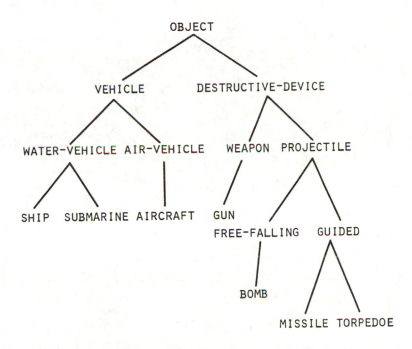

Figure 4-4:   The Generalization Hierarchy

for which a record exists in the database, include the **AIRCRAFT-CARRIER**, **FRIGATE, DESTROYER**, and **CRUISER**, among others. Some of the sub-types of the **SHIP** are shown in Figure 4-5. This portion of the hierarchy (along with the sub-types of the other leaves of the hierarchy shown in Figure 4-4) was generated automatically by a system called **ENHANCE**, developed by McCoy (see (McCoy 82) for a description of how this was done).

Entities for which records exist in the physical database are the only kind of entities used in Chen's representation. In this work, these types of entities are termed *database entity classes*. Use of a generalization hierarchy broadens the range of meaning of the term *entity*. It can refer to a generalization of a database entity class, a database entity class, or a sub-type of a database entity class. This distinction between the kinds of entities is especially important when representing the distinguishing characteristics of

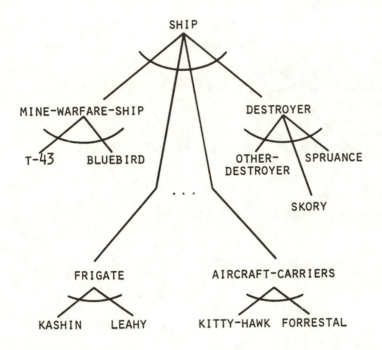

Figure 4-5:   Sub-Classes Formed for Entity Class SHIP

the sub-types of any entity (see Section 4.2.9 and 4.2.12). In order to talk about this distinction without confusion, the following definitions are adopted:

Definition 4.2.5
Database entity class: An entity for which a record exists in the physical database.

Definition 4.2.6
Database entity subset: A sub-type of a database entity class.

Definition 4.2.7
Database entity generalization: **A** generalization of a database entity class.

Definition 4.2.8
Entity (redefined): Any node in the generalization hierarchy. This includes database entity classes, database entity subsets, and database entity generalizations.

Figure 4-5 shows that mutual exclusion on database entity subsets is also part of the generalization hierarchy. In fact, mutual exclusion is used throughout the generalization hierarchy. Mutual exclusion is used in a variety of knowledge representations (e.g., Smith and Smith 77; Brachman 79). A set of sub-types is mutually exclusive only if no member of any sub-type is also a member of another sub-type. If an entity has two sets of mutually exclusive sub-types, then an instance occurring in a sub-type of one set may also occur in a sub-type of the other set. For example, a DESTROYER (a member of one mutually exclusive set) may also be a US SHIP (a member of another mutually exclusive set), but a DESTROYER cannot also be a FRIGATE. Mutual exclusion is represented graphically by drawing an arc across the sub-type links of an entity.

Definition 4.2.9
Mutual exclusion: A set of sub-types is mutually exclusive if and only if no member of any sub-type is also a member of another sub-type.

4.2.6. The topic hierarchy
A hierarchy is also used on the database attributes in the TEXT system. Although this is not a feature common to many database models, it has been discussed and used in the AI literature (e.g., Schubert et al. 79; Brachman 79). It provides the same kinds of advantages for the generation system for describing attributes as the generalization hierarchy does for describing entities. In order to refer to each hierarchy without confusion, the hierarchy on attributes is termed a *topic hierarchy*, while the hierarchy on entities is termed the *generalization hierarchy*. The topic hierarchy in the TEXT system proved to be especially rich and extremely useful in describing commonalities between entities. Attributes such as MAXIMUM SPEED and MINIMUM SPEED were generalized to EXTREME SPEED, ENDURANCE SPEED and ECONOMIC SPEED generalized to REGULATED SPEED, and EXTREME SPEED and REGULATED SPEED generalized to SPEED

INDICES. Note how the topic hierarchy also allows the generation system to refer to attributes concisely. It can refer to SPEED INDICES without having to list all the attributes that it includes. The topic hierarchy used for the TEXT system is shown in Figure 4-6.

Both the generalization and the topic hierarchy allow for a more compact, as well as more abstract, representation of the data. In other words, *both* hierarchies allow for economies in the logical description of data as well as its physical storage. Use of the generalization hierarchy means that if both the SHIP and SUBMARINE have the attributes FUEL TYPE and FUEL CAPACITY, the attributes need not be duplicated for each entity but can be stored as attributes of their superordinate in the generalization hierarchy, WATER-VEHICLE (note that this would not be the case if there existed a third type of WATER-VEHICLE in the ONR database which did not have the attributes FUEL TYPE and FUEL CAPACITY). Furthermore, if an entity has the three attributes FUEL TYPE, FUEL CAPACITY, and REFUEL CAPABILITY, all three attributes need not be associated with the entity. Instead, the superordinate of the three attributes, FUEL INDICES, in the topic hierarchy can be attached to the entity. An example of the economy and abstraction gained by the combined use of these two hierarchies is shown in Figures 4-7 and 4-8. A sub-tree of GUIDED PROJECTILES is shown as well as the representation that would have to be used if the system did not include either of the two hierarchies.

Creating a generalization hierarchy and topic hierarchy for a new domain is not a process that can be easily systematized. The best instructions that can be given for this process are to look for commonalities across entities to find an inclusive superordinate for some subset of the entities. Examination of hierarchies used in other systems to get some ideas of possible breakdowns is also helpful. Creating an acceptable hierarchy is a subjective process; there is no single "correct" hierarchy for a set of objects.

McCoy (82) has done some work on simplifying the process of generating the generalization hierarchy by developing a system that will automatically generate sets of sub-types for database entity classes. Transferring her system to a new domain requires specification by the designer of a set of domain-specific axioms which her system uses to form sets of sub-types, termed *breakdowns*, and to determine distinguishing characteristics of each sub-type (discussed below). The domain-specific axioms can be as simple (e.g., a list of important database attributes) or as detailed (e.g., a table of sub-class divisions desired) as the designer likes. The development of this system relieves the designer of the process of creating the generalization hierarchy from the level of database entity classes down when transferring the TEXT system to a new domain.

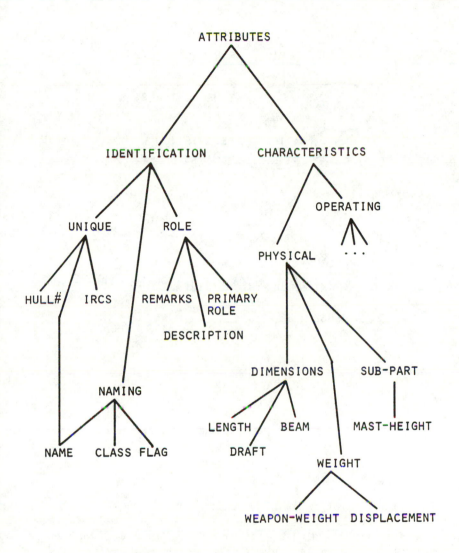

Figure 4-6: Part of the Topic Hierarchy

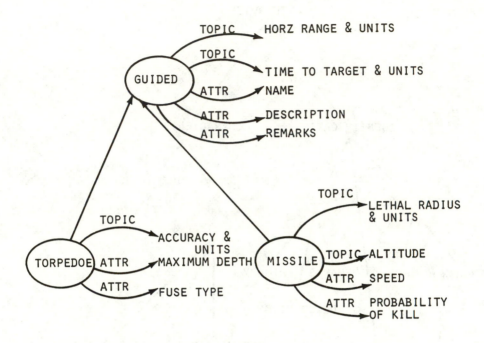

Figure 4-7:   Using Topic Hierarchy and Generalization Hierarchy

4.2.7. Relations

Although a complete generalization hierarchy on relations was not included in the TEXT system, some generic information was used. Relations between entities are termed relation instances. Some instances of the same relation occur between different entities. For example, SHIPs *carry* GUNs, they *carry* MISSILEs, and they *carry* TORPEDOEs. Thus, the carry relation (called "ON" in the database) occurs between SHIPs and GUNs, SHIPs and MISSILEs, and SHIPs and TORPEDOEs. The similarity across these three different instances of the relation is captured by using a generic relation *ON* which has information about appropriate fillers of roles, attributes that each instance has (in this case, "QUANTITY"), and cardinality information (e.g., whether the relation is one-to-many, etc.).

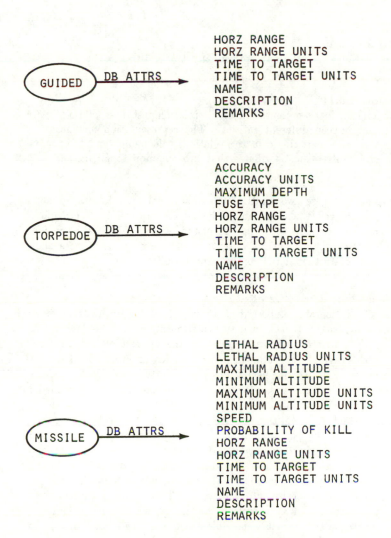

Figure 4-8: Without Using Either Hierarchy

Definition 4.2.10

Relation instance: A *relation* between any two entities.

Definition 4.2.11

Generic relation: A representation of all relation instances of the
same name between different entities. The representation includes
entities that may participate in the relation, role names and their
values, cardinalities, and attributes that are common to all instances.

By representing these two kinds of information about relations, greater
variety can be achieved when describing them. Generic relations provide
general information common to a class of instances and therefore allow for
economy of description in a generated text when necessary. Instances allow
for the provision of further detail in the generated text.

4.2.8. Distinguishing descriptive attributes

The use of the hierarchies described above allows for an abstract view of
the data not provided by the Chen entity-relationship model; it describes the
data in other than strictly database terms. In the interest of including more
of this real-world view of the data, an additional feature was added to the
TEXT knowledge base. Distinguishing descriptive attributes (DDAs), which
are attribute name - value pairs, provide a view of the data not included in
the database system point of view.

DDAs are attached to entities at each split in the hierarchy. They
describe the basis for the partition in the hierarchy and are related to what
Lee and Gerritsen call *partition-attributes* (Lee and Gerritsen 78). Lee and
Gerritsen make an assumption, however, that doesn't always hold. They
assume that there exists a single database attribute whose value in the
database differentiates an entity into sub-types. This is not always the
case.[28] For the database entity subsets of an entity, which have a large
number of identical attributes, it is possible to find a single attribute, or set
of attributes, whose value can partition the entity. For database entity
generalizations, however, a single database attribute whose value can be used

---

[28]Lee and Gerritsen's assumption may result from the fact that they are
not working with an existing database and can choose to include whatever
attributes and values they like in the database itself. In this research, a
meta-level representation is described for an existing database and it must
therefore be constructed within the confines of the values represented in the
database.

to partition the class may not exist. OBJECTS, for example, only have the attribute REMARKS which does not allow for a meaningful distinction. Yet, the partition of OBJECTS into VEHICLES and DESTRUCTIVE DEVICES is clearly a useful one. Above the database entity class level the different database attributes that each sub-type possesses, however, do indicate the basis for the partition. In this example, all VEHICLES possess attributes indicating their speed and fuel indices, while DESTRUCTIVE DEVICES possess attributes indicating their lethal indices.

A single attribute and value are formulated for database entity generalizations which provide an additional characterization of the partition. The choice of attribute and value is supported by the different database attributes that each sub-type possesses. These attributes correspond to the partition attributes of Lee and Gerritsen. The form of the DDA for entities which occur above the level of database entity classes in the hierarchy is different from the form for entities which occur below that level since values of database attributes differentiate database entity subsets while variation in database attributes possessed differentiates database entity generalizations. These two forms are described in more detail in the sections below.

4.2.9. DDAs for database entity generalizations

Each sub-type of a database entity generalization is given the same DDA name, but a different value which describes one way in which the entities are characteristically different. For example, the two main classes of entities in the ONR database, VEHICLE and DESTRUCTIVE DEVICE, both have DDA names of FUNCTION. The VEHICLE's FUNCTION is TRANSPORTATION (DDA value) and the DESTRUCTIVE DEVICE has a FUNCTION of LETHALITY (DDA value).

DDAs consist of a single word attribute name and value (hyphenation is sometimes used). DDA names are either selected from a set of standard functional terms (e.g., function, role) or from any of the cases (e.g., agent, patient, to-location, from-location, etc. See (Palmer 81) for a discussion of various verb cases) of higher-level DDA names or values in the generalization hierarchy. For example, one case of the VEHICLE's DDA value, TRANSPORTATION, is travel-medium. TRAVEL-MEDIUM is the DDA name for WATER-VEHICLE and AIR-VEHICLE.

Definition 4.2.12
Distinguishing Descriptive Attribute (DDA)
(Part I): An attribute-value pair associated with each entity in the
hierarchy describing a characteristic difference between the entity
and its siblings such that

$$attribute\ (entity) = attribute\ (sibling)$$
for all mutually exclusive
siblings of entity
$$value\ (entity) \sim= value\ (sibling)$$
for all mutually exclusive
siblings of entity

4.2.10. Supporting database attributes
Distinguishing descriptive attributes for database entity classes and their
generalizations are supported by existing database attributes that illustrate the
reasons for the chosen DDA name-value pair. This allows the generation
system both to describe the database information in real world terms via the
DDAs and to relate these descriptions to information actually contained in
the database. The VEHICLE's transportation function is supported by the
fact that all VEHICLEs in the ONR database have attributes describing their
TRAVEL-MEANS, such as SPEED, FUEL TYPE, FUEL CAPACITY, etc.
DESTRUCTIVE DEVICEs, on the other hand, have database attributes
providing information on LETHAL INDICES (e.g., PROBABILITY OF KILL,
LETHAL ACCURACY, etc.).

Definition 4.2.13
Supporting database attribute: A subset of an entity's attributes such
that:

if E1 is a generalization of E2 and
    DDA-name (E1,E2) = A1
    DDA-value (E1,E2,A1) = V1
then y is a supporting database attribute of E2
if y is a database attribute of E2 and y
implies DDA-value (E1,E2,A1) = V1

The topic hierarchy on attributes is very useful here, since it is rare that
all entities in a class have exactly the same database attribute. For example,

ships have MAXIMUM SPEED, ENDURANCE SPEED, and ECONOMIC SPEED, the SUBMARINE has OPERATING SPEED, and the AIRCRAFT has CRUISE SPEED. While none of these database attributes have exactly the same name, they each provide information about the speed capabilities of the various VEHICLEs. In this case, it would be useful to associate the superordinate in the topic hierarchy, SPEED INDICES, with the entity VEHICLE and the specific types of SPEED with the SHIP, SUBMARINE, and the AIRCRAFT. This capability is similar to *role differentiation* as described by Brachman (Brachman 79).

In order to do so, a distinction is made between cases like this, where entities share related, but not identical attributes, and cases where entities share identical attributes. Each supporting database attribute is linked to its entity via either *some-type-of* or *have*. *Have* indicates that all entities in the generic class possess each database attribute occurring under the given topic in the topic hierarchy (or the database attribute if a leave in the hierarchy is given). *Some-type-of* indicates that all entities in the generic class possess attributes related by the given topic in the topic hierarchy. Thus, VEHICLE SOME-TYPE-OF SPEED INDICES indicates that each VEHICLE in the ONR database has some of the attributes occurring under SPEED INDICES in the topic hierarchy.

The computational interpretation for this intuitive description of some-type-of follows a fairly rigid set of rules that can be used by a designer when determining how to associate the supporting database attributes drawn from the topic hierarchy with entities in the generalization hierarchy for a new domain. Working from the leaves of the topic hierarchy up, the following rules should be applied to each entity in the generalization hierarchy:

For each superordinate attribute in the topic hierarchy:

1. If each sub-type of entity is determined to *have* every attribute under a superordinate attribute, then use "entity *have* superordinate attribute".

2. If each sub-type of entity is determined to *have* at least one attribute under a superordinate attribute and no sub-type shares attributes under the superordinate attribute, then "entity some-type-of superordinate attribute".

3. If each attribute under a superordinate attribute is shared by two or more sub-types of entity in either *have* or *some-type-of* then "entity *some-type-of* superordinate attribute".

4. If each sub-type of entity shares some attribute under a superordinate attribute in either *have* or *some-type-of* and there exists more than one attribute which is not shared, then "sub-type *some-type-of* attribute-i, sub-type *have* attribute-j, for each applicable attribute-i, attribute-j".

Diagrams representing each of these cases are shown in Figures 4-9 - 4-12. The distinguishing descriptive attributes and their supporting database attributes for the subtree under VEHICLEs are shown in Figure 4-13.

4.2.11. Based database attributes

Database entity subsets have similar types of descriptive information associated with them. This descriptive information was generated automatically by McCoy's system along with the subset nodes. Each data-type associated with a subset has the same function as its counter-part in the upper half of the generalization hierarchy, but has a slightly different format.

Subsets are formed by McCoy's system on the basis of three sources of information: the knowledge base already formed by hand, actual database values, and a set of world knowledge axioms. The axioms fall into three classes: very specific, specific, and general. Very specific axioms dictate actual breakdowns that a database designer would like to see in the knowledge base. They specify both a sub-type name and a unique identifier (database attribute and value) of that sub-type. For example, sub-types of the SHIP may be formed on the basis of identifying characters in the HULL NO. All AIRCRAFT-CARRIERs, in fact, are identified by the first two characters of the HULL NO being CV. Specific axioms specify attributes

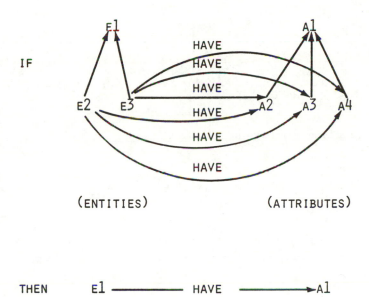

Figure 4-9: Attaching Supporting DB attributes - *have*

which are important for the particular database domain. For example, CLASS, FUEL TYPE, and FLAG (which specifies country), are important for a database containing information about military vehicles. Thus, a sub-type may be formed on the basis of the value of a SHIP's CLASS, such as KITTY-HAWK.

The uniquely identifying attribute on which the sub-type formation was based is called the *based database attribute* (counterpart to the supporting database attribute in the upper half of the hierarchy and to Lee and Gerritsen's partition attribute). They represent the defining attribute and value for the sub-type in the database. For the AIRCRAFT CARRIER, the based database attribute is HULL NO paired with an indication that the first two characters of the HULL NO must be CV. Since some sub-types may be based on more than one value, a disjunction may be used. Cruisers, for example, are identified by a HULL NO with first two characters of either CG or CL. The based database attribute, therefore, indicates the reason for the breakdown.

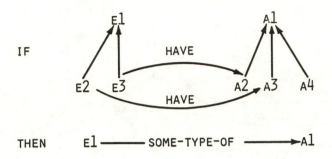

Figure 4-10: Some-type-of Interpretation (Part I)

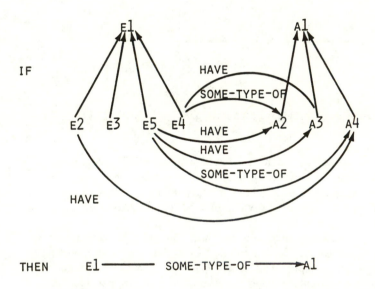

Figure 4-11: Some-type-of Interpretation (Part II)

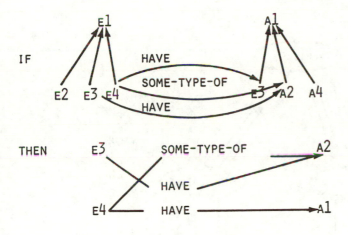

Figure 4-12:   Some-type-of and Have

Definition 4.2.14
Based database attribute: Attribute-value pair of database entity
subset whose value uniquely identifies an instance as belonging to a
given sub-type.

4.2.12. DDAs for database entity subsets

McCoy's system selects as DDAs those database attributes whose
collective value over the sub-type distinguishes that sub-type from every other
mutually exclusive sub-type of the parent. In some cases, a single database
attribute may be sufficient for forming a distinction. For example,
ENHANCE chose attribute LENGTH as the DDA for SHIP sub-type
AIRCRAFT-CARRIER since no other SHIP in the database has a LENGTH
as large as the AIRCRAFT CARRIER's. The DDA value for a sub-type
may be either a constant or a range. If all AIRCRAFT-CARRIERs have a
LENGTH between 1039 and 1063, but all other SHIPs have a LENGTH less
than 1039, then the range is sufficient distinction. If an attribute has a
constant value across a sub-type, and no other sub-type has the same value
for that attribute, then it is sufficient distinction.

In some cases, no single attribute may be sufficient for distinguishing one
sub-type from another. For example, an OCEAN-ESCORT may
hypothetically have either a smaller LENGTH or a smaller BEAM than every
other SHIP (i.e. - a DESTROYER may have a smaller LENGTH than the
OCEAN-ESCORT, but have a larger BEAM, while a FRIGATE may have a
smaller BEAM but a larger LENGTH). In such cases, a set of attributes and

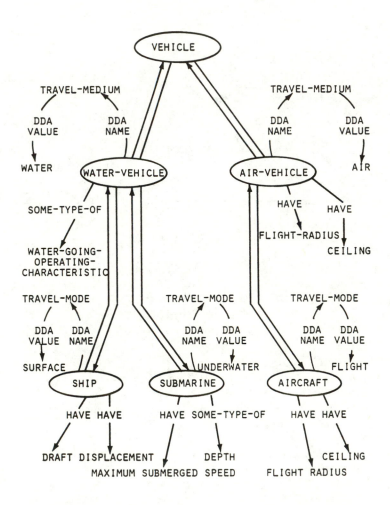

Figure 4-13:   DDAs and Supporting Database Attributes

their values provide the distinguishing characteristics of a sub-type. If more than a single set of attributes distinguishes one sub-type from all others, McCoy's system uses world knowledge axioms to select that set providing the most meaningful distinction (see McCoy 82).

Definition 4.2.15
DDA (part 2): Database attribute-value pairs that distinguish a database entity subset from all others such that:
No mutually exclusive sibling of entity has DDA-value (DDA-name sibling, parent) = DDA-value (DDA-name entity, parent)

OR

No mutually exclusive sibling of entity has DDA-value (DDA-name sibling, parent) within the range of DDA-value (DDA-name entity,parent).

4.2.13. Constant database attributes

A database entity subset inherits all the database attributes of its ancestors, and, as mentioned earlier, has no additional attributes of its own. The value of all of its database attributes is, however, further constrained by its sub-typing. A database entity subset contains a restricted range of values across all of its attributes. In order to be able to describe these restrictions, any attributes having constant values are recorded. In addition, the ranges of database attributes that appear as distinguishing descriptive attributes of other database entity subsets are also recorded. This is done so that comparisons can be made between these sub-types without an extensive amount of inferencing.

A database entity subset also inherits all the relations of its ancestors without having any additional relations of its own. Again, the values of the relation attributes are recorded as these are restricted in different ways across different database entity subsets. The SHIP, for example, has the relation ON with GUNS, MISSILES, and TORPEDOES. The DESTROYER, one database entity subset of SHIP, carries 2-40 MISSILES, and 8-99 TORPEDOES, while the PATROL SHIP carries 1-4 GUNS, and 2-8 MISSILES and 6-12 TORPEDOES.

A portion of one breakdown of the SHIP is shown in Figure 4-14. The descriptive information associated with two of the sub-classes is shown. Note that the set of distinguishing descriptive attributes is not the same for both sub-classes. While either LENGTH or DISPLACEMENT distinguishes the AIRCRAFT-CARRIER from all other SHIPS, the OCEAN-ESCORT has LENGTH in the same range as at least one other database entity subset of SHIP. DDAs for the OCEAN-ESCORT include DISPLACEMENT. Since LENGTH is a distinguishing descriptive attribute of another class, however, the values that the OCEAN-ESCORT's LENGTH ranges over are recorded as part of the constant values for its database attributes.

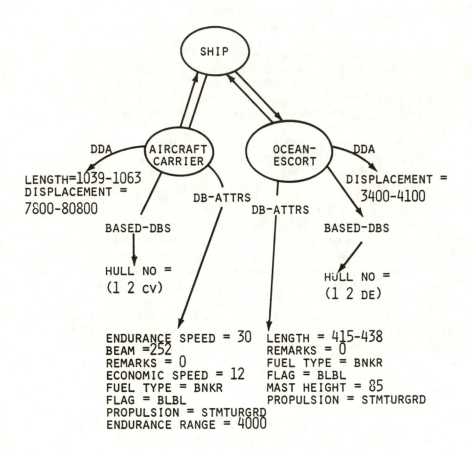

Figure 4-14:   Information for Database Entity Subsets

4.3. Selection of relevant knowledge

The first step in answering a question directed to the TEXT system is to partition off a subset of the knowledge base that contains information relevant to the given question. The resulting subset is termed the *relevant knowledge pool*. As discussed in Chapter Three, the relevant knowledge pool is used to provide a limit on what needs to be considered when determining the content of the answer. It is similar to what Grosz has termed "global focus" (Grosz 77) since its contents remain focused throughout the course of an answer. It models a speaker's narrowing of attention to information relevant to his current discourse purpose. This process is crucial to the success of later processes in the TEXT system.

Instead of developing a complex semantic reasoning engine, the approach taken in TEXT was to section off as much knowledge as could be considered relevant for the answer with the result that the system may err on the side of including too much information in the subset. Not all information in the subset need be included in the answer, however. The schemata determine exactly what information will be included from the relevant knowledge pool and in what order. Filling of the schema may end with information still remaining in the knowledge pool.

In determining which knowledge is relevant, a naive, infrequent user of the system is implicitly assumed. In situations where it is unclear whether more detail would be needed for this standard user, a choice was made not to include it. If a user-model were developed, the relevant knowledge pool could be dynamically expanded only in those specific situations where it is determined that more detail on a concept is needed for a particular user (see Section 3.2.1).

4.3.1. Requests for information and definitions

When responding to requests for information or for definitions, a relatively simple technique is used to partition the knowledge base. The area around the questioned object is sectioned off and all links of the questioned entity are preserved. These include links to its database attributes, its distinguishing descriptive attribute name and value, either its supporting database attributes or its based database attributes, its relations, its super-ordinates in the generalization hierarchy, and its sub-classes in the hierarchy. The siblings of the questioned object are included in the relevant knowledge pool with all links preserved in case they are needed for analogies.[29] Descendants are also included with all links preserved for the cases where an

---

[29]Currently, only numerical comparisons are performed between an entity and its siblings. Tracking of discourse, however, would allow the system to make analogies to siblings that have been recently discussed.

entity is defined (or information available about it provided) in terms of its constituency. The only links included for all other entities selected for the relevant knowledge pool (these include the questioned object's parent and all entities related through database relations) are those which lead to pieces of knowledge already included. The parent, for example, would be included with only its subset links (links to the questioned object and its siblings). It should be noted that inheritance on database attributes and relations is preserved for the questioned object. Figure 4-15 shows the relevant knowledge pool that would be constructed for the question "What kind of information do you have about ships?".

4.3.2. Comparisons

For questions about the difference between two entities, a slightly more complicated technique is used. The kind of information that is included in the relevant knowledge pool is dependent upon the conceptual closeness of the two entities in question. For two entities that are very similar, it is common to provide more detail when discussing their differences. When two objects are very different, a discussion of their differences could be endless and for this reason, the most salient distinction between the two is provided. This is a discussion of their generic class membership. Consider the questions shown in (1) and (2) below. Comparing the attributes of the part-time and full-time students (as in (3) below) can reasonably be part of an answer to question (1), but a comparison of the attributes of the raven and writing desk yields a ludicrous answer to question (2) (see (4) below). Instead, an indication that ravens belong to the class of animate objects, while writing desks are inanimate yields a better answer.

1. What is the difference between a part-time and a full-time student?

2. What is the difference between a raven and a writing desk?

3. A part-time student takes 2 or 3 courses per semester while a full-time student takes 3 or 4.

4. A writing desk has 4 legs while a raven has only 2.

4.3.3. Determining closeness

The TEXT system uses three categories in determining conceptual closeness. Two entities are classified as **very close** in concept if they are siblings in the generalization hierarchy. The ocean-escort and the cruiser are two entities in the ONR database that fall into this category since they are both sub-types of the SHIP. Two entities are classified as **very different** in

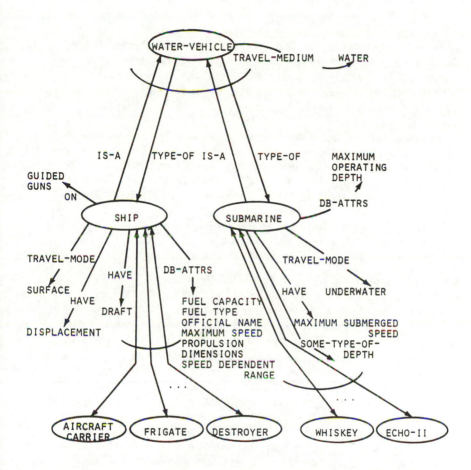

Figure 4-15: Relevant Knowledge Pool for Information and Definitions

concept if their common ancestor occurs at too high a level in the generalization hierarchy to provide useful information. An entity occurs at too high a level if it and all of its ancestors have no supporting database attributes for their distinguishing descriptive attributes. In other words, the concept is so vague that it has no database attributes that are common to all of its sub-entities. In the TEXT system, only the root node of the hierarchy happens to meet this description, although if the knowledge base was expanded to include more concepts this would not be the case. The DESTROYER and the BOMB are an example of two entities that are *very different* in concept since the only ancestor they share is OBJECT, the root node in the hierarchy.

Any two entities that don't fall into either of these classifications are categorized as *class difference*. These are entities that are not very close in concept but do have some similarities. An example of this type of category is the WHISKY and the KITTY HAWK. Although both are classes of water-going vehicles, the WHISKY is a submarine and the KITTY HAWK is a SHIP.

Figure 4-16 below depicts the generalization hierarchy which illustrates the basis for these three types of classification.

4.3.4. Relevancy on the basis of conceptual closeness

For entities that are *very close* in concept, all links of the questioned objects are included in the relevant knowledge pool. As was the case for requests for definitions or for information, this includes the entity's database attributes, distinguishing descriptive attributes, relations, and supporting or based database attributes. The entities' common parent and its links are also included in the pool. No other entities (except those dictated by the entities' links) are included in the relevant knowledge pool. The partition that is constructed in response to the question "What is the difference between an ocean-escort and a cruiser?" is shown in Figure 4-17.

In the case of entities which are *very different* in concept, only the superordinate links in the hierarchy and the reasons for the splits (distinguishing descriptive attributes) from the questioned objects to the nodes directly below the common ancestor are included. In order to avoid presenting long chains of superordinates when the common ancestor is very far away in the hierarchy, only the questioned objects, their parents, and the two nodes along the respective chains which are directly below the common ancestor are included in the knowledge pool. In addition, a search on common features of the questioned objects themselves is made in case there are any commonalities in database attributes, relations, or distinguishing descriptive attributes which were not common to all entities under the common ancestor. In practice, this rarely occurs for any two entities that are so different. The relevant knowledge pool that is constructed for the

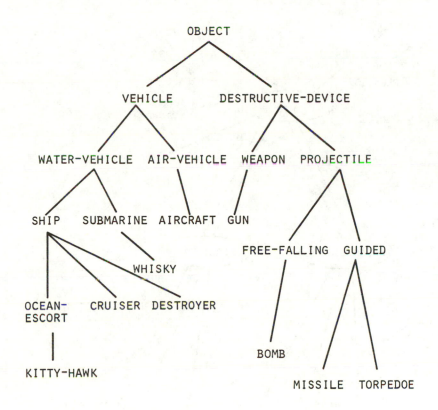

Figure 4-16:   The Generalization Hierarchy

question "What is the difference between a destroyer and a bomb?" is shown in Figure 4-18.

For entities that fall into the *class difference* categorization, the two questioned objects, their common ancestor, and the two children of the ancestor which are also ancestors of the questioned objects are included in the relevant knowledge pool. All links of each of these entities are included in the partition, with the exception of links that lead to other entities (e.g. some subset links of the common ancestor). No other entities are included. The relevant knowledge pool that is constructed for the question "What is the difference between the KITTY HAWK and the WHISKY?" is shown in Figure 4-19.

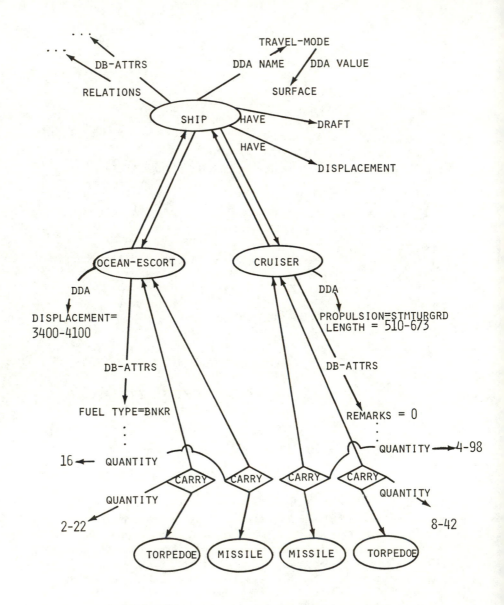

Figure 4-17: Relevant Knowledge Pool
for Category "very close"

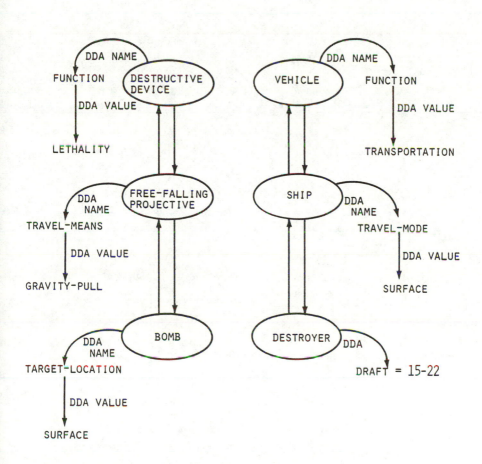

Figure 4-18:   Relevant Knowledge Pool
for Category "very different"

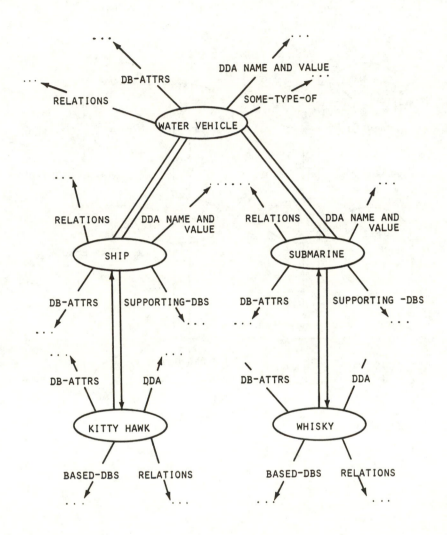

Figure 4-19: Relevant Knowledge Pool
for Category "class difference"

4.3.5. Conclusions

The TEXT system does not embody an exceptionally sophisticated treatment of semantic questions of relevance, with the exception of the treatment of comparisons. It does, however, provide a powerful computational and practical advantage for the generation process. By partitioning the knowledge base into a subset of relevant knowledge, the system need not scan the entire knowledge base when determining what to include in the current answer. This means less work computationally for the system and it avoids the possibility of including totally unrelated material by chance. Since all that is included in the relevant knowledge pool is not necessarily included in the answer, a simpler semantic procedure can be used in constructing the relevant knowledge pool. The contents of the actual answer are further constrained by the schema's predicates and the focus constraints.

The development of a user model would mean that the relevant knowledge pool could be dynamically expanded or restricted if the user was found to need more explanation of a particular concept. In the current system, only concepts that are directly questioned are explained in detail. It is assumed that the user will ask about other concepts presented in the answer if he is unsure of their meaning.

4.4. Schema implementation

The schemata were implemented using a formalism similar to an augmented transition network (ATN). An ATN is a graph representation of a grammar and allows for actions on its arcs which may set or test various registers. The ATN formalism was originally developed to parse sentences. When parsing a sentence, taking an arc involves consuming a word from the input string and augmenting a syntactic parse tree to include the new word and its category. Notable features of the ATN include recursion and backtracking (see Woods 70).

For TEXT, an ATN is used to build discourse instead of a parse tree. Taking an arc corresponds to the selection of a proposition for the answer and the states correspond to filled stages of the schema. No input string is consumed; instead the relevant knowledge pool is consumed, although it is not consumed in any order and it need not necessarily be completely exhausted when the graph is exited.

The most significant difference between the TEXT ATN implementation and a usual ATN, however, is in the control of alternatives. In the TEXT system, at each state all possible next states are computed and a function that performs the focus constraints is used to select one arc from the set of possibilities. Thus, although all possible next states are explored, only one is actually taken. The TEXT system originally used limited lookahead to avoid uncontrolled backtracking.[30] An arbitrary number of lookahead steps was used to eliminate traversing an arc which led to a blocked state (i.e., no propositions could be matched from this state). This feature was implemented, but it was found that, in practice, a blocked state was never reached. For reasons of efficiency, this feature was eliminated and the extra processing involved in lookahead avoided.

4.4.1. Arc types

The arc-types used in the schema implementation include:

1. **fill** <predicate> (to match predicate against the knowledge pool and retrieve propositions)

2. **jump** <state> (to jump to specified state)

3. **subr** <subr-state> (to proceed to start state of a subroutine graph. This arc type was included for a cleaner representation of

---

[30]This refers to backtracking an arbitrary number of states and not to the one step next state exploration described above.

the ATN graphs. They could have been implemented without this arc type)

4. **end-subr** (to return to state following subroutine call in main graph)

5. **push** <schema> (to recursively call a schema. All registers are saved)

6. **pop** (to return from a recursive schema call. All registers are restored).

4.4.2. Arc actions

The implementation allows for both pre-actions and post-actions to be associated with an arc. Pre-actions are performed before the arc is taken and include such things as resetting the relevant knowledge pool before taking a recursive push on a schema. Post-actions are performed after an arc has been taken and include adding a proposition to the message, updating the focus record, and proceeding to the next state.

Arcs may also have tests. A test is performed before deciding whether to take an arc. If a test succeeds, the arc is taken. One test used in the TEXT system is on the question-type, since schemata may be used for different purposes and sometimes a particular rhetorical technique is appropriate for one question-type and not for another.

4.4.3. Registers

The registers used in the TEXT system maintain information about the focus records, the message so far, and the question type. The registers include the following:

CF (current focus)
GF (global focus)
PFL (potential focus list)
kpool (the relevant knowledge pool)
current-discourse (the message so far)
question-type

4.4.4. Graphs used

Figures 4-20 - 4-23 show the ATN graphs that were used in TEXT to represent the identification, attributive, and constituency schemata. These graphs encode schemata which are modifications of the schemata that resulted from the analysis of text. Some of the predicates which occurred in the original schemata have been deleted, for the most part because information supporting those predicates does not occur in the knowledge base. The exact modifications that were made to the schemata are described in Section 2.4. Recall that the modified schemata used in the system are each a subset of the original and thus generate a more restricted range of text than do the original.

4.4.5. Traversing the graph

The ATN graph representing a schema is traversed to produce the textual content of a response. As a fill arc is taken, a proposition is selected and added to the answer. The traversal of the ATN requires some special treatment to account for the type of arcs that are used in this formulation as well as for the control of alternatives.

The first step in traversing the graph is accessing the start-state of the selected schema. Arcs are taken from the given state until the first fill-arc on each path is reached. If an outgoing arc from the state is a jump-arc, the jump is taken and all arcs from the next state taken until the respective fill-arcs are reached. Similar processing occurs for subr- and push-arcs. The predicates on each path-initial fill-arc are matched against the relevant knowledge pool and any matching propositions are retrieved. After the focus constraints select the most appropriate proposition, the post-actions on the arc whose predicate matched are performed and the successor function is applied to the next state.

In order to use subr-arcs and push-arcs, two stacks are maintained, a subr-stack and a push-stack. When a subroutine is taken, the return state is pushed onto the subr stack. When an end-subr is encountered, the first state on the subr-stack is taken. When a push is taken, the states are saved on the push-stack in the same manner. For a push, the registers (which include the focus records) are saved as well.

The use of the stacks is complicated by the fact that all outgoing arcs of a state are traversed until the first fill arc of each successor is encountered, although only one of these arcs is actually taken. If one of the outgoing arcs is a subr or push arc, the return state must be stacked, but if it is not the arc actually taken, then it is no longer needed on the stack. Further complications arise if more than one outgoing arc of the state is a subr or push arc. All return states must be remembered, but only one of

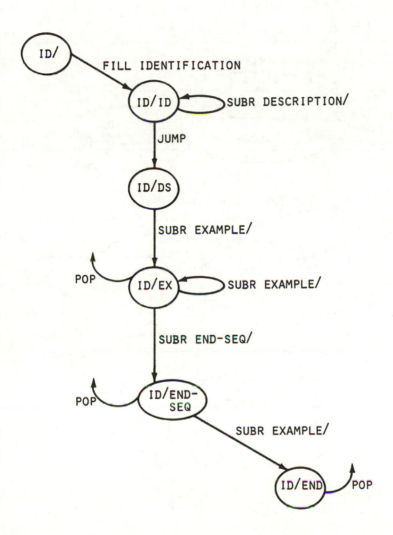

Figure 4-20: The Identification Schema Graph

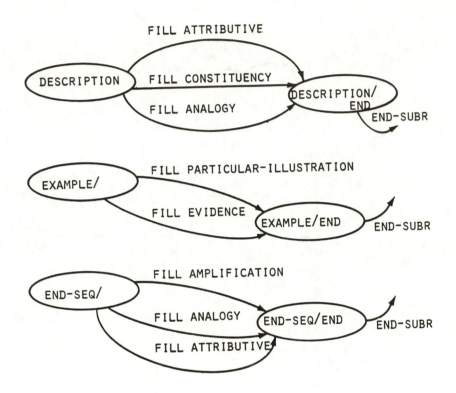

Figure 4-21: Identification Schema Sub-graphs

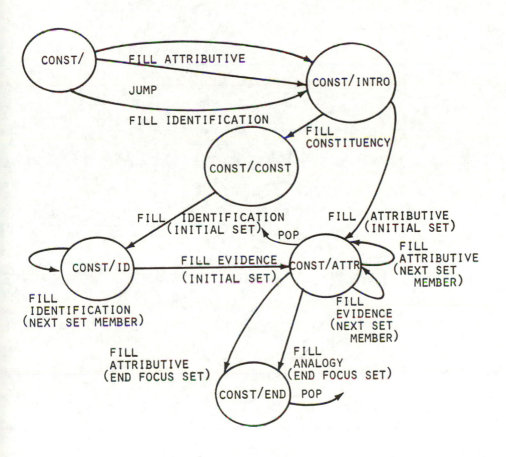

Figure 4-22: The Constituency Graph

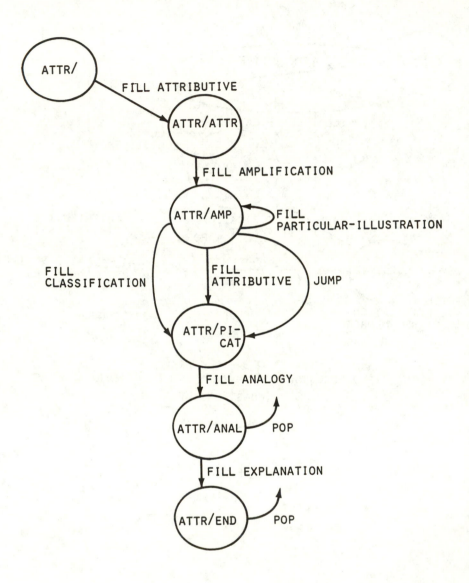

Figure 4-23: The Attributive Graph

them will actually be stacked.[31]

To handle this problem, a tentative-subr and a tentative-push stack are used to stack return states of outgoing arcs. Any stack actions that must be performed in traversing an arc are stored on the tentative stacks under the *destination state*, the state reached by traversing an arc. If a path of arcs must be taken from a single outgoing arc to reach a fill-arc, stack actions are carried along from the initial state of each arc to its destination state until the final destination state is reached. The tentative stacks look like association lists, with destination states as keys. After the focus constraints determine which arc (or path) should actually be taken, the stack actions associated with the destination state actually reached are retrieved from the tentative stacks and performed on the subr and push stacks. The tentative stacks are then cleared for the next step through the graph. Note that since only states are recorded on the stacks, the graphs must be written so that it is not possible to reach the same state via more than one subr-arc. This can be avoided through the use of jump-arcs.

As an example, consider the process of responding to the question "What is a ship?" which was described in some detail in Section 2.7. Suppose the system has matched the *identification* predicate against the knowledge pool and has selected the proposition *(identification SHIP WATER-VEHICLE (restrictive TRAVEL-MODE SURFACE) (non-restrictive TRAVEL-MEDIUM WATER))* as the first proposition of the answer. At this point, the system would be at state *id/id* in the graph representing the identification schema (shown in Figure 4-24). At this point in processing, either the *attributive*, *constituency*, or *analogy* arc can be taken next. These are represented by the *description/* subroutine. These steps are optional, however, and can be omitted entirely, in which case either the *evidence* or *particular-illustration* predicate would be selected.

A diagram of graph traversal and effects on the stack for the next step in processing (from state *id/id*) are shown in Figures 4-24 and 4-25. Processing calls for all arcs to be tested and the focus constraints dictate which one to take. In the diagram, the traversal of each possible next arc and the changes that are made to the stack are shown in steps 1 - 6. After an arc (or path) has been selected by the focus constraints (step 7), the post-actions on the arc are performed (the focus records are updated and the proposition added to the message) and the proposition is marked as used in the relevant knowledge pool. The successors of the destination-state are then found (step 8) and the process repeated until the schema is finally exited.

---

[31] The problem of remembering information computed down one path of a non-deterministic mechanism is a common one. In the original ATN implementation, a well-formed substring table was used to handle this problem. In Planner, the *finalize* predicate is used for this same purpose.

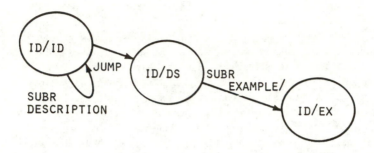

Figure 4-24: Portion of Identification Schema

4.4.6. The compare and contrast schema

The compare and contrast schema is shown in Figure 4-26 using the ATN formalism. Note that the three other schemata are used for the contrastive portion of the answer. The first step in the schema is to identify the commonalities of the two entities. During this portion, the two entities are treated as a set and the identification schema is used to describe the set as an entity. This step is optional if no commonalities exist, which is the case for entities which are very different in concept. At this point, a test for conceptual similarity determines the path followed and the schema used. The schema is called twice (once for each entity) and thus the contrast is set up over a several sentence sequence which corresponds to a single application of the embedded schema. An exception to this is the constituency schema which itself includes a description of the class difference and then focuses on each of the two entities in turn. The schema concludes with a direct comparison between the two entities via the inference predicate.

Using other schemata within a single schema requires the recursive machinery. Such use is achieved by pushing to that schema. The environment of the compare and contrast schema is saved and the knowledge pool reset for the sub-dialogue. In the case of a push to the attributive and identification schemata, the knowledge pool is reset to contain information about one of the entities for each push. When the sub-discourse is complete, a pop returns the process to the original discourse environment.

successors (id/id):
  outgoing arc = subr description/
                jump id/ds   tentative-subr-stack = nil
1) traverse subr-arc to description/
                            tentative-subr-stack =
                              ((description/ id/id))
2) traverse fill-arcs (3 of them) to description/end
   (carry fill-arc initial state to destination-state)
                            tentative-subr-stack =
                              ((description/end id/id)
                              (description/end id/id)
                              (description/end id/id)
                              (description/ id/id))
3) traverse jump-arc to id/ds (no stack actions)
4) traverse subr-arc to example/
                            tentative-subr-stack =
                              ((example/ id/ex)
                              (description/end id/id)
                              (description/end id/id)
                              (description/end id/id)
                              (description/ id/id))
5) traverse fill-arc to example/end (only one succeeds)
                            tentative-subr-stack =
                              ((example/end id/ex)
                              (example/ id/ex)
                              (description/end id/id)
                              (description/end id/id)
                              (description/end id/id)
                              (description/ id/id))
6) 5 matching predicates (as discussed in Section 2.7):
       attributive
       analogy
       constituency (WATER VEHICLE)
       constituency (SHIP)
       evidence
7) focus constraints dictate that the evidence arc
  is taken (destination-state = example/end)
                        subr-stack =
                          (id/ex)
                      tentative-subr-stack = nil
8) repeat for successors (example/end)

Figure 4-25:   Traversing the Graph

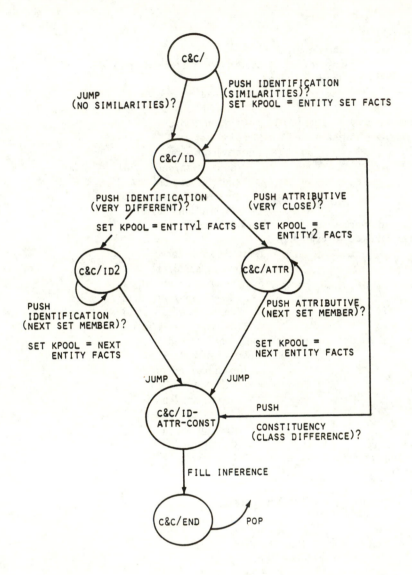

Figure 4-26:   The Compare and Contrast Graph

4.5. The tactical component

A tactical component in language generation systems typically takes as input an internal representation of what's to be said and uses a grammar to translate that representation into English. In the TEXT system, input to the tactical component is a deep structure representation of the message. The tactical component determines the surface ordering of the constituents and exactly which grammatical constructions are to be used. Without its implementation, it would be unclear whether the text planning devices used in the TEXT system are successful. In order to demonstrate that TEXT is successful, some uses of sophisticated linguistic devices were implemented in addition to basic syntactic constructions to show that the kind of information provided by the text planning components allows the tactical component to make decisions about their use. In particular, the tactical component uses focus information provided by the strategic component to select pronominalization, the passive construction over the active, and there-insertion. It uses information about rhetorical strategy to select various textual connectives. While this type of choice was discussed in the chapters on focusing and discourse structure, details are given in this chapter on how these choices are actually made.

The tactical component uses a functional grammar based on Kay's formalism (79). It was selected because of the ability to encode directly in the grammar tests on focus and theme for determining which syntactic construction to use, information which the strategic component supplies for this purpose. The functional grammar formalism is thus perfectly suited to the generation task as it allows the input representation to leave many of the details of the actual surface structure unspecified. These can then be filled in by the grammar. In the following sections, I describe TEXT's use of this formalism and delineate the range and limitations of its grammar and generated text.

4.5.1. Overview of functional grammar

In the functional grammar system, both the input and the grammar are represented in the same formalism, each as a list of attribute value pairs. Attribute value pairs represent the constituents and features of the desired sentence or grammar. To generate a sentence, the input, which represents the deep structure of the sentence, is *unified* with the grammar. This process is a modification of the unification process used in resolution theorem proving (Robinson 71). During this process, the actual surface structure of the sentence is determined. Syntactic structure that is missing in the input representation is filled in by the grammar. The final sentence is produced by linearizing the result of the unification process.

4.5.2. The grammar formalism

The basic unit of Kay's grammar is the *attribute value pair*. Attributes specify categories (syntactic, functional, or semantic) and values specify the legal fillers of those categories. Attributes are symbols and denote categories such as noun phrase, noun, protagonist, goal, subject, etc. Values may be either symbols or sub-grammars, which also consist of attribute value pairs. These basic building blocks are augmented by a discrete set of connecting devices which allow for the representation of complex syntactic structures.

A grammar is termed a *functional description* (FD). A single FD is used to encode the entire sentence grammar and it contains smaller FDs which describe the grammar of sentence constituents. For example, an FD for a sentence grammar might consist of three attribute value pairs: subject, verb, and object. FDs are represented diagrammatically by square brackets. Figure 4-27 shows a sample sentence grammar. Note that the sub-grammars are not specified so the grammar is not complete as it stands.

$$
S = \begin{bmatrix} \text{SUBJ} = [\text{ subject grammar}] \\ \text{VERB} = [\text{ verb grammar }] \\ \text{OBJECT} = [\text{ object grammar }] \end{bmatrix}
$$

Figure 4-27:   Sample Sentence Grammar

FDs may contain *alternatives* which specify that a particular category may be formed in more than one way. Another version of the sentence grammar, shown in Figure 4-28, specifies that the object is optional and that a sentence may therefore contain either two or three constituents. Alternatives are represented by curly braces. Note the use of the special symbol NONE, which indicates that this alternative will only be taken if there is no object in the input and if taken no object occurs in the output.

Patterns are used within an FD to specify the surface order of the constituents in the resulting string. A pattern is a list of attribute names which specifies the left to right order of the constituents. Since the value of an attribute may be another FD, which may in turn contain a pattern, the process of linearizing an FD using a pattern is a recursive one. An entry in a pattern list can correspond to a single word in the resulting string or to a string of words specified by another pattern. Patterns may contain two

$$S = \begin{bmatrix} \text{SUBJ} = [\text{ subject grammar }] \\ \text{VERB} = [\text{ verb grammar }] \\ \left\{ \begin{array}{l} \text{OBJECT} = \text{NONE} \\ \text{OBJECT} = [\text{ object grammar}] \end{array} \right\} \end{bmatrix}$$

Figure 4-28: Sample Sentence Grammar II

special symbols in addition to attribute names. *Dots* (...) are used to specify that 0 to n constituents from other patterns may appear between two attributes and *pound-signs* (#) specify that exactly one constituent from another pattern must occur between two attributes. These two symbols are used in handling alternatives which encode different orderings of the same constituent.

For example, dots are often used to allow for the inclusion or exclusion of optional constituents such as OBJECT in Figure 4-28 above. Consider Figure 4-29 below which is a version of the grammar shown in Figure 4-28 modified to contain two patterns. Unification of the patterns will result in (SUBJ VERB OBJECT) if an object exists in the input or the pattern (SUBJ VERB) if no object exists in the input.

Paths are used in Kay's formalism to refer to the value of one constituent from another constituent. A path is represented by angle brackets ($<>$) and specifies a list of attributes. The sample path $<a1\ a2 ... an\text{-}1\ an>$ points to the value of attribute *an* in the value of attribute *an-1*, and so forth. Up-arrow (^) is a special symbol in a path that can be used to point to the FD containing the current FD (i.e., upper-level FD). Paths can be used, among other things, for number agreement, person agreement, and traces. In Figure 4-30 below, the path is used to indicate that the number (NUMB) of the verb is equivalent to the number of the sentence subject ($<\text{^SUBJ NUMB}>$).

Description of some special symbols used in the grammar will be helpful before describing how it is used. Attribute names include the following symbols, as well as traditional category names :

$$S = \begin{bmatrix} \text{SUBJ} = [\text{subject grammar}] \\ \text{VERB} = [\text{verb grammar}] \\ \text{PATTERN} = (\text{SUBJ VERB} \ldots) \\ \left\{ \begin{array}{l} [\text{OBJECT} = \text{NONE}] \\ \\ \begin{bmatrix} \text{PATTERN} = (\ldots \text{OBJECT}) \\ \text{OBJECT} = [\text{object grammar}] \end{bmatrix} \end{array} \right\} \end{bmatrix}$$

Figure 4-29:   Sample Sentence Grammar III

$$S = \begin{bmatrix} \text{SUBJ} = \begin{bmatrix} \text{CAT} = \text{NP} \\ \text{NUMB} = \text{ANY} \end{bmatrix} \\ \text{VERB} = \begin{bmatrix} \text{CAT} = \text{VERB} \\ \text{V} = [\text{CAT V}] \\ \text{NUMB} = <\hat{\ } \text{ SUBJ NUMB}> \end{bmatrix} \\ \text{OBJ} = \quad [\text{CAT NP}] \end{bmatrix}$$

Figure 4-30:   The Use of a Path

- *cat* (category): The value indicates the syntactic category of the FD.

- *pattern*: Its value is the list of elements determining the surface order.

- *lex* (lexical entry): Its value specifies a particular lexical element or set of elements.

Two special symbols are used for values: *any* and *none*. *Any* is a wild-card and indicates that the value of the attribute can be any non-null value. *None* specifies that the attribute must not occur in the output. A sample grammar can now be given for a noun phrase. The grammar allows for an optional adjective and an optional prepositional phrase and is shown in Figure 4-31.

$$
NP = \begin{bmatrix}
\begin{aligned}
&\text{CAT} = \text{NP} \\
&\text{PATTERN} = (\ ...\ \text{N}\ ...\ )
\end{aligned} \\
\left\{
\begin{aligned}
&[\text{ADJ} = \text{NONE}] \\[4pt]
&\begin{bmatrix}
\text{PATTERN} = (\text{ADJ}\ ...) \\
\text{ADJ} = \begin{bmatrix} \text{CAT} = \text{ADJ} \\ \text{LEX} = \text{ANY} \end{bmatrix}
\end{bmatrix}
\end{aligned}
\right\} \\
\left\{
\begin{aligned}
&[\text{PP} = \text{NONE}] \\[4pt]
&\begin{bmatrix}
\text{PATTERN} = (...\ \text{PP}) \\
\text{PP} = \begin{bmatrix}
\text{PATTERN} = (\text{PREP NP}) \\
\text{CAT} = \text{PP} \\
\text{PREP} = \begin{bmatrix} \text{CAT} = \text{PREP} \\ \text{LEX} = \text{ANY} \end{bmatrix} \\
\text{NP} = [\text{CAT} = \text{NP}]
\end{bmatrix}
\end{bmatrix}
\end{aligned}
\right\}
\end{bmatrix}
$$

Figure 4-31:   Sample NP grammar

4.5.3. A functional grammar

Kay's grammar is termed "functional" because it assigns equal status to terms which describe the functional roles elements play in a sentence (e.g., protagonist) and to terms which describe the syntactic category an element belongs to (e.g., noun phrase). An FD may describe legal strings of the language using both these terminologies. In the TEXT system, Kay's functional categories *protagonist* (PROT), sometimes called *agent* in case formalisms, and *goal* (GOAL), sometimes called *object*, were adopted. *Beneficiary* (BENEF) is used for verbs which take an indirect object. A sentence grammar is defined for passive and active sentences by identifying the subject of the sentence as the protagonist if the voice is active or as the goal if the voice is passive. An example of this simple grammar for actives and passives is shown below in Figure 4-32. Note that verbs in this example do not take an indirect object. This was done to simplify the example. Further simplification was achieved by assuming that a protagonist is obligatory. Each category mentioned in the FD (e.g., VERB, PP) must be defined by a grammar elsewhere.

In this grammar, the value of voice is used as a test for determining the values of subject and object. Use of this functional notation simplifies the input considerably. Assuming that the sentence grammar of Figure 4-32, the noun phrase grammar shown in Figure 4-31, and unspecified verb and prepositional phrase grammars constitute the system grammar, the input need only specify the values for protagonist and goal and indicate whether the sentence is to be in active or passive form. Unification of the input with the sample grammar would result in an identification of subject and object, the construction of the prepositional by-object when needed, and indicate the surface order of the constituents. The sample input shown below in Figure 4-33 would result in the sentence "The old man was bitten by the dog" when unified with the sample grammar.

Kay's formalism also allows for the specification of concepts such as *topic* and *comment* directly in the grammar. This feature is particularly attractive since the assignment of values to these categories can be used to determine the order of constituents within the sentence. In such a case, the grammar indicates that the subject of the sentence is the topic. This scheme means that the process which creates the input need not be cognizant of the difference between syntactic concepts such as active and passive. Use of topic-comment articulation within the grammar itself means that the input can be specified in functional and semantic terms and that the grammar can use these functional roles in determining the values of the syntactic categories and their ordering within the sentence. Figure 4-34 shows how the input given in Figure 4-33 would have to be changed to specify the topic.

This type of formalism is particularly appealing for the TEXT system since the output of the strategic component contains focus information and

PATTERN = (SUBJ VERB OBJ)
PROT = [CAT NP]
GOAL = [CAT NP]

$$
\left\{
\begin{array}{l}
\begin{bmatrix}
\text{VOICE} = \text{ACTIVE} \\
\text{SUBJ} = <\text{PROT}> \\
\text{VERB} = [\text{CAT VERB}] \\
\text{OBJ} = <\text{GOAL}>
\end{bmatrix} \\[2em]
\begin{bmatrix}
\text{VOICE} = \text{PASSIVE} \\
\text{SUBJ} = <\text{GOAL}> \\
\text{OBJ} = \begin{bmatrix} \text{CAT} = \text{PP} \\ \text{PREP} = \begin{bmatrix} \text{LEX} = \text{BY} \\ \text{CAT} = \text{PREP} \end{bmatrix} \\ \text{NP} = <\hat{}\ \text{PROT}> \end{bmatrix} \\[3em]
\text{VERB} = \begin{bmatrix} \text{PATTERN} = (\text{V1 V2}) \\ \text{V1} = \begin{bmatrix} \text{CAT} = \text{VERB} \\ \text{LEX} = \text{BE} \\ \text{TENSE} = <\hat{}\ \text{VERB TENSE}> \end{bmatrix} \\ \text{V2} = \begin{bmatrix} \text{CAT} = \text{VERB} \\ \text{LEX} = <\hat{}\ \text{VERB LEX}> \\ \text{TENSE} = \text{PASTP} \end{bmatrix} \end{bmatrix}
\end{array}
\right\}
$$

Figure 4-32: Grammar for Actives and Passives

argument assignments for predicates, but embodies no syntactic information. Focus information can be used in the same way as topic/comment articulation to select between syntactic constructions. Currently, tests on focus information are made in the dictionary and the sentence voice selected at that point. Input to the tactical component, therefore, looks like the sample input shown in Figure 4-33. These tests could be incorporated as part of the grammar.

$$
\begin{bmatrix}
\text{PROT} = [\text{N} === \text{DOG}] \\[1em]
\text{VERB} = \begin{bmatrix} \text{V} === \text{BITE} \\ \text{TENSE} = \text{PAST} \end{bmatrix} \\[1em]
\text{GOAL} = \begin{bmatrix} \text{ADJ} === \text{OLD} \\ \text{N} === \text{MAN} \end{bmatrix} \\[1em]
\text{VOICE} = \text{PASSIVE}
\end{bmatrix}
$$

Figure 4-33: Sample Input

$$
\begin{bmatrix}
\text{PROT} = \ [\text{N} === \text{DOG}] \\[1em]
\text{VERB} = \ \begin{bmatrix} \text{V} === \text{BITE} \\ \text{TENSE} = \text{PAST} \end{bmatrix} \\[1em]
\text{GOAL} = \ \begin{bmatrix} \text{ADJ} === \text{OLD} \\ \text{N} === \text{MAN} \end{bmatrix} \\[1em]
\text{TOPIC} = \text{<PROT>}
\end{bmatrix}
$$

Figure 4-34: Sample Input with Topic

4.5.4. The unifier

A sentence is produced in Kay's formalism by unifying the grammar with the input, which is specified in the same formalism as the grammar. The input to the unifier is a deep structure representation of what is to be generated. The output is a surface syntactic representation of the sentence which is linearized using the patterns it contains.

During the unification process, variables (values of *any*) are replaced by values from the input and alternatives in the grammar are eliminated. The process involves unifying the value of each attribute in the grammar FD with the value of the attribute of the same name in the input FD. If the grammar value is an alternative, all options are unified and the first successful result taken. If either value is a symbol, then unification succeeds when the two values are equal, when one value is a wild card (*any*) and the other value is non-null, or when either of the values is nil. If both values are FDs then the two FDs are unified. If an attribute occurring in the grammar does not occur in the input, the attribute and its value are added to the result. In all other cases, unification results in failure. After the FD is unified with the grammar, each constituent of the FD is unified with the appropriate sub-grammar. Unification is a fully recursive non-deterministic process. For further clarification on Kay's unification process, see (Kay 79). Unification in the TEXT system was modeled after Kay's design, but liberties were taken in solving problems peculiar to the TEXT system.

4.5.5. The TEXT system unifier

The unifier for the TEXT system was designed and partially implemented by Bossie (81). Some of the special features of the TEXT system unifier which depart in concept from Kay's include the ability to handle unattached attributes in the input, the treatment of gapping, and the use and implementation of paths in the grammar. A brief description of each of these features is given followed by an example of the unification procedure. For more details on the TEXT system implementation of the unifier, see (Bossie 81).

The ability to handle unattached attributes in the input means that the input deep structure representation of the sentence can be less well-defined than would otherwise be required. Since the input need not specify exactly where constituents are attached, less work needs to be put into the dictionary (which is hand-encoded) where the translation from message formalism to deep structure is made. This feature is particularly useful for the description of noun phrases. The fact that noun phrases can take any number of adjectives is described recursively in the grammar. That portion of the noun phrase following the determiner is described by the rule: NNP -> ADJ NNP / NOUN. This is shown in functional notation in Figure 4-35.

If more than one adjective is desired in the output, each adjective need not be attached to its NNP category in the input. Instead, adjectives can simply be listed as part of the containing noun phrase. During the process of unification, the nodes corresponding to NNP are added to the structure. Recursion on the category NNP stops when all adjectives in the input have been used. Figure 4-36 shows some sample input along with the output that would be generated by the unifier if the given input were unified with the grammar shown in Figure 4-35. Note that === is used in the input to abbreviate the attribute value pair LEX = <value>.

$$
\text{NNP} = \left[\begin{array}{l}
\text{CAT} = \text{NNP} \\
\\
\left\{ \begin{array}{l}
\left[\begin{array}{l}
\text{PATTERN} = \text{(ADJ NNP)} \\
\text{ADJ} = \left[\begin{array}{l} \text{CAT} = \text{ADJ} \\ \text{LEX} = \text{ANY} \end{array} \right] \\
\text{NNP} = \quad [\text{CAT NNP}]
\end{array} \right] \\
\\
\left[\begin{array}{l}
\text{PATTERN} = \text{(N)} \\
\text{N} = \left[\begin{array}{l} \text{CAT} = \text{NOUN} \\ \text{LEX} = \text{ANY} \end{array} \right] \\
\text{ADJ} = \text{NONE}
\end{array} \right]
\end{array} \right\}
\end{array} \right]
$$

Figure 4-35: Encoding Multiple Adjectives

The implementation of gapping in the **TEXT** system also departs from Kay's design (see Kay 79). In the **TEXT** system, the feature "(gap +)" (an attribute value pair) is added to the FD of any constituent that corresponds to a gap in the final sentence. Since a gap is a hole that would have been filled by some other constituent in the sentence, a path is also added to the FD as the value of the attribute. The constituent that the path points to is used when resolving questions of number agreement. Although the attribute denoting the constituent that is gapped appears in the pattern, the linearizer checks for the presence of the gap feature before linearizing the value of any constituent in the pattern. If the gap is present, nothing is added to the string for that constituent.

The use of paths, as specified by Kay, was found to be incompatible with the use of recursive structures (such as the NNP above) and the loose specification of attributes. Kay uses the *up-arrow* (^) to specify the FD in which the current FD is embedded. If a path is used in the input to specify the value for a gap occurring in a relative clause, it is unclear how many levels up (or down) in the recursive structure built by the unifier the NP occurs. For example, in "The old man who walks by my house every day", the gap acting as subject of the relative clause is co-referential with the noun phrase "the old man". The structure for the noun phrase could be built by the unifier in several ways. The unifier may group the head noun and relative clause under an nnp which is modified by an adjective or the unifier may group the adjective and the head noun under an nnp which is modified

$$\text{INPUT} = \begin{bmatrix} \text{ADJ} === \text{BIG} \\ \text{ADJ} === \text{OLD} \\ \text{N} === \text{SHOE} \end{bmatrix}$$

$$\text{OUTPUT} = \begin{bmatrix} \text{CAT} = \text{NNP} \\ \text{PATTERN} = (\text{ADJ NNP}) \\ \text{ADJ} = \begin{bmatrix} \text{CAT} = \text{ADJ} \\ \text{LEX} = \text{BIG} \end{bmatrix} \\ \\ \text{NNP} = \begin{bmatrix} \text{CAT} = \text{NNP} \\ \text{PATTERN} = (\text{ADJ NNP}) \\ \text{ADJ} = \begin{bmatrix} \text{CAT} = \text{ADJ} \\ \text{LEX} = \text{OLD} \end{bmatrix} \\ \\ \text{NNP} = \begin{bmatrix} \text{CAT} = \text{NNP} \\ \text{PATTERN} = (\text{N}) \\ \text{N} = \begin{bmatrix} \text{CAT} = \text{NOUN} \\ \text{LEX} = \text{SHOE} \end{bmatrix} \end{bmatrix} \end{bmatrix} \end{bmatrix}$$

Figure 4-36: Input and Result of Unification

by a relative clause. In one case three up-arrows are required to refer to the head noun and in the other case, only two. When designing the input, there is no way of knowing which of these structures will be built, and therefore how many up-arrows to include in the input.

To accommodate for this phenomenon, a *up-arrow (*^) is used, which refers to the closest higher level FD which contains the attribute following *up-arrow. *Up-arrow (multiple upward path) indicates that the search is made upwards through the FD until the desired attribute is found. The same problem can occur when following a path downward through an FD. For this reason, a breadth-first search through the FD is done for the next attribute in a path. This means that if the next attribute in the path occurs in the current level FD, processing of paths will proceed as Kay suggests. If it is not in the current level FD, a search for the attribute is made through the value of each attribute in the current level FD.

4.5.6. Unifying a sample input with a sample grammar

A subset of the grammar used for TEXT is shown in Figure 4-38. Note that it consists of a list of alternatives where each alternative is a different syntactic category. The lexicon is considered part of the grammar. A sample noun phrase input is shown in Figure 4-37. Pre-processing adds the attributes *lex* to the input to obtain I2, shown in Figure 4-37, to replace the abbreviation "===". Unification processing is controlled by the grammar. Processing begins by scheduling each alternative in the grammar for unification with the input.

The first success halts the unification of following alternatives. The first alternative in the sample grammar is the NP FD. Each attribute in the FD is unified with the input. The first attribute is *cat*. Its value in the input is retrieved and is found to match the grammar's value (np). The attribute and value are returned to the input and the second attribute checked. *Pattern* has a null value in the input and since nil and a given symbol are defined as success (Section 4.5.4), the attribute and the value "(.. nnp)" are added to the input. An alternative is found next and each choice is scheduled for unification. The first FD ([article = NONE]) fails since the symbol NONE only matches against nil or NONE and the value for *article* in the input is [lex = def]. The second alternative is then attempted.

$$
I = \begin{bmatrix} cat = np \\ article === def \\ n === man \end{bmatrix}
$$

$$
I2 = \begin{bmatrix} cat = np \\ article = [lex = def] \\ n = [lex = man] \end{bmatrix}
$$

Figure 4-37:   Sample Input and Preprocessed Input

The value of *pattern* in the grammar "(article ...)" is matched against the value of *pattern* in the input "(... nnp)". Although the two patterns can be unified in any of the following ways, the first success is selected and used as the value for the input:

pattern = (article nnp)
            (article ... nnp)

The result of unifying the value of article in the grammar with the value

$$
\text{Grammar} = \left\{
\begin{array}{l}
\left[
\begin{array}{l}
\text{cat} = \text{np} \\
\text{pattern} = (\text{... nnp}) \\
\\
\left\{
\begin{array}{l}
[\text{article} = \text{none}] \\
\\
\left[
\begin{array}{l}
\text{pattern} = (\text{article ...}) \\
\text{article} = \left[
\begin{array}{l}
\text{cat} = \text{article} \\
\text{lex} = \text{any}
\end{array}
\right]
\end{array}
\right]
\end{array}
\right\} \\
\\
\text{nnp} = [\text{cat} = \text{nnp}]
\end{array}
\right] \\
\\
\left[
\begin{array}{l}
\text{cat} = \text{nnp} \\
\text{pattern} = (\text{... n}) \\
\text{n} = \left[
\begin{array}{l}
\text{cat} = \text{noun} \\
\text{lex} = \text{any}
\end{array}
\right] \\
\left\{
\begin{array}{l}
[\text{adj} = \text{NONE}] \\
\\
\left[
\begin{array}{l}
\text{adj} = \left[
\begin{array}{l}
\text{cat} = \text{adj} \\
\text{lex} = \text{any}
\end{array}
\right] \\
\text{nnp} = [\text{cat} = \text{nnp}] \\
\text{pattern} = (\text{adj nnp})
\end{array}
\right]
\end{array}
\right\}
\end{array}
\right] \\
\\
\left[
\begin{array}{l}
\text{cat} = \text{adj} \\
\left\{
\begin{array}{l}
\text{lex} = \text{old} \\
\text{lex} = \text{big}
\end{array}
\right\}
\end{array}
\right] \\
\\
\left[
\begin{array}{l}
\text{cat} = \text{noun} \\
\left\{
\begin{array}{l}
\text{lex} = \text{cat} \\
\text{lex} = \text{man}
\end{array}
\right\}
\end{array}
\right] \\
\\
\left[
\begin{array}{l}
\text{cat} = \text{article} \\
\left\{
\begin{array}{l}
\text{lex} = \text{indef} \\
\text{lex} = \text{def}
\end{array}
\right\}
\end{array}
\right]
\end{array}
\right\}
$$

Figure 4-38: Grammar

of article in the input results in the value of *lex* in the grammar ("any") being replaced by the value of *lex* in the input ("def").

The final attribute in the NP FD is then matched against the input. Again, nnp has a null value in the input and therefore the grammar's attribute and value are added to the input. The FD that results from this stage of unification is shown in Figure 4-39.

Processing proceeds at this point by unifying the value of every

$$\begin{bmatrix} \text{cat} = \text{np} \\ \text{pattern} = (\text{article nnp}) \\ \text{n} = [\text{lex} = \text{man}] \\ \text{nnp} = [\text{cat nnp}] \\ \text{article} = \begin{bmatrix} \text{lex} = \text{def} \\ \text{cat} = \text{article} \end{bmatrix} \end{bmatrix}$$

Figure 4-39:   Intermediate FD

constituent in the input FD's pattern against the grammar.[32] If the FD had no pattern, unification would halt successfully with the FD shown in Figure 4-38 without its pattern. The value of the first constituent, *article*, is unified with the grammar and successfully results in the same value (it matches against the fifth alternative in the grammar and returns successfully since [lex = def] is one of the alternatives).

The value of the second attribute in the pattern is then unified with the grammar. Note that the second attribute in the pattern is *nnp* and its value in the input is [cat = nnp]. The first alternative in the grammar fails since "cat = np" is in the grammar and "cat = nnp" is in the input. The second alternative in the grammar succeeds. After unifying the categories (*cat*), the first alternative of the nnp FD in the grammar is matched against the input. Since there is no *adj* in the input, the first attribute value pair of the alternative *adj = none* succeeds and is added to the value of the input. *Pattern* also succeeds and is added. The value for *n* is then searched for. Although it is not a member of this particular FD, it is an unattached attribute, since it is not a constituent of the FD it is contained in, and is therefore available for use (see Bossie 82 for a discussion of the treatment of unattached attributes). Thus, the value of the attribute *n* in the grammar is unified with the value of *n* in the input and results in success. The value of nnp after this stage in the unification process is shown in Figure 4-40.

The values of the attributes in this FD's pattern are then unified with the grammar (not described here). The result of the nnp unification is then added to the resulting FD (unattached attributes were removed when used) and the final FD is shown in Figure 4-41. This FD is linearized to produce the string "the man". For further details on the unification process see (Bossie 81).

---

[32]Attributes name both constituents and features of the grammar (e.g., *n* is a constituent, but *numb* is a feature). See (Bossie 81) for a description of the use of constituents.

$$nnp = \begin{bmatrix} cat = nnp \\ pattern = (n) \\ adj = NONE \\ n = \begin{bmatrix} cat = noun \\ lex = man \end{bmatrix} \end{bmatrix}$$

Figure 4-40: Unified nnp

$$output = \begin{bmatrix} cat = np \\ pattern = (article\ nnp) \\ article = \begin{bmatrix} cat = article \\ lex = def \end{bmatrix} \\ nnp = \begin{bmatrix} pattern = (n) \\ adj = NONE \\ n = \begin{bmatrix} cat = noun \\ lex = man \end{bmatrix} \end{bmatrix} \end{bmatrix}$$

Figure 4-41: Final FD

4.5.7. Grammar implementation

In this section, the capabilities of the TEXT system grammar are described and sample output from the system given which illustrates the use of each syntactic construction. Sentence constructions include the simple active, simple passive, and there-insertion. Sentences (1),(2), and (3) are sentences generated by the TEXT system which use these three constructions:

1. The torpedo has an underwater target location. (active)

2. Torpedoes are carried by water-going vehicles. (passive)

3. There are two types of entities in the ONR database: destructive devices and vehicles. (there-insertion)

Verbs in the sentence grammar either take no object or a direct object (the grammar was implemented to handle indirect objects as well, but no use was made of this type of verb in the TEXT system). Output from the TEXT system showing the use of verbs with no object and a single object is

147

given in sentences (1) and (2) below (the portion of the sentence illustrating the example is italicized). Modifiers of a verb phrase can include adverbs and prepositional phrases. The use of verb complements was also implemented. Sample output for these constructions is shown in sentences (3)-(5), with the relevant portion in italics.

1. *An aircraft travels* by flying. (no object)

2. The entity has DB attributes REMARKS. (direct object)

3. A submarine is a water-going vehicle that *travels underwater.* (adverb)

4. A ship is a water-going vehicle that *travels on the surface.* (verb prepositional phrase)

5. A submarine is classified as a whisky *if its CLASS is WHISKY.* (verb complement)

A sentence may take a sentential-adverb, as in sentence (1) below. The use of "for example" is triggered by the predicate particular-illustration and is selected in the dictionary. Amplification is another predicate which can trigger the use of a sentential adverb (e.g., also). A sentence may be followed by a sub-list as in sentence (2) below, which exemplifies what was stated in the sentence. The use of a sub-list is triggered by the constituency predicate. When the sub-list is selected, a colon is attached to the preceding part of the sentence.

1. Mine warfare ships, for example, have a displacement of 320 and a LENGTH of 144. (sentential adverb)

2. There are 2 types of guided projectiles in the ONR database: torpedoes and missiles. (sentence sublist)

Noun phrases are perhaps the most complex syntactic category in the grammar. Adjectives, relative clauses, and prepositional phrases are all modifiers of a noun that can appear any number of times within a single noun phrase and were therefore implemented recursively. Relative clauses are fairly complex since they make use of paths and the gap feature. Examples of these three constructions are shown in sentences (1)-(3) below. A noun phrase also has several optional constituents which can appear only once, if at all. These include determiners, parentheticals, and the use of sub-lists. The input need only specify whether a determiner is definite or indefinite and the appropriate lexical item will be selected. A default definite determiner is assumed if none is specified in the input.

1. The torpedo and the missile are *self-propelled guided projectiles.* (adjectives)

2. *All aircraft carriers in the ONR database* have REMARKS of 0, FUEL TYPE of BNKR, ... (prepositional phrases on nouns)

3. The vehicle has *DB attributes that provide information on SPEED INDICES and TRAVEL MEANS.* (relative clause)

Parentheticals are used to provide further specification of a noun phrase for two reasons: providing examples and specifying members of a class. Examples are used when a noun phrase specification may not be sufficient for a user to understand. In most cases a single example is presented because the complete set is too large to list. Parentheticals are also used to list the database attributes that an entity has under a single topic in the topic hierarchy. A noun phrase is used for the topic and the specific attributes are parenthesized. The use of parentheticals for examples is shown in Sentence (1) below where only two of the sub-types of the aircraft are mentioned. Sentence (2) shows the use of a parenthetical to list the attributes of FUEL indices which the aircraft possesses.

1. Aircraft are categorized by PROPULSION (for example, jet) and FLAG (for example, US aircraft).

2. Other DB attributes of the aircraft include FUEL (FUEL CAPACITY and FUEL TYPE) and FLAG.

Noun phrase sub-lists are used to specify elements of a category. The category is described using a generic description, but only some members of the generic class actually participate in the relation. These are specified by using a list construction. In the noun phrase "Jane's friends, John, Sue, and Mary", "Jane's friends" constitutes the generic description while the list "John, Sue and Mary" specifies the relevant elements. Sentence (1) below shows an example of noun phrase sub-list construction from the TEXT system output:

1. Its surface-going capabilities are provided by the DB attributes DISPLACEMENT and DRAFT. (noun sub-list)

The tactical component is currently capable of using conjunction for sentences, noun phrases, and prepositional phrases. Conjunction is represented in the grammar through the use of recursive structures. Each category that allows for conjunction must be modified to contain an alternative which tests for the presence of a conjoining term. Its presence triggers the construction of two categories, *np-list* and *np* for a noun phrase, separated by the conjoining term. *Np-list* recurses on itself until no more *nps* are found in the input. The alternative added to the noun phrase FD and the additional syntactic category added to the grammar in order to produce sentences with conjunction for noun phrases are shown below in Figure 4-42.

Alternative added to the NP FD

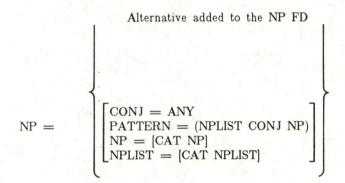

$$\text{NP} = \left\{ \begin{bmatrix} \text{CONJ} = \text{ANY} \\ \text{PATTERN} = (\text{NPLIST CONJ NP}) \\ \text{NP} = [\text{CAT NP}] \\ \text{NPLIST} = [\text{CAT NPLIST}] \end{bmatrix} \right\}$$

Additional category (NPLIST) added to the grammar

$$\begin{bmatrix} \text{CAT} = \text{NPLIST} \\ \left\{ \begin{array}{l} [\text{NP} = \text{NONE}] \\ \begin{bmatrix} \text{PATTERN} = (\text{NPLIST NP}) \\ \text{NPLIST} = [\text{CAT NPLIST}] \\ \text{NP} = [\text{CAT NP}] \\ \text{PUNCTUATION} = \text{AFTER} = \text{","} \end{bmatrix} \end{array} \right\} \end{bmatrix}$$

Figure 4-42:   Conjunction Additions

It should be noted that the lexical value of the conjoining term must be specified by the input. "And" and "or" are the two most common types of lexical conjunction, but at the sentence level other types of conjunction may be necessary (e.g., "but", "although", etc.). Although the TEXT strategic component currently does not make any selection of these types of conjunction, the grammar could produce these types of sentences if they were specified. The use of a sublist within an NP or a sentence calls for the standard use of conjunction. Some examples of this have already been seen. Two additional examples are provided in Sentences (1) and (2) below, the first using *and* and the second using *or*.

1. All aircraft carriers in the ONR database have *REMARKS of 0, FUEL TYPE of BNKR, FLAG of BLBL, BEAM of 252, ENDURANCE RANGE of 4000, ECONOMIC SPEED of 12, ENDURANCE SPEED of 30, and PROPULSION of STMTURGRD.* (conjunction in nps using and)

2. The missile has a target location *in the air or on the earth's surface.* (conjunction in pps using or)

Future work on conjunction in the tactical component should include a more general treatment of conjunction. Currently, a test for conjunction must be added to each syntactic category for which it is needed. Although the test is fairly simple, a more general method would be to let the presence of the conjoining term trigger the use of conjunction for whatever category was present in the FD of the input.

The tactical component is also capable of producing possessives. A possessive is a constituent of the noun phrase in the TEXT grammar and is itself a noun phrase (although a limited one in the TEXT grammar since the full range of modifiers on possessives was not accounted for). Possessives affect the immediately succeeding noun phrase since it can no longer take a determiner. Sentence (1) below contains a noun phrase with possessive.

1. *The missile's target location* is indicated by the DB attribute DESCRIPTION ... (possessive)

Punctuation is also handled within the grammar. Sentence final periods are the only exception to this rule. If a particular syntactic construction requires the use of punctuation (i.e., commas for lists, colons for sub-lists following sentences, parentheses for parentheticals), a punctuation feature is added to the constituent specifying the type of punctuation to be used and whether it should occur before or after the constituent. The punctuation element is concatenated to the appropriate word (the last word of the constituent if "after" is specified; the last word of the preceding constituent if "before" is specified) during the process of linearization. In Figure 4-42, the use of a comma was specified by the punctuation feature.

4.5.8. Morphology and linearization

Morphological suffixes to words are added during the linearization process. A list of attributes specifying the linear order of the constituents is obtained from an FD by retrieving its pattern. The value of the first attribute of the list is then accessed. If the value is an FD, its pattern is accessed. If it is a lexical entry, the morphological routines are called, the lexical entry processed, and the resulting word added to the sentence string. Certain word categories, such as adjectives and adverbs, need no morphological processing. Nouns, on the other hand, do require processing. They must be pluralized if they contain the feature "NUMB = PLUR". This requires adding "s" or "es" to the root noun provided in the input ("es" is added if the noun ends in "s"). For nouns taking an irregular plural, the plural is provided explicitly under the word's entry in the lexicon.

Verbs are conjugated as dictated by the features "TENSE" and "NUMB" in the verb FD. Present tense triggers the concatenation of "s" for third person singular only, to the root verb. Past tense triggers the concatenation of "ed" for all persons. Because of the database application, a default tense of "present", person of "third", and number of "singular" is assumed if any of these features are missing. The conjugations for irregular verbs, such as "be" and "have", are provided explicitly in the lexicon under their entries.

4.5.9. Extensions

In the TEXT system, tests for pronominalization and syntactic constructions are made in the dictionary. In the dictionary, predicates are mapped into verbs and their arguments into the sentence constituents; the output is an underlying syntactic structure for the sentence. If a test on the focus information indicates that a sentence should be passivized, the attribute value pair "voice == passive" is added to the underlying structure. In the dictionary, tokens in the message are replaced by their associated English words. During this replacement stage, a check for pronominalization is made and if the test is satisfied, a pronoun is used.

Eventually these tests should be incorporated into the grammar, where they belong. The functional grammar used in the TEXT system was selected because of the ability to encode tests on concepts such as focus or topic/comment directly into the grammar.

4.5.10. Disadvantages

The major disadvantages of the functional grammar and unifier involve implementation issues. Since the unifier is non-deterministic, the production of a single sentence from the given deep structure is incredibly time-consuming. The unifier is, *at best*, ten times slower than the strategic component. A representative processor time for the unifier to produce an answer is 730.75 CPU seconds, while the strategic component uses 54 CPU seconds. Average elapsed time for the tactical component is approximately 15 to 20 minutes, while the strategic component is about 2 minutes. Code for the tactical component, furthermore, was compiled while the strategic component code was not.

These results are understandable, however, when considering that the main purpose for implementing the tactical component was to demonstrate the success of the strategic component and extensive effort was not put into its implementation.

Some improvements in the design of the TEXT tactical component unifier could result in significant speed-ups. Using the syntactic category provided in the input[33] to retrieve the appropriate alternative directly from the grammar, rather than testing each alternative individually as is currently done, would be one such improvement. The same approach could be used when unifying a lexical entry against the lexicon.

A second problem with the unifier also results from the fact that it is non-deterministic. Debugging the grammar during its design stages is made more difficult by the fact that an error doesn't show up until far from the place where it first caused the problem. This situation is common to many non-deterministic processes and could be improved through the incorporation of testing diagnostics in the unifier.

4.5.11. Advantages

Use of Kay's formalism in the TEXT tactical component was successful on two accounts. The first, mentioned earlier, is that the grammar allows for equal treatment of functional and syntactic categories. This means that the input to the tactical component can be formulated by a process having little information about syntax. The dictionary designer can easily specify the protagonist and goal of a predicate, but more detailed syntactic information, such as syntactic category and surface position, can be deduced by the tactical component. It should be noted that the TEXT system grammar was not developed fully enough to allow for complete semantic specification by the input. For example, a modifier of a noun must be specified by *adj*, a syntactic classification. Further simplification of input specification was achieved by Bossie by allowing for the presence of unattached constituents.

Augmenting the grammar also turned out to be a fairly easy task in Kay's formalism. When a new type of syntactic category is needed, another alternative can be added to the grammar specifying the structure. Only the alternatives which encode the syntactic categories of which the new category is a constituent need to be modified. All other alternatives remain unchanged. The use of alternatives results in a clearly modular design for the grammar.

Future incorporation of the use of focus information into the grammar is another favorable aspect of the grammar. Although not currently implemented in the TEXT tactical component, the grammar allows for easy incorporation of tests on focus to select an appropriate syntactic construction.

---

[33] The syntactic category of only the top-level FD needs to be provided in the input (cat = s). The syntactic category of each of the sentence's constituents is deduced during the process of unification.

The advantages cited in this section far outweigh the disadvantages described in the previous section, which could, in fact, be minimized through an increased implementation effort.

4.6. The dictionary

The dictionary stands as interface between the strategic and tactical components. Its task involves: 1) the substitution of English words for tokens in the message produced by the strategic component, and 2) the selection of a deep structure for each proposition in the message. Note that the deep structure of the sentence is dependent on its verb (e.g., whether it takes zero, one, or two objects, a complement, etc.) which is in turn dependent on the predicate of the proposition. Once a verb has been selected to translate the predicate, the semantic arguments of the deep structure are filled in with the instantiated arguments of the predicate. During this process, English words are substituted for the instantiated arguments.

The use of a dictionary for this purpose was based on McDonald's design of the linguistic component (McDonald 80). A separate component is used rather than assuming that the message formalism is already in the deep structure representation because there may be cases where the choice of referents for the same message will vary depending upon the situation in which the message is used. In other words, the use of particular lexical items requires decisions to be made about the best possible choice given the circumstances (e.g., who the audience is, what has already been said, etc.). Similar decisions may need to be made about the verb, which will change the deep structure of the generated sentence.

In the TEXT system, these decisions have been simplified since no research was done on referential choice. A single token may translate into different syntactic categories, and thus different words, depending on how it is used in the proposition. The words selected to translate a token for one syntactic category, however, remain the same regardless of the situation in which the token is used. Knowledge about the user and the previous discourse is not used (or available) to select different lexical items. Use of a dictionary component, however, allows for easy extension in this area if this information were made available.

4.6.1. Design

An underlying message is translated into natural language in TEXT by passing each proposition of the message separately to the dictionary. The dictionary thus takes a single proposition as input, consisting of a predicate and its instantiated arguments (see Appendix D for discussion of the TEXT message formalism). Dictionary output is the deep structure representation for the English sentence to be generated, specified in Kay's (79) functional notation (see Section 4.5.2 for details on the grammar formalism). The output is passed to the tactical component which uses the grammar to produce an English sentence. This process is repeated until the full text is produced.

The dictionary consists of a list of entries for each token in the knowledge base. The selection of lexical translations for each token in a given proposition begins with the predicate. Its entry is accessed, the verb of the sentence selected, and the arguments of the predicate mapped to the case roles of the verb. Then the entries for each argument are accessed to return the lexical translations for the remainder of the proposition. Each of those entries may, in turn, call other entries if needed. After entries for each token in the proposition have been accessed, the complete deep structure is returned and the tactical component invoked.

4.6.2. Structure of dictionary entries

Each entry in the dictionary consists of a key (which is the token to be translated) and a function. On determining a lexical translation for a knowledge base token, the entry is accessed via the key and the associated function is evaluated. This function may take arguments as input and returns an appropriate structure, including lexical terms. Note that to fill in all lexical items in the structure another dictionary entry may have to be accessed.

A very simple dictionary entry for the entity GUIDED is shown below. In this entry, GUIDED is the key and the remainder of the entry is its associated function. The function takes no arguments since the translation for the entity is always the same. Note that the lexical items are not simply returned as a string; each lexical item is assigned to its syntactic category and thus a portion of the entire underlying structure of the sentence is returned.

```
[GUIDED (lexpr (x)
        (prog (nil)
              (return '((adj === guided)
                        (n === projectile]
```

A slightly more complicated entry is shown below. The entry for the distinguishing descriptive attribute value SURFACE is shown. It takes a single argument, a marker from the calling entry which indicates what type of syntactic translation is called for.[34] The entry tests the value of the marker to determine what kind of translation to provide. *Nil* is returned if the value can not be translated using the given form.

---

[34]The type of syntactic category required depends upon the argument's function in the sentence. One function may call for a noun phrase and another, an adjective.

```
[SURFACE
 (lexpr (x)
         (prog (marker)
               (setq marker (arg 1))
               (return
                 (cond ((equal marker 'adj)
                        '((adj === surface)))
                       ((equal marker 'mod)
                        '((adj === surface-going)))
                       ((equal marker 'n)
                        '((n === surface)))
                       ((equal marker 'pp)
                        '((pp ((cat pp)
                               (prep === on)
                               (n === surface)
                               (article === def)))))
                       ((equal marker 'verb) nil))
                 (t nil]
```

A single calling function, *entry-for*, is used to access entries in the dictionary. *Entry-for* searches the dictionary, an associated list, for its first argument, the token to be translated (the key). It then applies the function associated with its first argument to its remaining arguments and returns the result. This function may in turn call *entry-for* to access other entries in the dictionary if a variable in the translation exists. Thus, the entry for the predicate *attributive* is a function which selects the verb *have* (for certain uses of attributive) and calls other entries using *entry-for* for each of the predicate's arguments since these arguments do not remain constant for each use of the *attributive* predicate.

4.6.3. General entries

Entries common to all instances of a single data-type are used wherever possible. These entries can be used when the same decisions have to be made for each instance of a data-type. A single entry is written, encoding these decisions, which calls another entry to fill in the word, or words, that differ.

The data-type *entity*, for example, always translates as a noun phrase. A certain number of decisions are common to the translation of any entity: Does it have any modifiers? Should those modifiers be translated as relative clauses or as adjectives?[35] Is this a case of a list of entities, in which case conjunction is required, or is a single entity being translated? Does this use of the entity require indefinite or definite reference? Rather than repeat these decisions under the entry for each entity, a single entity entry is used which calls an entry for the particular entity being translated. The separate entity entries, therefore, encode no decisions, and simply return the lexical entry for the noun constituent of the entity (in some cases, translation of an entity also calls for a modifier, as was the case in the guided projectile example given above).

General entries are also used for the translation of database attributes. Database attributes often appear in a list since two or more attributes are usually discussed at a time. One test common to all translations of database attributes, therefore, is on the necessity of conjunction. All translations of database attributes must also test whether an attribute is a topic or a leaf in the topic hierarchy (see Section 4.2) since a different structure will be used for the two cases. If several, but not all, attributes under a topic (the topic is termed *duplicate* attribute in this situation) are described, a parenthetical is used to list the sub-nodes after the topic. The message formalism, the dictionary output, and the eventual translation for this case is shown on the next page.

---

[35]In the TEXT system, a restrictive modifier (i.e., that restricts the class of items the entity refers to) calls for the use of a relative clause. A non-restrictive modifier (i.e., that describes all instances of the class that the entity denotes) results in the selection of an adjective.

Dictionary input for *duplicate* attribute:

(duplicate (FUEL (FUEL_CAPACITY FUEL_TYPE)))

Dictionary output for *duplicate* attribute:

[(n === FUEL)
  (parenthetical ((conj === and)
              (np ((n === FUEL_CAPACITY)))
              (np ((n === FUEL_TYPE]

Eventual translation:
The ship has DB attributes DIMENSIONS, *FUEL (FUEL CAPACITY and FUEL TYPE)*, ...

Currently, in the TEXT system, the knowledge base token for each database attribute is used directly in the produced sentence, rather than translating each attribute separately. Translation of a set of database attributes, therefore, only uses the general entry in the dictionary and separate entries for each attribute are not needed. This shortcut was taken since the knowledge base tokens for attributes are English-like (e.g., SPEED INDICES, MAXIMUM SPEED, FUEL CAPACITY). The extra time needed to add entries for each attribute in the topic hierarchy to the dictionary would result in some added fluency in the text but it should be noted that such fluency would result solely from hand-encoding.

Database attribute value pairs are also translated using a general entry in the dictionary. An example of the use of attribute value pairs within a sentence is shown below. Each attribute value pair is translated as "<attr> of <value>" (dictionary output for the given translation is also shown) and inserted within a conjunction if more than one pair is present. Database values are used as lexical items in the sentence as were database attributes. Again, a slightly smoother translation would result if dictionary entries provided translations for all character values in the database (e.g., consider

"FLAG of BLBL" vs. "of US nationality" since BLBL stands for the country "US"). This would, however, be a large and tedious task that must be done by hand.

Dictionary input:

> (attributive db AIRCRAFT-CARRIER (FLAG BLBL) ....)

Dictionary output:

> [(n === FLAG)
> (pp ((prep === of)
>   (n === BLBL))]

Eventual translation:
All aircraft carriers in the ONR database have *FLAG of BLBL*, ...

4.6.4. An example

Tracing the translation of a proposition through the dictionary will clarify the process. The following proposition, in which the data-type is indicated by the token *def*, attributes the distinguishing descriptive attribute TARGET-LOCATION = UNDERWATER to the TORPEDOE. GUIDED is present in the proposition since it is the TORPEDOE's parent and the given attribute distinguishes the TORPEDOE from all other children of GUIDED. It is not used in the translation.

> (attributive def TORPEDOE GUIDED TARGET-LOCATION UNDERWATER)

The translation process begins by accessing the entry under the predicate *attributive*, passing the proposition as argument. The attributive entry tests the data-type used to make the attribution and accesses a second entry based on that type. (In this case, the type is distinguishing descriptive attribute. For a complete list of predicate data types see Appendix D.) During this stage, a check is also made on whether the particular distinguishing descriptive attribute can be translated as a verb. TARGET-LOCATION has no verb translation. (FUNCTION is an example of a distinguishing descriptive attribute that can be translated as a verb.) A new entry is accessed based on these decisions, called *attr-def*. The discrimination net used to reach this decision is shown in Figure 4-43.

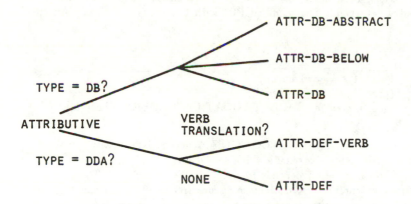

Figure 4-43:   Discrimination net for *Attributive* entry

In the entry *attr-def*, the verb "have" is selected for the sentence. The semantic cases of "have" are filled by arguments in the proposition. Protagonist (prot) is filled by the entity TORPEDOE (since this is the item to which information is being attributed) and the goal is filled by the distinguishing descriptive attribute name-value pair, TARGET-LOCATION = UNDERWATER. The deep structure for the sentence having been determined, the translations for the sentence cases are accessed by looking up the entries for the corresponding proposition arguments in the dictionary. The FD constructed at this stage is shown below. Lists in this FD headed by *entry-for* are slots that will be filled in by the value returned after accessing the dictionary for the entry which follows *entry-for*.

```
[(verb ((v === have))
(prot (entry-for entity TORPEDOE))
(goal (entry-for TARGET-LOCATION UNDERWATER]
```

The value for the protagonist is obtained by applying the function

associated with *entity* in the dictionary to the argument TORPEDOE. As
discussed in Section 4.6.3, a general entry (*entity*) is used for translating all
entities. In the entity entry, a test for conjunction is made and fails since
only one entity, the TORPEDOE, is passed. No modifiers are passed and
therefore no adjectives or relative clauses are added to the result. These
decisions having been made, the entry for TORPEDOE is accessed and the
lexical entry returned. The modified FD, with the value for protagonist filled
in, is shown below.

[(verb ((v === have)))
(prot ((n === torpedo)))
(goal (*entry-for* TARGET-LOCATION UNDERWATER n)]

The entry under TARGET-LOCATION is accessed next with
distinguishing descriptive attribute value UNDERWATER and marker *n* as
arguments. Its translation depends upon a variety of factors. The first is its
function in the sentence. A distinguishing descriptive attribute can be used
as a modifier of an entity or as a noun phrase itself. In this case, the
distinguishing descriptive attribute functions as the goal of the sentence, a
noun phrase (the reason for passing marker *n*). Secondly, the distinguishing
descriptive attribute name can be translated without the value or with it. In
this case, the value is given and therefore must be taken into account in the
translation. Given these decisions, the distinguishing descriptive attribute
name is translated as the head noun and the distinguishing descriptive
attribute value as its modifier. The head noun is selected in this entry, but
since more than one value may be passed as an argument for TARGET-
LOCATION (e.g., the MISSILE has TARGET-LOCATION = SURFACE-
AIR), the entry for the particular value passed is called to determine the
type of modifier (i.e., adjective versus prepositional phrase) as well as the
lexical items used. The modified FD is shown below and the choices that
were made to arrive at this FD are shown as a discrimination net in Figure
4-44.

Since the distinguishing descriptive attribute name is being used in goal
position and has not been previously mentioned, the indefinite determiner is
selected. Although focus information could be used to make this selection, no
explicit checking of focus is made here. Instead, use of indefinite is always
made for this particular construction, since it is assumed that this proposition
would not be generated if target location had already been mentioned.

```
[(verb ((v === have)))
(prot ((n === torpedo)))
(goal ((entry-for UNDERWATER 'adj 'pp)))
        (article === indef)
        (n === location)
        (adj === target) ]
```

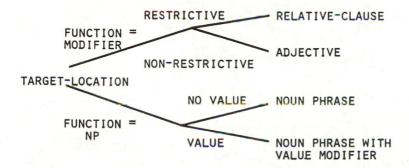

Figure 4-44:   Discrimination net for entry TARGET-LOCATION

All distinguishing descriptive attribute value entries translate their values according to their function in the sentence, as was the case for distinguishing descriptive attribute name entries. In this case, the second and third arguments indicate that the value is to function as modifier, and, more specifically, as an adjective if possible (the preference since it would entail less text) and a prepositional phrase if not. UNDERWATER translates as an adjective and this result is added to the FD to produce the final dictionary output shown below. The choices taken in the entry are shown in Figure 4-45.

Dictionary Output:

$$[(verb ((v === have)))$$
$$(prot ((n === torpedo)))$$
$$(goal ((adj === underwater)$$
$$(article === indef)$$
$$(n === location)$$
$$(adj === target)))]$$

Eventual Translation:

The torpedo has an underwater target location.

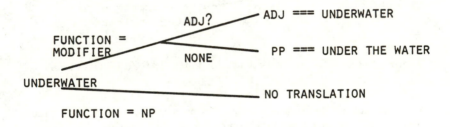

Figure 4-45: Discrimination net for UNDERWATER entry

4.6.5. Creating the dictionary

Creating the dictionary is a tedious, time-consuming task since it must be generated by hand. Furthermore, it acts as a bottleneck in the generation process since a message in internal representation cannot be generated in English until the English translations for the tokens it contains have been entered in the dictionary. The dictionary also limits the fluency of the generated text. If the translations of knowledge base tokens are not well thought out, the resulting text will be awkward and unnatural. Thus, the larger the range of generated text (i.e., the more messages that can be constructed), the more time must be invested in writing the dictionary. In order to use more sophisticated lexical items in the generated text, more thought must be invested in the creation process.

Planning the dictionary involves systematic analysis of each data-type in the knowledge base and the message formalism. The first step involves determining the unmarked semantic structure corresponding to each predicate used in the message formalism. For predicates that can be instantiated by more than one type of data in the knowledge base a semantic structure must be determined for each instantiation type. Following this stage, each data-type in the knowledge base (see Section 4.2 for a description of the different data-types used in the TEXT system) must be analyzed to determine: 1) its possible functions in the sentence (which will be multiple since it may be used by different predicate translations in different ways), 2) what syntactic category should correspond to each of its functions, and 3) what lexical items should be used within the categories.

A set of interactive functions was developed for the TEXT system to aid in the creation of the dictionary. Each data-type was analyzed separately to determine the variety of sentential roles it could fill and then interactive functions were written to prompt for the conditions for each role and the lexical items to be used for each instance of the data-type. The functions use the responses given to construct the entry in proper format. Automating the process in this way is particularly helpful since the functions can scan the knowledge base for each instance of the data-type and prompt the dictionary designer for each translation. This relieves the designer of the tedious task of scanning the knowledge base by hand and ensures that a translation for each instance will be included.

Interactive functions were written for the distinguishing descriptive attribute names, distinguishing descriptive attribute values, the supporting database attributes, entities, relations and for the predicates. Since database attributes and database attribute value pairs do not require lexical translation, a single general entry could be written to handle these cases. Each function prompts the user for the following parts of the entry: 1) its parameters, 2) the setting of its parameters, 3) conditions for translation (these may be omitted if the conditions are the same for each instance of a data-type), and 4) the lexical translations for each condition. The user is prompted for the lexical translations for each instance of the data-type in the knowledge base.

The interactive functions used for creating the entries for distinguishing descriptive attribute name, for example, request translations for each sentential role the distinguishing descriptive attribute could serve. As mentioned earlier, these are non-restrictive modifier, restrictive modifier, noun phrase with modifying distinguishing descriptive attribute value, or noun phrase without modifying distinguishing descriptive attribute value. Since it is assumed that the desired sentential role can be passed to the entry as argument (the predicate entry assigns instantiated arguments of the predicate to semantic arguments in the deep structure and therefore can pass this information on when the distinguishing descriptive attribute name entry is called), the entry builder need only prompt for translations and not conditions. The translations that are needed are relative clause, adjective, and noun phrase. Note that any of these may depend in part or in whole on the translation of the value that is passed. In such cases, the designer can enter the function *entry-for* and its arguments instead of a syntactic category and lexical item.

The function first notifies the user of the distinguishing descriptive attribute name currently being worked on. Separate functions are then called for each of the categories that the name can be translated as. Each of these functions knows about the possible constituents of the respective category and prompts the user for lexical values for each of these. The noun phrase building function, for example, is aware that a noun phrase can consist of a head, optional modifiers, determiner, and number. Complex constituents of the noun phrase, such as relative clause and prepositional phrase, are built by their own functions which prompt the user for their constituents. Note that for any constituent the user can enter either a value or a function. If a function is entered, it will be evaluated at the time the entry is accessed to produce the constituent value. Functions can be used either for calling other entries in the dictionary or for testing the arguments of an entry to determine the appropriate value.

As another example, consider the predicate entry. It consists of tests on its type and calls to separate entries which construct the deep structure for the sentence which corresponds to the particular predicate type. The entry is constructed by prompting the user to supply the tests on type as well as both the entry-name and its arguments for each type. As discussed in Section 2.6, a predicate may be instantiated by more than one data-type in the database. The attributive predicate, for example, may be instantiated by attributing database attributes to an entity or by describing an entity's distinguishing descriptive attribute. Each of these types translates into a different deep structure for the sentence. A separate entry is written for each predicate type for clarity.

In constructing the predicate type entry, the user is prompted for the verb and the semantic cases of the sentence. The predicate type determines the verb of the sentence and thus a lexical value is usually entered for this constituent. The protagonist and goal of the sentence are most often filled by the instantiated arguments of the predicate and thus a call to the entry for the appropriate predicate argument is usually assigned to these slots in the deep structure. The user is also prompted for a sentential adverb. Textual connectives are associated with the underlying predicate of the sentence. Thus, the predicate *particular illustration* uses the sentential adverb *for example* while the *inference* predicate triggers the use of the connective *therefore*. Currently in the TEXT system, if a sentential adverb is associated with a predicate type in the translation, it is always used in the sentence. Some more sophisticated uses of textual connectives might involve testing focus information across sentence boundaries. A connective would be required when a sudden shift in focus was made and would not be used in other cases (see Chapter Three, Section 3.3.2 for a discussion of this phenomenon).

4.6.6. Conclusions

Hand-encoding of the dictionary requires a considerable amount of time and effort. While some improvement in the fluency of the generated text can be gained by increasing the effort that goes into hand-encoding the dictionary, a deliberate decision was made not to make this effort because of its lack of theoretical value. In general, it is important to demonstrate that an approach, such as the dictionary, is viable by implementing a limited number of examples and indicating how the effort can be extended through increased implementation effort. Perhaps even more important to the future success of the field is to identify areas such as these, where extensive hand-encoding is required, as hard areas where future research must attempt to remove hand effort from the loop.

Another effect of hand-encoding is that the dictionary designer is free to encode as complex (or as ad-hoc) translations as he likes. This means that the generated text can be made to appear arbitrarily sophisticated. One of the problems along these lines in the TEXT system implementation was the separation of semantic and syntactic information about the sentence structure. Ideally, the dictionary should use only semantic terms in constructing the deep structure. Although Kay's formalism allows for the input to be specified in purely semantic form, the TEXT system grammar wasn't developed fully enough to handle this. To accommodate this lack, the dictionary had to specify some of the sentence structure in syntactic form (this accounts for the use of adjective and noun in dictionary output).

Steps for automating the creation of the dictionary were taken in the TEXT system by writing interactive functions which prompt the designer for lexical values. Additional work in this area needs to be done if generators are to be made portable. Research on reasoning about referential choice is part of the process needed to increase the sophistication of this component (e.g., Appelt 81; Cohen 81a). If the dictionary has access to a user model and pragmatic information about lexical choice, the designer would have to do less work in selecting appropriate lexical items for the translation.

4.7. Practical considerations

Although the TEXT system was implemented to test the generation principles developed in this dissertation, it addresses a real need in natural language database systems. It is just this fact that raises the question of how practical the system is for use in a real-world application. Faster response time is obviously one problem that must be solved before the TEXT system can be considered practical. Practicality, however, involves more than just questions of speed. In this section, the following two questions are discussed: 1) Does the system appropriately address the needs of the user for the questions covered? and 2) Does the system cover all the questions that a user might want to ask about database structure?

4.7.1. User needs

By providing a facility that can respond to questions the user has been shown to have about database structure (Malhotra 75), the TEXT system clearly addresses the needs of the user in ways that previous systems did not attempt. By providing a natural language response that describes concepts as they are viewed by the database system and at the same time incorporating into the response real-world knowledge about the concepts that the user may be familiar with, the system provides a comprehensible text for the naive and casual user of the database system. Some questions that need to be addressed before the system can be said to be truly appropriate in all response situations involve repetition within a single session and the length of the responses generated.

Currently the system may repeat information that it has just provided in a previous response. If the user is constantly presented with information he has already seen, he will become bored and frustrated with the system. Although the problem of when to omit information because of its presence in previous discourse and when to repeat it is not a simple question (e.g., it may be affected by how much time has passed since the information was first presented), it is an issue that must be addressed before the system can be called truly practical (some issues involved in this problem are discussed in detail in Chapter Five).

One of the main issues that this dissertation addresses is the generation of multi-sentential text, a problem that was only superficially addressed by previous research in natural language generation. Now that the generation of longer text is feasible, a serious examination of when length is needed must be done. Shorter answers do not suffice in situations where the user's question does not clearly delimit the conditions for determining an appropriate answer. For example, when providing definitions, there may be more than one piece of information which can be used to identify a term, while in answering a question like "Who is the president of the programming division?'', a name alone will suffice. Consistently long and wordy answers, however, may tax a user's patience.

In order to make decisions about how much information is sufficient for answering a particular user, an explicit model of the user's beliefs (Allen and Perrault 80) is necessary. In cases where a user is clearly unfamiliar with the terms involved, a more detailed explanation is necessary. If more detail is not provided, the user will be unhappy with the system performance when he can not understand the response. When it is clear that the user understands the concepts involved, longer text is unnecessary and cumbersome. An example of this situation was discussed in Chapter Two, where the definition of a Hobie Cat was given. If the user was ascertained to be unfamiliar with the world of sailing, a detailed explanation of catamarans was provided. If the user was knowledgeable about sailing, however, the Hobie Cat could be simply identified as a brand of catamaran.

4.7.2. Question coverage

The TEXT system addresses three classes of questions that were discovered by Malhotra during experimentation with user interaction with natural language database systems. These three question types were questions that Malhotra found users frequently asked to familiarize themselves with the database before asking questions about the data itself. Other classes of questions which Malhotra identified in his experimentation were not covered in this system because the typical knowledge base used in natural language database systems does not encode the kind of information needed to answer such questions. These include questions about the system's capabilities, such as "Can the system handle ellipsis?", questions about system processes such as "How is manufacturer's cost determined?", and questions involving counterfactuals, such as "If John Brown were promoted to systems analyst, what would his salary be?". Mays (82) has developed a knowledge representation that provides the information necessary to handle questions about time and processes. Discovery of other classes of questions that should be handled and the knowledge needed to answer those questions requires more experimentation with users of natural language database systems.

4.7.3. Conclusions

The TEXT system was developed in part to increase the practicality of natural language database systems by allowing users to ask questions to familiarize themselves with the database system. The system as it stands, however, is not ready to be used in a real life situation. In order to make the system fully practical for everyday use, it must be augmented so that it can avoid repetition of information within a single session, so that it can provide shorter or longer answers depending on the user's needs, and so that it can answer other classes of questions as well as requests for definitions, requests about available information, and questions about the differences between entities. In providing the ability to answer questions of these types, the TEXT system has opened up possibilities for areas of future research which are needed to create a truly practical system.

5
Discourse history

Tracking the discourse history involves remembering what has been said in a single session with a user and using that information when generating additional responses. The discourse history can be used to avoid repetition within a single session and, more importantly, to provide responses that contrast with previous answers. Although the maintenance of a discourse history record was not implemented in the TEXT system, an analysis of the effects such a history could have on succeeding questions as well as the information that needs to be recorded in order to achieve those effects was made. In the following sections some examples from each class of questions that the system handles are examined to show how they would be affected by the various kinds of discourse history records that could be maintained.

5.1. Possible discourse history records

Several different discourse history *types*, each containing a different amount of information, are possible. One history type could simply note that a particular question was asked and an answer provided by maintaining a list of questions. On the other hand, the system could record both the question asked and the actual answer provided in its history. The answer itself could be maintained in any of a number of ways. The history could record the structure and information content of the answer (for TEXT, this would be the instantiated schema). Another possibility would be to record some representation of the surface form of the answer, whether its syntactic structure or the actual text. Given that my goal is to identify how the previous discourse affects the structure and content of the current answer, I will not be considering this last option, although it is important for those interested in the effect of previous discourse on the wording of the current answer. This leaves two history types to consider:

1. A list of questions asked.

2. A list of questions asked and answers provided, where the structure and content of each answer is recorded as an instantiated schema.

In the following sections, it is shown, through examples, that by simply maintaining a list of the questions asked in the session the capabilities of the system can be substantially improved by avoiding repetition. In some cases, access to the exact information that was provided earlier can be used to create a text that contrasts with or parallels the earlier ones. The distinction between these two history types and their affect on improvement is important. A system can use this distinction to determine what to examine in the past discourse for a given question if it knows which type of history is needed to improve each class of questions. Moreover, if there are space limitations, a designer will be aware of how much quality is sacrificed if a full history is not maintained. The differences between the effects that can be achieved with both history types are described for each question class below.

5.2. Questions about the difference between entities

Questions about the difference between entities are greatly affected by the previous discourse. Within this class of questions, the type of information that needs to be recorded depends on how close in concept the two entities are. First consider entities that are very different in concept. For these entities, I claim it is sufficient to know what questions have already been asked. If one of the entities in question was recently defined, then information *that would normally be conveyed* about that entity in response to the difference question does not have to be included in the current answer as it must have been presented in the recent definition. Since only generic information is provided about each entity for the difference question if the entities are very different, the system can correctly assume that information would have been provided in the definition and can thereby avoid repetition. Knowing which structure was used for the previous response does not improve the current response since the structure and content of the earlier response have little in common with the current response.

Consider the question "What is the difference between a destroyer and a bomb?". The answer currently provided by the system, which does not take the previous discourse into account, is shown below in (A). If the question "What is a bomb?" had been recently answered as shown in (B), then the question about the difference between entities would be more appropriately answered as shown in (C). (Note that this is a hypothetical answer, not one generated by the system.) In order to answer the question this way, the system only needs to know that it recently provided the definition of a bomb. Only generic class information about the bomb is presented in (A) and since this information is provided in the definition (B), it can be omitted from the new response (C). Other information presented about the bomb in the definition (B) does not pertain to or affect the original answer (A).

(A)   What is the difference between a destroyer and a bomb?
A destroyer is a surface ship with a DRAFT between 15 and 222. A
ship is a vehicle.   A bomb is a free falling projectile that has a
surface target location.   A free falling projectile is a lethal
destructive device.   The bomb and the destroyer, therefore, are very
different kinds of entities.

(B)   What is a bomb?
A bomb is a free falling projectile that has a surface target location.
The bomb's target capabilities are provided by the DB attribute
LETHAL RADIUS & UNITS.   Other DB attributes of the bomb
include NAME and WEIGHT & UNITS.   The MK-84, for example,
has a LETHAL RADIUS of 200 FT and a WEIGHT of 2000 LBS.

(C)   What is the difference between a bomb and a destroyer?
A destroyer is a surface ship with a DRAFT between 15 and 222.
A ship is a vehicle.   Since the bomb is a destructive device, it is a
very different kind of entity than the destroyer.

In responding to questions about entities that are very similar, the
previous discourse information can have an even greater effect.   In this case,
if a definition of one of the entities in question has been provided previously,
the system can use that earlier answer to select directly contrasting
information about the second entity. In places where the previous answer
provided characteristic features of one entity, the new answer should provide
characteristic features of the other.   Thus, the predicates selected for the
previous answer can determine the predicates to be instantiated for the
current answer. The new answer should include an inference made about the
two entities, as did the original answer.

If the system knew that the previous question had been answered, but
didn't have access to the instantiated schema, it could eliminate repetition
about the previously defined entity, but it could not necessarily select
appropriate information about the other entity when contrasting it against
the first.   Note that this is the case since the two entities are very similar
and therefore have many common features which can be contrasted. The
destroyer and the bomb, on the other hand, have no features in common.
Thus, an improvement over the current state of the system could be achieved
by recording the question only, but no guarantee that the most appropriate
information for comparison would be selected could be made.

Consider, as an example, the question "What is the difference between

an ocean-escort and a cruiser?''. The answer currently produced by the
TEXT system is shown below in (D). If the answer shown in (E) had been
recently generated in response to the question ''What is an ocean-escort?'',
then the answer shown in (F) would be a more appropriate response to the
question about the difference between the two entities. Note that the
definition provided in (E) controls exactly which information is provided in
(F). In order to provide a response like that shown in (F), the system would
have to have access to a fully instantiated schema of the previous question.

(D) What is the difference between an ocean-escort and a cruiser?
The cruiser and the ocean escort are surface ships. The ship's
surface-going capabilities are provided by the DB attributes
DISPLACEMENT and DRAFT. The ship has DB attributes
MAXIMUM SPEED, PROPULSION, FUEL (FUEL CAPACITY and
FUEL TYPE), DIMENSIONS, SPEED DEPENDENT RANGE and
OFFICIAL NAME. Ocean escorts have a DISPLACEMENT between
3400 and 4100. All ocean escorts in the ONR database have
REMARKS of 0, FUEL TYPE of BNKR, FLAG of BLBL, MAST
HEIGHT of 85 and PROPULSION of STMTURGRD. Ocean escorts
carry between 2 and 22 torpedoes, 16 missiles, and between 1 and 2
guns. A ship is classified as an ocean escort if the characters 1
through 2 of its HULL NO are DE. Cruisers have a PROPULSION
of STMTURGRD and a LENGTH between 510 and 673. All
cruisers in the ONR database have REMARKS of 0 and FUEL
TYPE of BNKR. Cruisers carry between 8 and 42 torpedoes,
between 4 and 98 missiles, and between 1 and 4 guns. A ship is
classified as a cruiser if the characters 1 through 2 of its HULL NO
are CL or the characters 1 through 2 of its HULL NO are CG.
The ocean escort, therefore, has a smaller LENGTH and a smaller
DISPLACEMENT than the cruiser.

(E) What is an ocean-escort?
An ocean escort is a surface ship with a DISPLACEMENT between
3400 and 4100. A ship is classified as an ocean escort if the
characters 1 through 2 of its HULL NO are DE. All ocean escorts
in the ONR database have REMARKS of 0, FUEL TYPE of BNKR,
FLAG of BLBL, MAST HEIGHT of 85 and PROPULSION of
STMTURGRD.

(F)   What is the difference between an ocean-escort and a cruiser?
A cruiser is a surface ship with PROPULSION of STMTURGRD
and a LENGTH between 510 and 673.   A ship is classified as a
cruiser if the characters 1 through 2 of its HULL NO are CL or the
characters 1 through 2 of its HULL NO are CG.   All cruisers in the
ONR database have REMARKS of 0, DISPLACEMENT between
4600 and 5200, and FUEL TYPE of BNKR.   The cruiser, therefore
has a larger DISPLACEMENT and a larger LENGTH than the
ocean escort.

Difference questions about entities that are very close in concept are also
affected if discussion of the common superordinate of the two entities
occurred in the previous discourse.   Thus, the question "What is the
difference between an ocean escort and a cruiser?" will be affected if
discussion of ships, the superordinate of both ocean escorts and cruisers,
occurred recently.[36] If a request for available information or for a definition
of the ship was made and answered, then there is no need to provide much
detail on the common features of the ocean escort and the cruiser, since they
will have been provided in the previous answer.   In such a case, the two
objects in question need only be identified as ships, before discussing their
differences.   The modified answer is shown in (G).

---

[36]The system must also be able to discriminate between those questions
which occurred so long ago in the previous discourse that they would not
affect the current answer and those that should.

(G)   What is the difference between an ocean-escort and a cruiser?
The cruiser and the ocean escort are surface ships. Ocean escorts
have a DISPLACEMENT between 3400 and 4100. All ocean escorts
in the ONR database have REMARKS of 0, FUEL TYPE of BNKR,
FLAG of BLBL, MAST HEIGHT of 85 and PROPULSION of
STMTURGRD. Ocean escorts carry between 2 and 22 torpedoes, 16
missiles, and between 1 and 2 guns. A ship is classified as an ocean
escort if the characters 1 through 2 of its HULL NO are DE.
Cruisers have a PROPULSION of STMTURGRD and a LENGTH
between 510 and 673. All cruisers in the ONR database have
REMARKS of 0 and FUEL TYPE of BNKR. Cruisers carry
between 8 and 42 torpedoes, between 4 and 98 missiles, and between
1 and 4 guns. A ship is classified as a cruiser if the characters 1
through 2 of its HULL NO are CL or the characters 1 through 2 of
its HULL NO are CG. The ocean escort, therefore, has a smaller
LENGTH and a smaller DISPLACEMENT than the cruiser.

Difference questions which involve entities which are neither very close
nor very dissimilar in concept are less definitively affected by the previous
discourse.   There are two ways in which the previous types of difference
questions are affected: by the elimination of generic information about the
discussed entity from the current answer (both for very different and for very
close entities) and by the inclusion of directly contrasting information (for
very close entities only).   For entities which fall between these two extremes
of closeness, only some generic information can be eliminated from the answer
and directly contrasting information can not *necessarily* be included in the
answer.
    Normally, for this class of questions, the generic information that is
included in the answer is the common superordinate of the two entities in
question as well as the immediate superordinate of each.   A definition only
includes identification of the immediate superordinate and thus knowledge
that a request for a definition occurred recently means that only the
immediate superordinates should be omitted.   The common superordinates
must still be identified.
    As an example, consider the question "What is the difference between a
whisky and a kitty hawk?", answered currently by the system as shown in
(H). The definition of a whisky (I) identifies the whisky as a submarine.
That information can be deleted in the new answer (J), but the fact that
both entities are water-going vehicles must still be mentioned. Similarly, the
new answer must also identify the kitty hawk as a ship.
    If the discourse history contained the full answer, however, the system

could eliminate additional specific facts about the entity that was recently identified. It might also be able to select directly contrasting information about the other entity *if such information is available*. Since the two entities are not very close in the hierarchy, the likelihood of sharing common attributes is reduced and thus directly contrasting information may not be available.

Consider again the question "What is the difference between a whisky and a kitty hawk?". In the second half of the new answer (J) information about the whisky is completely omitted from the answer and the description of the kitty hawk parallels the second and third sentence of the whisky definition (I). Note that many attributes mentioned for the whisky are not included in the description of the kitty hawk (e.g., MAXIMUM OPERATING DEPTH, NORMAL OPERATING DEPTH) since this information is not available for ships.

(H) What is the difference between a whisky and a kitty hawk?
The whisky and the kitty hawk are water-going vehicles. The water-going vehicle's water-going capabilities are provided by the DB attributes under WATER GOING OPERATION (for example, DRAFT). The water-going vehicle has DB attributes FUEL (FUEL CAPACITY and FUEL TYPE) and OFFICIAL NAME. Its transporting capabilities are provided by the DB attributes under TRAVEL MEANS (for example, FUSE TYPE). There are 2 types of water-going vehicles in the ONR database: submarines and ships. A kitty hawk is a surface ship with a OFFICIAL NAME of KITTY HAWK, a HULL NO of CV-63, a IRCS of BL13, a FUEL CAPACITY of 7060, a ECONOMIC RANGE of 10000, a DRAFT of 36 and a MAST HEIGHT of 195. A whisky is an underwater submarine with a PROPULSION TYPE of DIESEL and a FLAG of RDOR. A ship is classified as a kitty hawk if its CLASS is KITTY HAWK. A submarine is classified as a whisky if its CLASS is WHISKY. The whisky and the kitty hawk, therefore, are 2 different kinds of entities.

(I) What is a whisky?
A whisky is an underwater submarine with a PROPULSION TYPE of DIESEL and a FLAG of RDOR. A submarine is classified as a whisky if its CLASS is WHISKY. All whiskies in the ONR database have REMARKS of 0, FUEL CAPACITY of 200, FUEL TYPE of DIESEL, IRCS of 0, MAXIMUM OPERATING DEPTH of 700, NORMAL OPERATING DEPTH of 100 and MAXIMUM SUBMERGED SPEED of 15.

(J)   What is the difference between a whisky and a kitty hawk?
The whisky and the kitty hawk are water-going vehicles.   The
water-going vehicle's water-going capabilities are provided by the DB
attributes under WATER GOING OPERATION (for example,
DRAFT).   The water-going vehicle has DB attributes FUEL (FUEL
CAPACITY and FUEL TYPE) and OFFICIAL NAME.   Its
transporting capabilities are provided by the DB attributes under
TRAVEL MEANS (for example, FUSE TYPE).   There are 2 types
of water-going vehicles in the ONR database: submarines and ships.
A kitty hawk is a surface ship.   A whisky is an underwater
submarine.   A ship is classified as a kitty hawk if its CLASS is
KITTY HAWK.   All kitty hawks in the ONR database have a
OFFICIAL NAME of KITTY HAWK, a HULL NO of CV-63, a
IRCS of BL13, a FUEL CAPACITY of 7060, a ECONOMIC
RANGE of 10000, a DRAFT of 36 and a MAST HEIGHT of 195.
The whisky and the kitty hawk, therefore, are 2 different kinds of
entities.

The previous discourse could also be used to establish a *context* against
which a request for the differences between objects could more appropriately
be evaluated.   Context can be used to determine which set of differences is
more relevant to the user.   For example, in responding to the question
"What is the difference between British Airways and TWA?"[37] it is more
appropriate to include the difference in cost when the user has indicated he
wants to travel from the US to London while it is more appropriate to note
the difference in intermediate stops when the user has previously noted he
wants to fly to Bangladesh.   In such a case, the previous context indicates
what the user's goals are and therefore what set of differences is relevant for
the response.

5.3. Requests for definitions

A response to a request for a definition requires less explicit modifications
on the basis of the preceding discourse.   Analogies can be made, however, to
a similar object recently discussed in the user session.   Similarity can be
determined on the basis of the generalization hierarchy.   If the entity
currently being questioned is a sibling in the hierarchy of an entity recently
discussed, then differences and similarities between the entities can be
discussed.   This would require use of the one-sided contrastive schema

---

[37]Example is due to Peter Buneman.

described in Chapter Two. It dictates that reference to the earlier discussed entity is made first, detailed discussion of the entity in question follows, paralleling information presented earlier, and finally, a direct comparison between the two entities made.

Consider the question "What is an aircraft-carrier?". If the question "What is a destroyer?" had been answered recently as shown in (K), the response to the request for the definition of an aircraft carrier would be affected. The answer currently generated by the TEXT system is shown in (L). If the answer were contrasted against the definition of the destroyer, it might hypothetically look like that shown in (M). It makes an analogy to the destroyer immediately and then presents information about the aircraft carrier similar to that presented for the destroyer. Finally, a direct comparison is made.

(K) What is a destroyer?

A destroyer is a surface ship with a DRAFT between 15 and 222.
A ship is classified as a destroyer if the characters 1 through 2 of
its HULL NO are DD. All destroyers in the ONR database have
REMARKS of 0 and FUEL TYPE of BNKR.

(L) What is an aircraft carrier?

An aircraft carrier is a surface ship with a DISPLACEMENT
between 78000 and 80800 and a LENGTH between 1039 and 1063.
Aircraft carriers have a greater LENGTH than all other ships and a
greater DISPLACEMENT than most other ships. Mine warfare
ships, for example, have a DISPLACEMENT of 320 and a LENGTH
of 144. All aircraft carriers in the ONR database have REMARKS
of 0, FUEL TYPE of BNKR, FLAG of BLBL, BEAM of 252,
ENDURANCE RANGE of 4000, ECONOMIC SPEED of 12,
ENDURANCE SPEED of 30 and PROPULSION of STMTURGRD.
A ship is classified as an aircraft carrier if the characters 1 through
2 of its HULL NO are CV.

(M) What is an aircraft carrier?

An aircraft carrier, like a destroyer, is a surface ship. It has a
DISPLACEMENT between 78000 and 80800 and a LENGTH
between 1039 and 1063. A ship is classified as an aircraft carrier if
the characters 1 through 2 of its HULL NO are CV. All aircraft
carriers in the ONR database have REMARKS of 0, FUEL TYPE of
BNKR, DRAFT between 36 and 37, FLAG of BLBL, BEAM of 252,
ENDURANCE RANGE of 4000, ECONOMIC SPEED of 12,
ENDURANCE SPEED of 30 and PROPULSION of STMTURGRD.
An aircraft carrier has a larger DRAFT and a larger
DISPLACEMENT than the destroyer. It has a greater LENGTH
than all other ships.

5.4. Requests for information

Responses to requests for information are affected if a question was
recently asked about an ancestor of the entity in question. In such cases, all
information available about the ancestor is also available for the entity, but
it doesn't need to be repeated. Additional information which is particular
only to the entity currently in question and restrictions on general
information provided for the entity's ancestor can be discussed. Since the
content of the response is affected in the same way for all questions and the
structure is not affected, a record that the question about the ancestor had
been asked is sufficient for modifying the response. All information inherited

from the ancestor, which is not further restricted for the entity, can be omitted from the response. In this case, therefore, having access to the instantiated schema for the previous response does not provide any advantage over having access to the question alone.

An example of this situation is shown in (N) - (P) below. The response to the question "What do you know about aircraft?" is shown as it is currently generated by the TEXT system in (N). If the answer to the question "What do you know about vehicles?" (O) was generated previously, the answer could be modified as shown in (P). In (P), attributes that were identified in (O) as being associated with vehicles are further specified for the aircraft. Thus, ROLE, an attribute of all vehicles, is specified for the aircraft as consisting of PRIMARY ROLE, DESCRIPTION, and REMARKS.

(N)   What do you know about aircraft?
The aircraft has DB attributes that provide information on FLIGHT RADIUS, CEILING, FUEL and ROLE.   Other DB attributes of the aircraft include CRUISE SPEED, MAXIMUM SPEED, PROPULSION and NAME.   An aircraft's ROLE includes PRIMARY ROLE, DESCRIPTION and REMARKS, its FLIGHT RADIUS includes CRUISE RADIUS and COMBAT RADIUS, its CEILING includes COMBAT CEILING and MAXIMUM CEILING and its FUEL includes REFUEL CAPABILITY, FUEL CAPACITY and FUEL TYPE.   Aircraft are categorized by PROPULSION (for example, jet) and FLAG (for example, US aircraft).   Aircraft are carried by ships. An aircraft travels by flying.   hinge

(O)   What do you know about vehicles?
The vehicle has DB attributes that provide information on SPEED INDICES and TRAVEL MEANS.   There are 2 types of vehicles in the ONR database: aircraft and water-going vehicles.   The water-going vehicle has DB attributes that provide information on TRAVEL MEANS and WATER GOING OPERATION.   The aircraft has DB attributes that provide information on TRAVEL MEANS, FLIGHT RADIUS, CEILING and ROLE.   Other DB attributes of the vehicle include FUEL (FUEL CAPACITY and FUEL TYPE) and FLAG.   hinge

(P)   What do you know about aircraft?
An aircraft's ROLE includes PRIMARY ROLE, DESCRIPTION and REMARKS, its FLIGHT RADIUS includes CRUISE RADIUS and COMBAT RADIUS, its CEILING includes COMBAT CEILING and MAXIMUM CEILING and its FUEL includes REFUEL CAPABILITY, FUEL CAPACITY and FUEL TYPE.   Other DB attributes of the aircraft include CRUISE SPEED, MAXIMUM SPEED, PROPULSION and NAME.   Aircraft are categorized by PROPULSION (for example, jet) and FLAG (for example, US aircraft).   Aircraft are carried by ships.   An aircraft travels by flying.

5.5. Summary

Some ways in which the responses the system currently generated might be affected by the previous discourse have been illustrated in this chapter. By simply maintaining a list of the questions already asked in the session, the system could achieve a significant improvement in the responses provided in various contexts, avoiding unnecessary repetition in generated responses. Question classes most significantly affected in this way include:

- questions about the difference between entities which are very different

- difference questions about entities neither conceptually close nor very different

- requests for available information

In some cases, additional improvement in the responses provided could be achieved if a record were maintained of the instantiated schemata that were generated. It was shown that although repetition could be avoided by consulting the list of questions asked, no guarantee can be made that appropriate comparative information could be provided if the instantiated schemata were not available. Questions whose responses are most affected by this type of discourse history are:

- questions about the difference between conceptually close entities

- in some cases, difference questions about entities neither conceptually close nor very different

- requests for definitions

This analysis has identified in very precise terms the effects that previous discourse can have on the generation of responses as well as the information needed in order to achieve such effects. The results can be generalized to other question types by noting that if the previous response overlaps sufficiently in type of content with the current response, then access to the content of that earlier response will allow the generation of a contrastive response that may make use of analogies. Otherwise, knowledge of previous questions asked will allow the system to avoid repetition.

6
Related generation research

Interest in the generation of natural language is beginning to grow as more systems are developed which require the capability for sophisticated communication with their users. This chapter provides an overview of the development of research in natural language generation. Other areas of research, such as linguistic research on discourse structure, are also relevant to this work, but are overviewed in the pertinent chapters.

The earliest generation systems relied on the use of stored text and templates to communicate with the user. The use of stored text requires the system designer to enumerate all questions the system must be able to answer and write out the answers to these questions by hand so that they can be stored as a whole and retrieved when needed. Templates allow a little more flexibility. Templates are English phrases constructed by the designer with slots which can be instantiated with different words and phrases depending upon the context. Templates may be combined and instantiated in a variety of ways to produce different answers. One main problem with templates is that the juxtaposition of complete English phrases frequently results in awkward or illegal text. A considerable amount of time must be spent by the designer experimenting with different combinations to avoid this problem.

Both of these methods require a significant amount of hand-encoding, are limited to handling anticipated questions, and cannot be extended in any significant way. They are useful, however, for situations in which a very limited range of generation is required particularly because the system can be as eloquently spoken as the designer.

Since these approaches are best viewed as engineering techniques which are often used to get a limited generation capability up and running fast, I do not discuss them further and focus instead on efforts which address some of the more interesting questions in generation: How can a system determine the phrasing of a response? How can a system communicate its intent? How can a system determine what it should say? How can a system organize its response? Later research in natural language generation, which addresses some of these issues,can be divided into the following areas of research: tactical components, planning and generation, knowledge needed for generation, and text generation. Research in each of these areas is overviewed in the following sections. The use of generation in natural language database systems is also briefly discussed in order to illustrate the extent of generation possible in natural language database systems before the TEXT system was implemented.

6.1. Tactical components - early systems

Some of the earliest work done in generation which used a grammar of English was by Simmons and Slocum (72). Their grammar was encoded in a formalism similar to an ATN (Woods 70) and was used to generate English sentences from semantic networks. Their system generated single sentences, whose content had already been specified in the semantic network formalism, and not texts. It should be noted, furthermore, that the semantic nets specified not only the propositional content of the sentence, but also the words and syntactic structures to be used. While their system produces different sentences for the same semantic net, they did little work on the reasons for using one of those sentences as opposed to any of the others. This is, however, one of the main concerns for TEXT: how information arising from decisions about what to say influences how it should be said.

Goldman (75) developed a system (MARGIE) which generates English from conceptual dependency networks. Goldman also used an ATN formalism to handle syntactic procedures, but he concentrated his research effort on developing a process to select particular words and idioms for a sentence. Goldman's generator can operate in any of three modes: question-answer, inference, or paraphrase. In paraphrase mode, Goldman's generator can output all possible ways it knows of for expressing a particular conceptual dependency net. Like Simmons and Slocum's system, however, each sentence is generated in isolation of the others and little work was done on reasons for generating one paraphrase over another. While Goldman did not address the questions of why to choose one word over another, it should be noted that he is one of the few people to have done any work on lexical choice and his formulation of the dictionary has influenced many later systems, including TEXT.

Davey's generation system (Davey 79) was an early system that was capable of more sophisticated output than some of the others. His system was implemented within the context of a tic-tac-toe game and provided a running commentary on the game. The capabilities of his system span, in some sense, both the strategic and tactical component. Although what needs to be said is given by the moves made by game participants, Davey's system maps those moves into concepts similar to the predicates used by the TEXT system (e.g. "counter-attack", "foiled threat", etc.) and uses those concepts, though limited to the tic-tac-toe context, to select connectives such as "however" and "but". Thus, Davey's system, like TEXT, can use the content and rhetorical structure to influence the surface text, but, unlike TEXT, does this on the basis of domain-dependent concepts. His grammar is based on a functional systemic grammar derived from Hudson (71), indicating he was also interested in the problem of choice. An important aspect of Davey's program is the capability for omitting details from the text which an "audience model" revealed was not necessary to provide.

6.2. Tactical components - later works

More recently, McDonald (McDonald 80) has done a considerable amount of work in natural language generation. McDonald's generator (called MUMBLE), given a "message", translates that message into English. His system can also be classified as a tactical component since it does none of the initial planning of the content or organization of the message. He describes the generation process as consisting of an "expert", which knows about the domain, the "speaker", which decides what to say about the domain, and the "linguistic component", which decides what words and syntactic structures to use. McDonald's work addresses problems in the linguistic component.

McDonald's system departs significantly from earlier work because of its broad coverage of English syntax and because of the decision making process it uses to arrive at the lexical and syntactic choices made. The linguistic component consists of three major modules: the dictionary, the grammar, and the controller. The input message is expanded as an annotated tree which will eventually represent the complete surface structure of the sentence. Initially, however, it represents the structure dictated by the selected verb of the sentence and may contain untranslated message tokens. The controller makes a depth-first traversal of the tree, consulting the dictionary when message tokens are discovered. The dictionary uses a discrimination net to select a structure and lexical items for the tokens. The grammar is also invoked during the traversal of the tree to make decisions about surface syntactic structure. Both the dictionary and the grammar take into account decisions already made in the tree traversal, the previous discourse, and knowledge about the audience to make their decisions.

The main differences between McDonald's system and other systems include 1) the modeling of spoken, and not written, English. This motivated the use of an indelible left-to-right decision-making procedure that increases the program's efficiency; 2) production is driven by the message to be produced and not by the grammar, again increasing efficiency; and 3) the linguistic structure of text already produced is represented and can be used as the basis of later decisions about syntactic or lexical choices.

Some of these points contrast directly with design decisions made for TEXT. TEXT models the production of written, and not spoken, language, and thus the process need not be strictly left-to-right and indelible as re-editing and planning ahead are clearly part of the writing process. Furthermore, production at both the strategic and tactical level is not driven by the message to be produced. That is, neither process traverses either the underlying knowledge base or message, but instead imposes textual or syntactic structure on it. Such a decision increases the generation system's capability to produce better organized text, as well as a greater variety of descriptions, at the cost of efficiency. On the other hand, TEXT draws on some of the results of McDonald's work, notably the use of a separate linguistic component and dictionary.

Mathiesson (81) is working on the development of a systemic grammar (Halliday 76) for generation as part of the PENMAN project at ISI (Mann 83). This research group is concerned with the development of a linguistically justifiable grammar since this component places an ultimate limitation on the kind of English that can be produced. They are particularly interested in the systemic grammar as a viable alternative, which models a system of choices, and are investigating the kinds of demands such a grammar would make of a knowledge representation or text planning system.

The systemic grammar is very similar in concept to the functional grammar used in TEXT. One might view Mathiesson's and Mann's work as an attempt to specify in more detail, and for a wider variety of choices, the kind of information that is needed from a strategic component to make decisions about the surface text. Thus, their work and my own can be seen as two complementary approaches to the same problem, each making demands on and suggestions for the other.

6.3. Generation in database systems

Generation of natural language in database systems has been used for providing responses to questions asked and for paraphrasing users' questions as a means of verification. These generation systems have been primarily concerned with problems that arise in the tactical component since the content of the response is usually determined by the database system to which the natural language front end is interfaced and the content of the paraphrase is determined by the user's question.

Paraphrasing systems have relied on fairly simplistic generation techniques such as canned text and the use of templates. The PLANES system (Waltz 78) selected a template in order to paraphrase a formal query and filled in the slots with arguments from the query. The Rendezvous system (Codd 78) also used templates, although it allowed for the combination of various patterns to construct a single paraphrase. An exception to this type of generation can be found in the CO-OP paraphraser (McKeown 79) which used a transformational grammar to generate paraphrases and a distinction between given and new information in the user's question to generate a paraphrase that differed syntactically from the user's.

Response generation in database systems has also been handled through the use of fairly simple techniques. Very often, information has been presented in tabular form. In some cases the user's question is inverted to produce a sentence which can be used to introduce the information retrieved from the database. An exception to this is Grishman's system (Grishman 79) which addressed the problem of unambiguously presenting answers containing conjunction or quantifiers.

6.4. Planning and generation

Cohen (78) was interested in the interaction between planning and generation. He addressed the problem of planning speech acts in response to a user's question. Part of the problem involved determining which speech act (e.g. inform, request, etc.) was most appropriate for the response. The implemented system, OSCAR, was capable of selecting speech acts, specifying the agents involved, and the propositional content of the act, but it did not produce actual English output. It should be noted that Cohen did not address problems resulting when a speech act (e.g. inform) requires the presentation of a quantity of material and how this might be achieved. These problems are, however, addressed by the TEXT system. In recent work, Cohen (81a) proposes the use of the planning formalism for deciding upon appropriate referential descriptions.

Appelt (81) extended Cohen's ideas by examining the interaction between planning and generation at all stages of the generation process. He showed that the planning formalism could be used not only for planning speech acts, but for determining the syntactic structure and lexical items of the text as well. Appelt was particularly interested in the use of language to satisfy multiple goals (for example, the ability to inform, request, and flatter simultaneously). He hypothesized that planning for speech is no different than the kind of planning that is done for physical actions and that, in fact, communication often requires the use of physical actions as well (e.g. pointing). He claims, therefore, that a speaker's behavior is controlled by a goal satisfaction process, whereby a speaker may construct a plan for satisfying one or more goals from available actions and these plans may involve interactions between physical and linguistic actions.

Appelt's program, KAMP, is a hierarchical planner. At the highest level, illocutionary acts, such as inform or request, are decided upon. At the next level, the surface speech act, an abstract representation of what's to be said, is determined. The next stage, concept activation, involves selection of explicit descriptions. At the lowest level, the utterance act is specified and this requires determining the actual words and syntactic structures to be used in the generated text. Although KAMP sometimes found it necessary to generate two or three sentences at a time in order to satisfy multiple goals, it did not embody the kind of planning necessary to deal with the generation of multi-sentential text in general.

One of the major departures of Appelt's work is its refutation of the "conduit metaphor". While other generation systems have assumed a separation between the processes of deciding what to say and how to say it, Appelt's work is based on the hypothesis that decisions made in the lowest level of the language generation process can influence decisions about what to say. This was implemented in the KAMP system through the use of a backtracking mechanism which can retract decisions across all levels of the planner.

It should be noted that although research for the TEXT system has assumed a separation between processes in order to focus on the problems of deciding what to say and how to organize it effectively, the approaches taken towards these problems would not be adversely affected by the use of a control strategy that allows for backtracking across the boundaries of the strategic and tactical component. Backtracking would give the system an additional constraint, functioning in the same way as the focus constraints, on when to include a proposition in the text. If a proposition could not be appropriately expressed at a particular point in the text, control would revert to the strategic component which would decide what else it should say at this point.

In order to allow for such a control strategy, a minor change would be needed in the TEXT system flow of control. Instead of waiting until the text message is completely constructed before invoking the tactical component, the tactical component would be invoked for each proposition as it is added to the message. The use of backtracking in the ATN mechanism, which controls the construction of the message, could then be exploited to allow for new decisions in the text planning process to be taken when a proposition could not be appropriately translated by the tactical component.

6.5. Knowledge needed for generation

Other approaches to research in language generation have emphasized the kind of knowledge needed in order to generate appropriate descriptions.

Swartout (81) examined this problem in the context of a medical consultation system. He showed that, although knowledge may be conveniently represented in one way in order to efficiently arrive at a medical diagnosis, that representation may not allow for the generation of understandable explanations about the reasoning the system uses to arrive at its diagnosis. He developed a representation appropriate for explaining the expert system's reasoning which was used for the generation of explanations. His main concern, however, was with the knowledge representation and not with the generation processes.

Meehan was also interested in the problem of knowledge needed for generation as part of his work on story generation (Meehan 77). Meehan's system was capable of producing simple short stories about persons making plans to achieve goals and their frustrations in achieving those goals. Meehan was most concerned with the planning aspects of the program and the knowledge needed for characters to be able to perform plans, although his system could produce multi-sentence descriptions of the characters and their actions.

Both of these works addressed important issues in knowledge representation, recognizing that systems are limited in what they can say to what is included in the underlying knowledge base. While the type of knowledge both of these researchers considered is not applicable to a database system and thus is not directly applicable to TEXT, it does address an issue that continues to need attention in language generation. TEXT operates under exactly the same constraint (i.e., it cannot say more than it knows about) and it was for this reason that an augmented meta-level representation of the database was used.

6.6. Text generation

Mann and Moore (81) were two of the first to be interested in the problems that arise in the generation of multi-sentential strings. They developed a system called *Knowledge Delivery System* (KDS) which could produce a paragraph providing instructions about what to do in case of a fire alarm. Their system relies on hill-climbing techniques to produce optimal text and does not use knowledge about discourse structure. Another drawback to their system is the fact that it operates in the very limited domain of the fire-alarm system.

One advantage to KDS is its ability to do continual re-editing of the text to produce the final version. TEXT does not encode the means for evaluating its own text and clearly this is an important facility which must eventually be developed. KDS uses heuristics which are not linguistically justified to do its re-evaluation, however. An example heuristic from their system is "Place all time dependent propositions in a lower section." It is unclear both why this rule should hold and whether it is applicable in any other domain than the fire alarm domain. In contrast, TEXT makes its decisions about ordering on the basis of rhetorical strategies that are commonly used for particular discourse goals.

Of previous work on text generation, Goguen, Linde and Weiner's work (Goguen, Linde and Weiner 82; Weiner 80) is most similar to TEXT. They are also interested in the structure of text, although they focus on explanations in particular, and formulate their theory of explanation structure on the basis of an analysis of naturally occurring explanations. They propose an *explanation grammar* which is similar to schemata in that it dictates what orderings of propositions are possible, it captures the hierarchical structure of text, and the kernels of the grammar (e.g., statement, reason) are at the same level of granularity as the predicates used for TEXT.

Furthermore, they also incorporate the notion of focus of attention by maintaining a pointer to the proposition in focus at each point in the explanation.

They propose that a person may justify a statement in one of three ways:

1. by providing a reason
2. by providing supporting examples
3. by providing alternatives, all of which are shown as inadequate except the alternative which supports the statement.

Thus, they use basically four "predicates" (*statement, reason, example*, and *alternative*), along with a number of subordinators such as *and/or* and *if/then*. Since explanations are frequently embedded, a statement followed by a reason may in turn function as the reason for another statement. To account for this, their grammar rules generate tree structures, which may be transformed by transformational rules, to generate the hierarchical structure representing the surface explanation. At each point in the explanation, one node of the tree is singled out as the focused node.

While the approach I have taken in TEXT is compatible with Goguen, Linde and Weiner's (hereafter referred to only as Weiner), the theory of textual structure as captured in the schemata goes considerably beyond their formulation in the following ways:

- *Association of strategy with discourse goals*: The TEXT schemata capture structures that are commonly used for three discourse goals (define, describe, and compare) in contrast to a grammar for a single discourse goal (justify). Not only do schemata capture strategies for different discourse goals than considered by Weiner, but also for a wider variety of goals. Furthermore, structure is explicitly associated with purpose (i.e., the discourse goal), while it is not in Weiner's formulation.

- *A greater number of predicates*: More predicates were observed and used for generation (a total of ten) than were used by Weiner (who described four). This is in part because a greater number of discourse goals were considered. As a result, it means that a richer description of textual structure is possible in TEXT.

- *Influences on variability*: The schemata used for TEXT capture the notion of variability which is determined by other influences on the text. Influences such as focus of attention and underlying semantic information were taken into account and the hooks exist for incorporating additional influences, such as a user model.

- *Focus of attention*: The specification of focus of attention and its
  interaction with the schemata is much more detailed in TEXT. In
  TEXT, one argument of a proposition is identified as its focus,
  while in Weiner's work, an entire proposition is focused. Because
  of this finer level of specification, the influence of focus on surface
  structure can be taken into consideration. Finally, in TEXT a
  preferential ordering on how focus can shift is used which
  describes what should be done when a choice in how to focus
  exists.

More recently, researchers have begun to look at some of the strategies
needed to provide explanations. Stevens and Steinberg (81) have made an
analysis of texts used by the Navy for instruction about propulsion plants.
They identify nine types of explanations that were used which include such
strategies as describing the flow of information through the process, describing
the process components, etc. Although not part of a generation system, this
is exactly the type of information needed to extend the capabilities of the
TEXT system to other generation tasks. Forbus (81), in fact, has proposed a
system that would use qualitative simulation of processes to provide
explanations of this sort.

Jensen et al. (81) propose the development of a system capable of
generating standard business letters. They are particularly interested in the
generation of coherent text and suggest using predicates such as CAUSE,
EFFECT, etc. to aid in the selection of appropriate textual connectives. They
assume, however, that the content of the letters and the assignment of
predicates to propositions has already been determined, something which
TEXT is capable of doing itself.

7
Summary and conclusions

In this research, I have shown how principles of discourse structure, discourse coherency, and relevancy criterion can be used for the task of generating natural language text. Each of these areas is particularly important since the generation of text and not simply the generation of single sentences was studied. In this section, the principles and their incorporation as part of the text generation method are reviewed. Some limitations of the generation method are then discussed and finally, some possibilities for future research are presented.

7.1. Discourse structure

A central thesis of this research is based on the observation that descriptions of the same information may vary from one telling to the next. This indicates that information need not be described in the same way in which it is stored. For the generation process, this means that production of text does not simply trace the knowledge representation. Instead, standard principles for communication are used to organize a text. These rhetorical techniques are used to guide the generation process in the TEXT system. Since different rhetorical techniques are associated with different discourse purposes, it was shown that different descriptions of the same information can be produced depending upon the discourse situation. By incorporating commonly used techniques for communication into its answers, the system is able to convey information more effectively.

7.2. Relevancy criterion

It was pointed out that, when speaking, people are able to ignore large bodies of knowledge and focus on information that is relevant to the current discourse purpose. By constraining focus of attention to relevant information, a generation system is able to determine more efficiently what should be said next. By computing such constraints early in the generation process, the system doesn't need to consider everything it knows about when deciding what to include in the text. This partitioning of the knowledge base to a subset of relevant information was shown to be the equivalent of global focus since its contents remain focused throughout the course of an answer. Some techniques for determining relevancy were presented.

7.3. Discourse coherency

It was shown that each utterance further constrains the possibilities for what can be said next. Thus, as the discourse is constructed it can be used to narrow down the set of choices for what information is selected next. These constraints were implemented through the use of a mechanism which tracks immediate focus. Although immediate focus has been used effectively for the interpretation of discourse, extensions were needed if it was to be used for generation. These extensions required the specification of reasons for discriminating between the legal focus moves a speaker can make at any given point. One major result of this research, therefore, is an ordering on these legal focus moves. Use of immediate focus constraints in the generation process means that the system will choose to say next that which most closely ties in with the previous discourse and in this way discourse coherency is ensured.

7.4. Generality of generation principles

Although the generation principles developed here were used for the tasks of providing definitions, describing information, and comparing entities, these principles are applicable to all generation tasks. That is, in any situation where generation is required, the best results can be achieved if the system is capable of reasoning about the communicative strategies most appropriate for the generation task. Responding to the classes of questions handled here is not unique in requiring consideration of communicative techniques. In fact, the analysis of texts (Chapter Two) shows that the use of various techniques occurs across a wide spectrum of text types.

Moreover, any generation system which does not adopt this approach is forced into describing information in exactly the same way every time a description is required, regardless of the situation for which the description is required. In such a case, special care is required when designing the knowledge base to ensure that information is represented in a way that makes the production of understandable descriptions possible.

The use of focusing, as described in this work, is clearly applicable to all types of generation. The preferences developed for shifting and maintaining focus are in no way dependent upon the type of generation required or the domain. The use of focusing provides computational constraints on the generation process that are useful in all domains. Furthermore, any multi-sentential text that is produced must be coherent and focusing is one way of ensuring that.

Although the TEXT system was designed to generate answers to questions about database structure (a feature lacking in most natural language database systems), the same techniques and principles can be used in other application areas where generation of language is needed. Computer assisted instruction systems provide a good example of where generation of language could be enhanced by taking into account the best techniques for presenting information. The generation of explanations in expert systems is another area where communicative techniques could be used to improve the quality of text output.

7.5. An evaluation of the generated text

To illustrate how the generation principles have been successful in producing coherent texts, as well as to identify defects in the text, consider the text generated in response to the question "What is a guided projectile?" (shown in (1) below). This text is representative of the range of generation the system can produce and is as good a choice as any of its answers for an evaluation.

(1) 1) A guided projectile is a projectile that is self-propelled. 2) There are 2 types of guided projectiles in the ONR database: torpedoes and missiles. 3) The missile has a target location in the air or on the earth's surface. 4) The torpedo has an underwater target location. 5) The missile's target location is indicated by the DB attribute DESCRIPTION and the missile's flight capabilities are provided by the DB attribute ALTITUDE. 6) The torpedo's underwater capabilities are provided by the DB attributes under DEPTH (for example, MAXIMUM OPERATING DEPTH). 7) The guided projectile has DB attributes TIME TO TARGET & UNITS, HORZ RANGE & UNITS and NAME.

First notice the overall structure of the text, dictated by the constituency schema. The paragraph is bracketed by discussion of the guided projectile (first and last sentence). The inner portion of the text relates the guided projectile to its sub-classes and then discusses each of these in turn. The overall structure is thus nicely balanced, providing a clear organizational framework for the reader. A random order of the sentences would be much less appealing and even confusing for the reader.

Now consider the content of the text. The system has correctly, although not surprisingly, included only information that is directly or indirectly related to the guided projectile. This is the result of using the relevant knowledge pool. More important, of all the information that could have been included from information related to the guided projectile, the system has selected only that which directly supports its goal of defining the object. Of 11 pieces of information related to the guided projectile[38] the system has chosen to include only 5 pieces of information (i.e., its superordinate (sentence 1), its sub-classes (sentence 2), and 3 of its attributes (sentence 3)). Of 26 pieces of information associated with the missile and at least that many for the torpedo, the system has chosen to select only 2 for the torpedo and 4 for the missile (1 defining attribute and 1 database attribute for the torpedo and 2 defining attributes and 2 database attributes for the missile). This is due partly to the use of the constituency schema which dictates which techniques and information are appropriate for a definition. It determines that the superordinate of the guided projectile should be identified and its sub-classes described. Moreover, it determines that defining attributes of both the missile and torpedo should be included (sentences 3 and 4). The focus constraints also play a role in the selection of information. They ensure, for example, that when DB attributes are selected for sentences 5 and 6, only attributes are selected which support the definitional attributes presented in the previous sentences.

The surface text is influenced by the focus constraints such that constructions are selected that increase coherency. In this particular text, the use of there-insertion in sentence (2) was selected on the basis of an introduction of a set into focus. Similarly, the passive is used in sentences (5) and (6) to allow continued focus on the missile and torpedo. In some texts, the use of a particular rhetorical technique will force the selection of a sentential connective. This does not occur in this text.

Many of the defects of the text are due to limitations in the surface text generator (i.e., the tactical component). The text could be improved, for example, by combining sentences (2) and (3), emphasizing the contrast (e.g., "The missile has a target location in the air or on the earth's surface while the torpedo has an underwater target location."). Alternatively, the switch in

---

[38]An English translation of these 11 pieces is:

1. The guided projectile is a self-propelled projectile.
2. Attributes relating to self-propulsion include FUSE TYPE (possessed by the torpedo).
3. The DB attribute SPEED INDICES (possessed by the missile) also indicates properties of self-propulsion.
4. It has 6 DB attributes associated with it (counted here as 6 pieces of information): HORZ RANGE & UNITS, TIME TO TARGET & UNITS, HORZ RANGE, HORZ RANGE UNITS, TIME TO TARGET, TIME TO TARGET UNITS.
5. It is carried by water-going vehicles.
6. There are two types of guided projectiles: missiles and torpedoes.

focus back to the guided projectile could be more clearly signalled, at the same time linking the proposition to previously conveyed information by using a phrasing such as "The DB attributes common to all guided projectiles include ...". The generation of more sophisticated phrasings such as these requires further theoretical work for the tactical component, addressing the question of why these phrasings are preferable to others.

On the organizational level, improvement could be achieved by grouping together statements about the missile and statements about the torpedo. This would involve a change to the constituency schema so that the system could group together statements about an element of a set when more than one statement occurs. Such a change would allow the tactical component to pronominalize second references to both the missile and the torpedo, thus reducing some of the ponderous feeling of the text.

More significant improvements to the text can only be made by dramatically improving the capabilities of the system. Some of these facilities would include inferencing (e.g., if the system can recognize and state the target location of the missile and torpedo, it should be able to infer that although both weapons have a target location, the exact location differs), varying detail (e.g., do all readers need to know about missiles and torpedoes or would the information about the guided projectile alone be sufficient?), and finer determination of relevance (e.g., if the reader already knew about bombs, a guided projectile should be compared against this existing knowledge, requiring the system to elaborate further on the fact that guided projectiles are self-propelled, while bombs are not). Improvements to the system in these directions are discussed in the following sections.

7.6. Limitations of the implemented system

One limitation of the TEXT system is the lack of specific information about the particular users of the system. This information could be used to tailor responses for different individuals. Currently, the system assumes a static, casual and naive user and its responses are geared for that type of person. Inclusion of a user-model would allow for improvement in the quality of text produced.

Another limitation of the TEXT system is the lack of an inferencing capability. This means that the TEXT system is only capable of talking about information which is explicitly encoded in the knowledge base.[39] The inclusion of an inferencing capability would allow the system to generate additional information from what is known which might be appropriate in different situations.

---

[39]A few exceptions to this rule exist. For example, the system is capable of making numerical comparisons between entities.

Despite these limitations, a significant improvement in the quality of computer generated multi-sentential text was achieved by the TEXT system through the use of text structuring techniques and an account of focusing. By limiting the scope of the project, this research could focus on issues concerning the content and organization of the generated text. These two issues are complex ones that have not been appropriately handled by previous work in natural language generation. Thus, by developing a computational solution to these two questions, this work constitutes a major contribution to the field of natural language generation.

7.7. Future directions

Although the TEXT system embodies a thorough treatment of principles of discourse structure, coherency, and relevancy, other uses and development of these principles are possible. In this section, possibilities for future research in each of these three areas are considered.

7.7.1. Discourse structure

Examination of the recursive nature of the schemas and the hierarchical text structure that would result from recursion is one possibility for future work. This would require determining when a single sentence is sufficient for explanation and in what situations more detail is required. Thus, an examination of when recursion is necessary as well as an examination of how recursion is achieved are needed. Decisions about the necessity for detail rest in part on an assessment of the user's knowledge and therefore the development of a user model for generation would be required.

The hooks for adding the ability to vary the amount of detail are present in the current formulation of schemata. The machinery for performing recursion is implemented in the TEXT system as it stands. The tests for when to recurse on a predicate, however, are not very well developed. The default assumption is that no recursion will be performed and only in a few very specific cases, where the user's question alone indicates that more detail is necessary, is recursion invoked. The incorporation of conditions that trigger recursion will require a major extension of the theory. It requires an extensive examination of the effect of the user's knowledge state on the need for more detail and an analysis of how that information can be derived from the discourse. While previous work on representation of beliefs and goals (e.g., Moore 80; Allen and Perrault 80) would be helpful here, particular attention must be addressed to the problem of how much to say. In addition, schemata would need to be developed for the predicates which do not have associated schemata in the current formulation. This would require additional analysis of texts which serve the discourse purposes of these predicates.

Segmentation of the discourse is another possibility for future research. Segmentation involves decisions about where sentence and paragraph boundaries should occur. The delineation of paragraphs within a text depends in part on the amount of information presented about a given topic (a text of single sentence paragraphs, for example, would not be appropriate) and in part on semantic boundaries. Paragraphing, therefore, seems to be closely related to the recursive use of schemata. Where a predicate has been expanded as a schema, a sufficient amount of related information is presented to warrant the use of a paragraph. Extensions in this direction depend on the incorporation of full recursion into the theory, but will essentially fall out of that effort. Experimentation would need to be done to determine whether the hypothesis that paragraph structure can depend on recursive structure will produce satisfactory texts. The compare and contrast schema, which entails the use of other schemata, illustrates how this use of paragraphing would work. In the example below, a paragraph is formed in each place where a different schema has been invoked.

Identification schema

The cruiser and the ocean escort are surface ships. The ship's surface-going capabilities are provided by the DB attributes DISPLACEMENT and DRAFT. The ship has DB attributes MAXIMUM SPEED, PROPULSION, FUEL (FUEL CAPACITY and FUEL TYPE), DIMENSIONS, SPEED DEPENDENT RANGE and OFFICIAL NAME.

Attributive schema

Ocean escorts have a DISPLACEMENT between 3400 and 4100. All ocean escorts in the ONR database have REMARKS of 0, FUEL TYPE of BNKR, FLAG of BLBL, MAST HEIGHT of 85 and PROPULSION of STMTURGRD. Ocean escorts carry between 2 and 22 torpedoes, 16 missiles, and between 1 and 2 guns. A ship is classified as an ocean escort if the characters 1 through 2 of its HULL NO are DE.

Attributive schema

Cruisers have a PROPULSION of STMTURGRD and a LENGTH between 510 and 673. All cruisers in the ONR database have REMARKS of 0 and FUEL TYPE of BNKR. Cruisers carry between 8 and 42 torpedoes, between 4 and 98 missiles, and between 1 and 4 guns. A ship is classified as a cruiser if the characters 1 through 2 of its HULL NO are CL or the characters 1 through 2 of its HULL NO are CG.

Return to compare and contrast schema

The ocean escort, therefore, has a smaller LENGTH and a smaller DISPLACEMENT than the cruiser.

Other research on discourse structure could involve the development of different strategies or structures for use in describing other kinds of knowledge. Descriptions of processes, causes and effects, and temporal or spatial relations might require the use of different communicative techniques as well as different combinations of these techniques. This type of research is particularly important in the development of interaction with *dynamic databases*. While the questions handled by the TEXT system are appropriate for static databases, additional question-answering capabilities are necessary for dynamic natural language database systems that encode knowledge about changes that can occur. Answering these types of questions requires the ability to describe processes, cause and effect, and temporal sequences.

It is unclear in what ways strategies for answering these types of questions will be like the discourse strategies developed here. One major hypothesis I have made is that textual organization need not mirror the organization of the knowledge being described. Yet, clearly, part of a strategy for describing a temporal sequence may be to mirror the underlying time-line. Preserving temporal sequence is one way to give coherence to a text. Strategies for describing processes, cause and effect, and temporal sequence may well include directives that specify how to trace the underlying knowledge. While I strongly feel that these two different perspectives on textual strategy can and will be merged, exactly how this integration can come about remains to be seen.

7.7.2. Relevancy

In the TEXT system as currently implemented, global focus remains unchanged throughout the course of an answer. For longer sequences of text, global focus may shift. This is also related to the use of schema recursion (see Chapter Three). Where more detail is required, focus shifts to the details presented. The implementation of shifting focus would require capabilities for expansion and stacking of focus in addition to the full development of the recursive mechanism.

More sophisticated techniques for determining relevancy must also be examined. The methods used in TEXT for determining relevancy are relatively unsophisticated with the exception of those used in response to "difference" questions. Any complex analysis of relevancy must take into account the particular user and thus a user model will be required. Other techniques for determining relevancy might rely on an account of saliency (e.g., McDonald and Conklin 82).

The development of a theoretical basis for relevance is a large undertaking which researchers have only recently begun to examine. Because so little is known about what such a theory might look like it is difficult to speculate how it might interact with the theory of generation espoused here. If relevancy can be totally determined at the beginning of the question-answering process, then we can imagine a larger theory producing the relevant knowledge pool in place of the process that is now used. If relevance continually changes as the text is constructed, then a more sophisticated theory would likely interact with the recursive mechanism and global focus shifts.

7.7.3. Coherency

An open question for the use of focusing concerns the nature of the structures for maintaining and shifting focus. More complex structures may be needed for some situations. For example, a speaker may introduce an item into conversation, but specify that he will continue to talk about it at a later point. It is unclear whether the use of a simple stack is sufficient for modeling these types of explicitly orchestrated expectations (see (Reichman 81) for a discussion of speaker expectations). Another case where different structures may be necessary is illustrated by Joshi and Weinstein (81) who point out that certain syntactic structures are used to turn off past foci as candidates for future foci. They also show that shifts in focus to items that are functionally dependent on past foci may have a similar effect. Accounting for these additional structures should not negate the theory, however, but augment it.

As mentioned in Chapter Three, no account of the use of foci implicitly associated with focus was made since this requires the use of general world knowledge and an inferencing capability. Developing a method for selecting an appropriate implicit association to talk about next is a difficult and challenging task precisely because of its dependence on world knowledge. A more manageable, but equally necessary, task that must eventually be addressed is the specification of conditions and influences on when to shift focus to associated items rather than to explicitly mentioned items. Such a specification would likely be part of an extension to the preference ordering on immediate focus shifts.

7.7.4. User model

The addition of a user model to the generation system is another direction for future research. It was shown that a user model is needed for extensions in the use of both discourse structure and relevancy for generation. A user model is necessary for the use of full schema recursion, both for determining when more detail is necessary and for expanding the relevant knowledge pool to include that detail. A user model could also be used in determining which information to include in the relevant knowledge pool initially. In these cases, knowledge of what the user knows and believes can aid in determining exactly what information is relevant for the current user and in determining how much information is necessary given what he already knows. In order to incorporate information about users into the generation system, research on exactly what information about the users can be determined from the discourse and on how that information can be deduced needs to be done. This effort can draw on the rich body of existing work on formalisms and methods for reasoning about knowledge and belief (e.g., Moore 79; Allen 80; Appelt 82).

7.8. Conclusion

The TEXT system successfully incorporates generation principles into a method for generating coherent, effective English text of paragraph length. This work has illustrated that knowledge about discourse structure can be used to guide the generation process and that focus constraints can be used to ensure discourse coherency. It was shown, furthermore, that an interaction between these structural and semantic processes is required for the production of text. By addressing issues such as these in the generation of multi-sentential text, this work has opened up a number of possible avenues for future research.

Appendix A
Sample output of the TEXT system

```
$ lisp
Franz Lisp, Opus 34
->   64400 bytes read into 2c00 to 66fff
loading init.lsp
* changed def


1.(load-TEXT)
kb access files dskined
initial files of system dskined
TEXT strategic component loaded
Dictionary loaded
[fasl [kathy.tact]newu.o]
[fasl [kathy.tact]ucon.o]
Unifier functions loaded
Grammar loaded
[fasl [kathy.tact]linear.o]
Linearizer loaded
Unifier ready to use
TEXT tactical component loaded


fql loaded --- system ready to use
nil
2.(TEXT)
```

Welcome to TEXT

A system which answers questions about
database structure

TEXT allows you to familiarize yourself with a database
before asking questions of the database itself.

You may ask questions of the following type about the database structure:

    1. What do you know about <e>?
    2. What is a <e>?
    3. What is the difference between <e1> and <e2>?

by using the corresponding functions:

    1. (information <e>)
    2. (definition <e>)
    3. (differense <e1> <e2>)

where <e> represents an entity-class in the database.

As each answer is constructed, you have the option of seeing
various intermediary information printed.
Would you like to see tracing information? (y/n) n
Would you like to see the potential focus list? (y/n) n
Would you like to see the focus-stack? (y/n) n

To exit from TEXT, type EXIT.
To execute regular LISP functions type x <lisp function>.

You may begin asking questions.

(information)

Schema selected: constituency

proposition selected:
(attributive db OBJECT (name REMARKS))

focus: OBJECT

proposition selected:
(constituency OBJECT (VEHICLE DESTRUCTIVE-DEVICE))

focus: OBJECT

proposition selected:
(attributive db VEHICLE (based-dbs (SOME-TYPE-OF TRAVEL_MEANS)
(SOME-TYPE-OF SPEED_INDICES)))

focus: VEHICLE

proposition selected:
(attributive db DESTRUCTIVE-DEVICE (based-dbs (SOME-TYPE-OF
LETHAL_INDICES)))

focus: DESTRUCTIVE-DEVICE

Message through dictionary. Entering tactical component

Processor time used: 977 seconds
Time used for garbage collection: 500 seconds

All entities have DB attributes REMARKS. There are 2 types of entities in
the ONR database: destructive devices and vehicles. The vehicle has DB
attributes that provide information on SPEED_INDICES and
TRAVEL_MEANS. The destructive device has DB attributes that provide
information on LETHAL_INDICES.

Processor time used: 17314 seconds
Time used for garbage collection: 8819 seconds

#(information ECHO-II-SUBMARINE)

Schema selected: attributive

proposition selected:
(attributive def ECHO-II-SUBMARINE ((FLAG) (PROPULSION_TYPE))
(((FLAG (RDRD))) ((PROPULSION__TYPE (NUCL)))))

focus: ECHO-II-SUBMARINE

proposition selected:
(amplification db ECHO-II-SUBMARINE (((FLAG) (PROPULSION_TYPE))
((FLAG (RDRD))) ((PROPULSION_TYPE (NUCL))))))
(MAXIMUM_SUBMERGED_SPEED 20) (NORMAL_OPERATING_DEPTH
100) (MAXIMUM_OPERATING_DEPTH 700) (IRCS 0) (FUEL_TYPE
NUCL) (REMARKS 0))

focus: (((FLAG) (PROPULSION_TYPE)) (((FLAG (RDRD)))
((PROPULSION_TYPE (NUCL))))

proposition selected:
(classification ECHO-II-SUBMARINE 0 sub-classes)

focus: ECHO-II-SUBMARINE

proposition selected:
(analogy rels ECHO-II-SUBMARINE ON (GUN 0) (MISSILE (16 99))
(TORPEDO (16)))

focus: ECHO-II-SUBMARINE

proposition selected:
(explanation based-db ECHO-II-SUBMARINE (((FLAG)
(PROPULSION_TYPE)) (((FLAG (RDRD))) ((PROPULSION_TYPE
(NUCL))))) (CLASS ECHO II))

focus: ECHO-II-SUBMARINE

Message through dictionary. Entering tactical component

Echo IIs have a PROPULSION_TYPE of NUCL and a FLAG of RDRD.
All Echo IIs in the ONR database have REMARKS of 0, FUEL_TYPE of

NUCL, IRCS of 0, MAXIMUM_OPERATING_DEPTH of 700 and NORMAL_OPERATING_DEPTH of 100. There are no sub-classes of Echo II in the ONR database. Echo IIs carry 16 torpedoes, between 16 and 99 missiles and 0 guns. A submarine is classified as an Echo II if its CLASS is ECHO II.

#(definition GUIDED)

Schema selected: constituency

proposition selected:
(identification GUIDED PROJECTILE (restrictive TRAVEL-MEANS SELF-PROPELLED) (non-restrictive ROLE PROJECTED-OBJECT))

focus: GUIDED

proposition selected:
(constituency GUIDED (MISSILE TORPEDOE))

focus: GUIDED

proposition selected:
(attributive def MISSILE GUIDED TARGET-LOCATION SURFACE-AIR)

focus: MISSILE

proposition selected:
(attributive def TORPEDOE GUIDED TARGET-LOCATION UNDERWATER)

focus: TORPEDOE

proposition selected:
(evidence based-db MISSILE (TARGET-LOCATION SURFACE-AIR) (INDICATED-BY DESCRIPTION) (HAVE ALTITUDE))

focus: MISSILE

proposition selected.

(evidence based-db TORPEDOE (TARGET-LOCATION UNDERWATER) (SOME-TYPE-OF DEPTH))

focus: TORPEDOE

proposition selected:
(attributive db GUIDED (name NAME) (Topics HORZ_RANGE_&_UNITS TIME_TO_TARGET_&_UNITS))

focus: db-attribute

Message through dictionary. Entering tactical component

Processor time used: 758 seconds
Time used for garbage collection: 0 seconds

A guided projectile is a projectile that is self-propelled. There are 2 types of guided projectiles in the ONR database: torpedoes and missiles. The missile has a target location in the air or on the earth's surface. The torpedo has an underwater target location. The missile's target location is indicated by the DB attribute DESCRIPTION and the missile's flight capabilities are provided by the DB attribute ALTITUDE. The torpedo's underwater capabilities are provided by the DB attributes under DEPTH (for example, MAXIMUM_OPERATING_DEPTH). The guided projectile has DB attributes TIME_TO_TARGET_&_UNITS, HORZ_RANGE_&_UNITS and NAME.

Processor time used: 26229 seconds
Time used for garbage collection: 11531 seconds

#(definition SHIP)

Schema selected: identification

proposition selected:
(identification SHIP WATER-VEHICLE (restrictive TRAVEL-MODE SURFACE) (non-restrictive TRAVEL-MEDIUM WATER) (non-restrictive FUNCTION TRANSPORTATION))

focus: SHIP

proposition selected:
(evidence based-db SHIP (TRAVEL-MODE SURFACE) (HAVE DRAFT)
(HAVE DISPLACEMENT))

focus: (TRAVEL-MODE SURFACE)

proposition selected:
(attributive db SHIP (name OFFICIAL_NAME) (topics
SPEED_DEPENDENT_RANGE DIMENSIONS) (duplicates (FUEL
FUEL_TYPE FUEL_CAPACITY)) (attrs PROPULSION
MAXIMUM_SPEED))

focus: db-attribute

proposition selected:
(particular-illustration SHIP ((name OFFICIAL_NAME) (topics
SPEED_DEPENDENT_RANGE DIMENSIONS) (duplicates (FUEL
FUEL_TYPE FUEL_CAPACITY)) (attrs PROPULSION
MAXIMUM_SPEED)) (OFFICIAL_NAME DOWNES)
(ENDURANCE_RANGE 2200) (ECONOMIC_RANGE 4200) (LENGTH 438)
(BEAM 46) (DRAFT 25) (FUEL_TYPE BNKR) (FUEL_CAPACITY 810)
(PROPULSION STMTURGRD) (MAXIMUM_SPEED 29))

focus: ((name OFFICIAL_NAME) (topics SPEED_DEPENDENT_RANGE
DIMENSIONS) (duplicates (FUEL FUEL_TYPE FUEL_CAPACITY)) (attrs
PROPULSION MAXIMUM_SPEED))

Message through dictionary. Entering tactical component

Processor time used: 3184 seconds
Time used for garbage collection: 858 seconds

A ship is a water-going vehicle that travels on the surface. Its surface-going
capabilities are provided by the DB attributes DISPLACEMENT and
DRAFT. Other DB attributes of the ship include MAXIMUM_SPEED,
PROPULSION, FUEL (FUEL_CAPACITY and FUEL_TYPE),
DIMENSIONS, SPEED_DEPENDENT_RANGE and OFFICIAL_NAME.
The DOWNES, for example, has MAXIMUM_SPEED of 29, PROPULSION
of STMTURGRD, FUEL of 810 (FUEL_CAPACITY) and BNKR
(FUEL_TYPE), DIMENSIONS of 25 (DRAFT), 46 (BEAM), and 438

(LENGTH) and SPEED_DEPENDENT_RANGE of 4200
(ECONOMIC_RANGE) and 2200 (ENDURANCE_RANGE).

Processor time used: 31150 seconds
Time used for garbage collection: 11050 seconds

#(definition **AIRCRAFT-CARRIER**)

Schema selected: identification

proposition selected:
(identification AIRCRAFT-CARRIER SHIP (restrictive ((LENGTH)
(DISPLACEMENT)) (((LENGTH (1039 1063))) ((DISPLACEMENT (78000
80800))))) (non-restrictive TRAVEL-MODE SURFACE))

focus: AIRCRAFT-CARRIER

proposition selected:
(analogy ranges AIRCRAFT-CARRIER (((LENGTH (1039 1063)))
((DISPLACEMENT (78000 80800)))) (larger-than-all LENGTH (1039 1063))
(larger-than-most DISPLACEMENT (78000 80800)))

focus: (((LENGTH (1039 1063))) ((DISPLACEMENT (78000 80800))))

proposition selected:
(particular-illustration MINE-WARFARE-SHIP (((LENGTH (1039 1063)))
((DISPLACEMENT (78000 80800)))) (LENGTH (144)) (DISPLACEMENT
(320)))

focus: (((LENGTH (1039 1063))) ((DISPLACEMENT (78000 80800))))

proposition selected:
(amplification db AIRCRAFT-CARRIER (((LENGTH (1039 1063)))
((DISPLACEMENT (78000 80800)))) (PROPULSION STMTURGRD)
(ENDURANCE_SPEED 30) (ECONOMIC_SPEED 12)
(ENDURANCE_RANGE 4000) (BEAM 252) (FLAG BLBL) (FUEL_TYPE
BNKR) (REMARKS 0))

focus: (((LENGTH (1039 1063))) ((DISPLACEMENT (78000 80800))))

proposition selected:
(evidence based-db AIRCRAFT-CARRIER (((LENGTH) (DISPLACEMENT))
(((LENGTH (1039 1063))) ((DISPLACEMENT (78000 80800))))) (HULL_NO
(1 2 CV)))

focus: (((LENGTH) (DISPLACEMENT)) (((LENGTH (1039 1063)))
((DISPLACEMENT (78000 80800))))))

Message through dictionary. Entering tactical component

Processor time used: 3290 seconds
Time used for garbage collection: 0 seconds

An aircraft carrier is a surface ship with a DISPLACEMENT between 78000
and 80800 and a LENGTH between 1039 and 1063. Aircraft carriers have a
greater LENGTH than all other ships and a greater DISPLACEMENT than
most other ships. Mine warfare ships, for example, have a DISPLACEMENT
of 320 and a LENGTH of 144. All aircraft carriers in the ONR database
have REMARKS of 0, FUEL_TYPE of BNKR, FLAG of BLBL, BEAM of
252, ENDURANCE_RANGE of 4000, ECONOMIC_SPEED of 12 and
ENDURANCE_SPEED of 30. A ship is classified as an aircraft carrier if
the characters 1 through 2 of its HULL_NO are CV.

Processor time used: 43845 seconds
Time used for garbage collection: 18256 seconds

#(differense OCEAN-ESCORT CRUISER)

Schema selected: c&c-attributive

proposition selected:
(identification (OCEAN-ESCORT CRUISER) SHIP (non-restrictive TRAVEL-
MODE SURFACE))

focus: (OCEAN-ESCORT CRUISER)

proposition selected:

(evidence based-db SHIP (TRAVEL-MODE SURFACE) (HAVE DRAFT)
(HAVE DISPLACEMENT))

focus: (TRAVEL-MODE SURFACE)

proposition selected:
(attributive db SHIP (name OFFICIAL_NAME) (topics
SPEED_DEPENDENT_RANGE DIMENSIONS) (duplicates (FUEL
FUEL_TYPE FUEL_CAPACITY)) (attrs PROPULSION
MAXIMUM_SPEED))

focus: SHIP

proposition selected:
(attributive def OCEAN-ESCORT SHIP ((DISPLACEMENT))
(((DISPLACEMENT (3400 4100)))))

focus: OCEAN-ESCORT

proposition selected:
(amplification db OCEAN-ESCORT (((DISPLACEMENT)) (((DISPLACEMENT
(3400 4100))))) (PROPULSION STMTURGRD) (MAST_HEIGHT 85) (FLAG
BLBL) (FUEL_TYPE BNKR) (REMARKS 0))

focus: (((DISPLACEMENT)) (((DISPLACEMENT (3400 4100)))))

proposition selected:
(analogy rels OCEAN-ESCORT ON (GUN (1 2)) (MISSILE (16))
(TORPEDOE (2 22)))

focus: OCEAN-ESCORT

proposition selected:
(explanation based-db OCEAN-ESCORT (((DISPLACEMENT))
(((DISPLACEMENT (3400 4100))))) (HULL_NO (1 2 DE)))

focus: OCEAN-ESCORT

proposition selected:
{(attributive def CRUISER SHIP ((LENGTH PROPULSION)) (((LENGTH
(510 673)) (PROPULSION (STMTURGRD)))))

focus: CRUISER

proposition selected:
(amplification db CRUISER (((LENGTH PROPULSION)) (((LENGTH (510 673)) (PROPULSION (STMTURGRD))))) (FUEL_TYPE BNKR) (REMARKS 0))

focus: (((LENGTH PROPULSION)) (((LENGTH (510 673)) (PROPULSION (STMTURGRD)))))

proposition selected:
(analogy rels CRUISER ON (GUN (1 4)) (MISSILE (4 98)) (TORPEDOE (8 42)))

focus: CRUISER

proposition selected:
(explanation based-db CRUISER (((LENGTH PROPULSION)) (((LENGTH (510 673)) (PROPULSION (STMTURGRD))))) (HULL_NO (1 2 CA) (1 2 CG) (1 2 CL)))

focus: CRUISER

proposition selected:
(inference OCEAN-ESCORT CRUISER (HULL_NO (1 2 DE) (1 2 CA)) (smaller DISPLACEMENT) (smaller LENGTH) (PROPULSION (STMTURGRD) (STMTURGRD)))

focus: (OCEAN-ESCORT CRUISER)

Message through dictionary. Entering tactical component

Processor time used: 5949 seconds
Time used for garbage collection: 0 seconds

The cruiser and the ocean escort are surface ships. The ship's surface-going capabilities are provided by the DB attributes DISPLACEMENT and DRAFT. The ship has DB attributes MAXIMUM_SPEED, PROPULSION,

FUEL(FUEL_CAPACITY and FUEL_TYPE), DIMENSIONS, SPEED_DEPENDENT_RANGE and OFFICIAL_NAME. Ocean escorts have a DISPLACEMENT between 3400 and 4100. All ocean escorts in the ONR database have REMARKS of 0, FUEL_TYPE of BNKR, FLAG of BLBL and MAST_HEIGHT of 85. Ocean escorts carry between 2 and 22 torpedoes, 16 missiles and between 1 and 2 guns. A ship is classified as an ocean escort if the characters 1 through 2 of its HULL_NO are DE. Cruisers have a PROPULSION of STMTURGRD and a LENGTH between 510 and 673. All cruisers in the ONR database have REMARKS of 0. Cruisers carry between 8 and 42 torpedoes, between 4 and 98 missiles and between 1 and 4 guns. A ship is classified as a cruiser if the characters 1 through 2 of its HULL_NO are CL or the characters 1 through 2 of its HULL_NO are CG. The ocean escort, therefore, has a smaller LENGTH and a smaller DISPLACEMENT than the cruiser.

Processor time used: 80671 seconds
Time used for garbage collection: 32890 seconds

#(definition **WHISKY-SUBMARINE**)

Schema selected: identification

proposition selected:
(identification WHISKY-SUBMARINE SUBMARINE (restrictive ((FLAG) (PROPULSION_TYPE)) (((FLAG (RDOR))) ((PROPULSION_TYPE (DIESEL))))) (non-restrictive TRAVEL-MODE UNDERWATER))

focus: WHISKY-SUBMARINE

proposition selected:
(evidence based-db WHISKY-SUBMARINE (((FLAG) (PROPULSION_TYPE)) (((FLAG (RDOR))) ((PROPULSION_TYPE (DIESEL))))) (CLASS WHISKY))

focus: (((FLAG) (PROPULSION_TYPE)) (((FLAG (RDOR))) ((PROPULSION_TYPE (DIESEL)))))

proposition selected:
(attributive db WHISKY-SUBMARINE (MAXIMUM_SUBMERGED_SPEED 15) (NORMAL_OPERATING_DEPTH 100)

(MAXIMUM_OPERATING_DEPTH 700) (IRCS 0) (FUEL_TYPE
DIESEL) (FUEL_CAPACITY 200) (REMARKS 0))

focus: db-attribute

Message through dictionary. Entering tactical component

Processor time used: 1631 seconds
Time used for garbage collection: 0 seconds

A whisky is an underwater submarine with a PROPULSION_TYPE of
DIESEL and a FLAG of RDOR. A submarine is classified as a whisky if its
CLASS is WHISKY. All whiskies in the ONR database have REMARKS of
0, FUEL_CAPACITY of 200, FUEL_TYPE of DIESEL, IRCS of 0,
MAXIMUM_OPERATING_DEPTH of 700,
NORMAL_OPERATING_DEPTH of 100 and
MAXIMUM_SUBMERGED_SPEED of 15.

Processor time used: 23357 seconds
Time used for garbage collection: 8108 seconds

#(differense **MISSILE TORPEDOE)**

Schema selected: c&c-attributive

proposition selected:
(identification (MISSILE TORPEDOE) GUIDED (non-restrictive TRAVEL-
MEANS SELF-PROPELLED))

focus: (MISSILE TORPEDOE)

proposition selected:
(evidence based-db GUIDED (TRAVEL-MEANS SELF-PROPELLED) (HAVE
FUSE_TYPE (EXCEPTION MISSILE)) (SOME-TYPE-OF SPEED_INDICES
(EXCEPTION TORPEDOE)))

focus; (TRAVEL-MEANS SELF-PROPELLED)

proposition selected:

(attributive db GUIDED (name NAME) (topics HORZ_RANGE_&_UNITS
TIME_TO_TARGET_&_UNITS))

focus: GUIDED

proposition selected:
(attributive def MISSILE GUIDED TARGET-LOCATION SURFACE-AIR)

focus: MISSILE

proposition selected:
(amplification evidence based-db MISSILE (TARGET-LOCATION SURFACE-
AIR) (INDICATED-BY DESCRIPTION) (HAVE ALTITUDE))

focus: (TARGET-LOCATION SURFACE-AIR)

proposition selected:
(attributive db MISSILE (name) (topics TIME_TO_TARGET_&_UNITS
LETHAL_RADIUS_&_UNITS ALTITUDE) (attrs SPEED
PROBABILITY_OF_KILL))

focus: db

proposition selected:
(analogy rels MISSILE ON AIR-VEHICLE WATER-VEHICLE)

focus: MISSILE

proposition selected:
(attributive def TORPEDOE GUIDED TARGET-LOCATION
UNDERWATER)

focus: TORPEDOE

(amplification evidence based-db TORPEDOE (TARGET-LOCATION
UNDERWATER) (SOME-TYPE-OF DEPTH))

focus: (TARGET-LOCATION UNDERWATER)

proposition selected:

(attributive db TORPEDOE (name)(topics
TIME_TO_TARGET_&_UNITS HORZ_RANGE_&_UNITS
ACCURACY_&_UNITS) (attrs MAXIMUM_DEPTH FUSE_TYPE))

focus: db-attribute

proposition selected:
(analogy rels TORPEDOE ON WATER-VEHICLE)

focus: TORPEDOE

proposition selected:
(inference MISSILE TORPEDOE (same TRAVEL-MEANS) (different
TARGET-LOCATION) ((MISSILE (INDICATED-BY DESCRIPTION) (HAVE
ALTITUDE)) (TORPEDOE (SOME-TYPE-OF DEPTH))))

focus: (MISSILE TORPEDOE)

Message through dictionary. Entering tactical component

Processor time used: **4163** seconds
Time used for garbage collection: **441** seconds

The torpedo and the missile are self-propelled guided projectiles. The guided
projectile's propulsion capabilities are provided by the DB attributes under
SPEED_INDICES (for example, MAXIMUM_SPEED) and FUSE_TYPE.
The guided projectile has DB attributes TIME_TO_TARGET_&_UNITS,
HORZ_&_UNITS and NAME. The missile has a target location in the air
or on the earth's surface. The missile's target location is indicated by the
DB attribute DESCRIPTION and its flight capabilities are provided by the
DB attribute ALTITUDE. Other DB attributes of the missile include
PROBABILITY_OF_KILL, SPEED, ALTITUDE,
LETHAL_RADIUS_&_UNITS and TIME_TO_TARGET_&_UNITS.
Missiles are carried by water-going vehicles and aircraft. The torpedo has an
underwater target location. Its underwater capabilities are provided by the
DB attributes under DEPTH (for example,
MAXIMUM_OPERATING_DEPTH). Other DB attributes of the torpedo
include FUSE_TYPE, MAXIMUM_DEPTH, ACCURACY_&_UNITS,
HORZ_RANGE_&_UNITS, and TIME_TO_TARGET_&_UNITS.
Torpedoes are carried by water-going vehicles. The torpedo and the missile,
therefore, have the same travel means, although they have different target
locations, reflected in the database by the torpedo's attribute DEPTH and
the missile's attributes ALTITUDE and DESCRIPTION.

Processor time used: 44786 seconds
Time used for garbage collection: 15608 seconds

(differense DESTROYER BOMB)

Schema selected: c&c-identification

proposition selected:
(identification DESTROYER SHIP (restrictive ((DRAFT)) (((DRAFT (15 222))))) (non-restrictive TRAVEL-MODE SURFACE))

focus: DESTROYER

proposition selected:
(identification SHIP VEHICLE (non-restrictive FUNCTION TRANSPORTATION))

focus: SHIP

proposition selected:
(identification BOMB FREE-FALLING (restrictive TARGET-LOCATION SURFACE) (non-restrictive TRAVEL-MEANS GRAVITY-PULL))

focus: BOMB

proposition selected:
(identification FREE-FALLING DESTRUCTIVE-DEVICE (non-restrictive FUNCTION LETHAL-KILL))

focus: FREE-FALLING

proposition selected:
(inference DESTROYER BOMB very-different-entities)

focus: (DESTROYER BOMB)

Message through dictionary. Entering tactical component

Processor time used: 1916 seconds
Time used for garbage collection: 497 seconds
A destroyer is a surface ship with a DRAFT between 15 and 222. A ship is a vehicle. A bomb is a free falling projectile that has a surface target location. A free falling projectile is a lethal destructive device. The bomb and the destroyer, therefore, are very different kinds of entities.

Processor time used: 18672 seconds
Time used for garbage collection: 8901 seconds

Appendix B
Introduction to *Working*

The paragraphs from the first topic group in the Introduction to *Working* (Terkel 72) are reproduced below.

INTRODUCTION

This book, being about work, is, by its very nature, about violence -- to the spirit as well as to the body. It is about ulcers as well as accidents, about shouting matches as well as fistfights, about nervous breakdowns as well as kicking the dog around. It is, above all (or beneath all), about daily humiliations. To survive the day is triumph enough for the walking wounded among the great many of us.

The scars, psychic as well as physical, brought home to the supper table and the TV set, may have touched, malignantly, the soul of our society. More or less. ("More or less," that most ambiguous of phrases, pervades many of the conversations that comprise this book, reflecting, perhaps, an ambiguity of attitude toward The Job. Something more than Orwellian acceptance, something less than Luddite sabotage. Often the two impulses are fused in the same person.)

It is about a search, too, for daily meaning as well as daily bread, for recognition as well as cash, for astonishment rather than torpor; in short, for a sort of life rather than a Monday through Friday sort of dying. Perhaps immortality, too, is part of the quest. To be remembered was the wish, spoken and unspoken, of the heroes and heroines of this book.

There are, of course, the happy few who find a savor in their daily job: the Indiana stonemason, who looks upon his work and sees that it is good; the Chicago piano tuner, who seeks and finds the sound that delights; the bookbinder who saves a piece of history; the Brooklyn fireman, who saves a piece of life ... But don't these satisfactions, like Jude's hunger for knowledge tell us more about the person than about his task? Perhaps. Nonetheless, there is a common attribute here: a meaning to their work well over and beyond the reward of the paycheck.

For the many, there is a hardly concealed discontent. The blue-collar blues is no more bitterly sung than the white-collar moan. "I'm a machine," says the spot-welder. "I'm caged," says the bank teller, and echoes the hotel clerk. "I'm a mule," says the steelworker. "A monkey can do what I do," says the receptionist. "I'm less than a farm implement," says the migrant worker. "I'm an object," says the high-fashion model. Blue collar and white call upon the identical phrase: "I'm a robot." "There is nothing to talk about," the young accountant despairingly enunciates. It was some time ago that John Henry sang "A man ain't nothin' but a man." The hard, unromantic fact is: he died with his hammer in his hand, while the machine pumped on. Nonetheless, he found immortality. He is remembered.

Appendix C
Resources used

The TEXT system was implemented in CMU lisp (an extension of Franz Lisp) on a VAX 11/780. The TEXT system source code occupies a total of 1176 K of memory with the following breakdown:

- Knowledge base and accessing functions (not including database and database interface functions): 442K

- Strategic component: 573K

- Tactical component: 145K

The system, including the knowledge base, was loaded in entirety into memory for use of the TEXT system. Only the database remains on disk. No space problems were encountered during implementation with one exception: the particular Lisp implementation available does not allow for resetting the size of the recursive name stack. This meant that certain functions which were originally written recursively had to be rewritten iteratively since the name stack was not large enough to handle them.

Processing speed is another question altogether. Currently the response time of the TEXT system is far from being acceptable for practical use. The bulk of the processing time, however, is used by the tactical component. Since it was not the focal point of this dissertation, no major effort was made to speed up this component. To answer a typical question posed to the TEXT system, the strategic component (including dictionary interface) uses 3290 CPU seconds, an elapsed time of approximately one and a half minutes, while the tactical component uses 43845 CPU seconds, an elapsed time of approximately 20 minutes. Times vary for different questions. These statistics were obtained when using the system in a shared environment. An improvement in speed could be achieved by using a dedicated system. It should be noted, furthermore, that the strategic component is not compiled, while the tactical component is. Thus, a further speed-up of the strategic component could be achieved through compilation. This length of response time is clearly unacceptable for practical use. The tactical component was designed as a non-deterministic, recursive process and this accounts for its slow speed. A sufficient investment of time in implementation effort, however, could result in a considerable saving in speed.

Appendix D
Predicate semantics

Table 1 below shows the message formalism for each predicate, including its given argument, its formalism, and an instantiated example of the formalism. For predicates that may be instantiated by several different data types, this information is given for each type.

The fill arc uses this information for testing whether a match exists by checking whether information for the given argument as defined by the other arguments of the formalism exists in the relevant knowledge pool. If such information does exist then the arguments are instantiated with the matching knowledge base tokens and the resulting proposition is added to the message.

TABLE 1 -- Predicate Semantics

Attributive

given-argument: entity

type: db-attributes[40]

>   **sub-type**: attributes only
>   (attributive db <entity> <naming-attr>
>   <topic-attr> <duplicate-attrs> <db-attrs>)
>
>   **example**:
>   (attributive db SHIP (name NAME) (topics
>   DIMENSIONS) (duplicates (FUEL (FUEL_TYPE
>   FUEL_CAPACITY))) (attrs MAXIMUM_SPEED))

---

[40]Any type of DB attribute (naming-attrs, topic-attrs, etc.) is optional. If none are present in the knowledge pool, nil is returned.

sub-type: attributes and values

(attributive db <entity> (<attr1 val2>) ...
(<attrn> <valn>))

example:

(attributive db AIRCRAFT-CARRIER
(PROPULSION STMTURGRD)(ENDURANCE_SPEED 30)
(ECONOMIC_SPEED 12)(ENDURANCE_RANGE 4000)
(BEAM 252) (FLAG BLBL) (FUEL_TYPE BNKR)
(REMARKS 0))

type: distinguishing descriptive attribute
(attributive def <entity> <parent>
<attr-name> <attr-value>)

example:

(attributive def MISSILE GUIDED TARGET-LOCATION
SURFACE-AIR)

(attributive def ECHO-II-SUBMARINE SUBMARINE
((FLAG) (PROPULSION_TYPE)) (((FLAG (RDRD)))
((PROPULSION_TYPE (NUCL)))))

Evidence

given-argument: entity
optional distinguishing descriptive attribute

(evidence based-db <entity> <def-attr>
<based-db1> ... <based-dbn>)

example:

(evidence based-db MISSILE TARGET-LOCATION
(indicated-by DESCRIPTION) (HAVE ALTITUDE))

Constituency

given-argument: entity

       (constituency <entity> (<sub-class1> ...
                               <sub-classn>))

example:

       (constituency WATER-VEHICLE (SHIP SUBMARINE))

Identification

given-argument: entity

       (identification <entity> <super-ord>
       (restrictive <attr-name> <attr-value>)[41]
       (non-restrictive <attr-name> <attr-value>))[42]

example:

       (identification SHIP WATER-VEHICLE
          (restrictive TRAVEL-MODE SURFACE)
          (non-restrictive TRAVEL-MEDIUM WATER))

Amplification

given-argument: entity
                  plus either a descriptive attribute, database
                  attribute, or relation on which to amplify

type: amplification on db-attributes

    sub-type: attributes only
         (amplification db <entity> <old-db>
            <naming-attr> <topic-attrs> <duplicate-attrs>
            <db-attrs>   )

---

[41]Restricts the class of superordinates to only those having the given attribute-value pair.

[42]All superordinates, and thus entities, have the given attribute-value pair.

example:

> (amplification db AIRCRAFT (topics ROLE FUEL
> CEILING FLIGHT_RADIUS) (name NAME)
> (attrs PROPULSION MAXIMUM_SPEED
> CRUISE_SPEED))

sub-type: attributes and values
(amplification db <entity> <old-db>
   (<attr1> <val1>) ... (<attrn> <valn>))

example:

> (amplification db AIRCRAFT-CARRIER (((LENGTH
> (1039 1063))) ((DISPLACEMENT (78000 80800))))
> (PROPULSION STMTURGRD)(ENDURANCE_SPEED 30)
> (ECONOMIC_SPEED 12) (ENDURANCE_RANGE 4000)
> (BEAM 252) (FLAG BLBL)(FUEL_TYPE BNKR)
> (REMARKS 0))

type: amplification on descriptive attributes

sub-type: new descriptive attribute

> (amplification def <entity> <old-def>
>   <parent> <attr-name> <attr-value>)

example:

> (amplification def MISSILE (TARGET-LOCATION
> SURFACE-AIR) AIR FUNCTION
> SELF-PROPELLED-TO-TARGET)

sub-type: evidence for descriptive attribute

> (amplification evidence <entity> <old-def>
>   <parent> <based-db1> ... <based-dbn>)

example:

> (amplification evidence SHIP (TRAVEL-MODE
> SURFACE) (HAVE DRAFT) (HAVE DISPLACEMENT))

type: amplification on relations

(amplification rel <entity> <old-relations>
  <new-relations>)

example:

(amplification rel SHIP (POSSESSION-06
  POSSESSION-03) (CARRY-01))

Analogy

given: entity plus an optional database attr-range pair[43]

type: relation

sub-type: no values
  (analogy rel <entity> <rel-name>
    <related-entities>)

example:
  (analogy rel SHIP ON GUIDED GUNS)

sub-type: with values

  (analogy rel <entity> <rel-name>
    <related-entity value pairs>)

example:

(analogy rel AIRCRAFT-CARRIER ON (6 GUNS)
  (3 MISSILES) (17 TORPEDOE))

type: range-comparison
  (analogy range <entity> <entity ranges>
    <comparison-attr1> ... <comparison attrn>)

example:

(analogy range AIRCRAFT-CARRIER (((LENGTH
  (1039 1063))) ((DISPLACEMENT (78000 80800))))
  (larger-than-all LENGTH) (larger-than-most

---

[43]A database attr-range pair is a database attribute associated with a
constant numeric range which indicates the values over which the attribute
ranges for the particular entity.

DISPLACEMENT))

Particular-illustration

given-argument: entity

either database attributes, attr-range pairs, or abstract attributes[44]

type: database attributes

(particular-illustration <entity> <given db-attrs>
    <attr value>1 ..... <attr value>n)

example:

(particular-illustration SHIP ((name NAME)
(topics SPEED_DEPENDENT_RANGE DIMENSIONS)
(duplicates (FUEL (FUEL_TYPE FUEL_CAPACITY)))
(attrs (MAXIMUM_SPEED)))
(OFFICIAL_NAME DOWNES)
(ENDURANCE_RANGE 2170)
(ECONOMIC_RANGE 4170) (LENGTH 438) (BEAM 46)
(DRAFT 25)(FUEL_TYPE BNKR)
(FUEL_CAPACITY 810)(PROPULSION STMTURGRD)
(MAXIMUM_SPEED 29))

type: attribute range pairs

(particular-illustration <new-entity>
    <old-attr-range> <attr range>1 ... <attr range>n)

example:

(particular-illustration MINE-WARFARE-SHIP
(((LENGTH (1039 1063))) ((DISPLACEMENT (78000
80800)))) (LENGTH (144)) (DISPLACEMENT (317)))

type: abstract attrs

(particular-illustration abstract <entity>
    <abstract-attrs> <attr1> ... <attrn>)

---

[44]Abstract attributes are those occurring in the topic hierarchy. They represent a set of related database attributes.

example:

(particular-illustration abstract (topics
ROLE FUEL CEILING FLIGHT_RADIUS) (ROLE
REMARKS DESCRIPTION PRIMARY_ROLE) (FUEL
FUEL_TYPE FUEL_CAPACITY
REFUEL_CAPABILITY)
(CEILING MAXIMUM_CEILING COMBAT_CEILING)
(FLIGHT_RADIUS COMBAT_RADIUS
            CRUISE_RADIUS))

Explanation

given-argument: entity

type: distinguishing descriptive attribute
            (explanation def <entity> <parent> <attr-name>
            <attr-value>)

example:

(explanation def AIRCRAFT AIR-VEHICLE
    TRAVEL-MODE FLIGHT)

type: based database attributes
            (explanation based-db <entity> <attr-value pair>
            <based-db>)

example:

(explanation based-db ECHO-II-SUBMARINE
(((FLAG) (PROPULSION_TYPE) (((FLAG (RDRD)))
((PROPULSION_TYPE (NUCL)))))) (CLASS ECHO II))

Classification

given-argument: entity

type: greater than one breakdown[45]

> (classification <entity> (<based-db-attr
>   <sample sub-type>)1 ... (<based-db-attr>
>   <sample-sub-type>)n)

example:

> (classification AIRCRAFT (FLAG (example
>   BLBL-AIRCRAFT)) (PROPULSION (example
>   JET-AIRCRAFT)))

type: one breakdown

> (classification <entity> (<based-db-attr>
>   (<sub-type1> ... <sub-typen>)))

example:

> (classification AIRCRAFT-CARRIER (CLASS
>   (KITTY-HAWK-SHIP FORRESTAL-SHIP)))

Inference

given-argument: 2 entities

type: very close

> **sub-type**: below database entity class
>   (inference <entity1> <entity2>
>   <comparison1 db-attr1> ...
>   <comparisonn db-attrn>)

> **example**:
>   (inference OCEAN-ESCORT CRUISER
>   (smaller DISPLACEMENT)
>   (larger LENGTH))

> **sub-type**: database entity class and above

---

[45]If an entity has two or more sets of mutually exclusive sub-types, only the attributes on which each set was based (and an example of a sub-type) are given in order to avoid putting too much information into a single sentence.

```
(inference <entity1> <entity2>
  (same <attr-name>) (different
  <attr-name>)(<entity1> <based-db1>)
  (<entity2> <based-db2>) )
```

example:
```
(inference MISSILE TORPEDOE
  (same TRAVEL-MEANS (different
  TARGET-LOCATION) (MISSILE
  (INDICATED-BY DESCRIPTION)
  (HAVE ALTITUDE) ) (TORPEDOE
  (SOME-TYPE-OF DEPTH)) )
```

type: very-different
```
(inference <entity1> <entity2>
  very-different-entities)
```

example:
```
(inference DESTROYER BOMB
  very-different-entities)
```

type: class difference

sub-type: below database entity class

```
(inference <entity1> <entity2>
  two-kinds-of-entity)
```

example:
```
(inference WHISKY-SUBMARINE KITTY-
  HAWK-SHIP two-kinds-of-entity)
```

sub-type: database entity class and above

```
(inference <entity1> <entity2>
  (same <attr-name>) (different
  <attr-name>) )
```

example:
    (inference GUN BOMB (same FUNCTION)
      (different ROLE))

Bibliography

(Akmajian 73). Akmajian, A., "The role of focus in the interpretation of anaphoric expressions." in Anderson and Kiparsky (eds.), *Festschrift. for Morris Halle*, Holt, Rinehart and Winston, New York, N.Y., 1973.

(Allen and Perrault 80). Allen, J. F. and C. R. Perrault, "Analyzing intention in utterances," *Artificial Intelligence 15*, 3, 1980.

(Appelt 81). Appelt, D. E., Planning Natural Language Utterances to Satisfy Multiple Goals, Ph.D. dissertation, Stanford University, Stanford, Ca., 1981.

(Barth 79). Barth, J. *The Floating Opera*. 1979.

(Bossie 81). Bossie, S., A tactical component for text generation: sentence generation using a functional grammar, University of Pennsylvania, Technical Report MS-CIS-81-5, Philadelphia, Pa., 1981.

(Brachman 79). Brachman, R., "On the epistemological status of semantic networks." in N. Findler (ed.) *Associative Networks: Representation and Use of Knowledge by Computer*, Academic Press, N. Y., 1979.

(Chafe 76). Chafe, W. L., "Givenness, contrastiveness, definiteness, subjects, topics, and points of view." in C. N. Li (ed.), *Subject and Topic*, Academic Press, N. Y., 1977.

(Chafe 77). Chafe, W. L., "Creativity and verbalization and its implications for the nature of stored knowledge." in R. O. Freedle (ed.), *Discourse Production and Comprehension*, Vol. 1, Ablex Publishing Co., N. J., 1977, pp. 41-55.

(Chafe 79). Chafe, W. L., "The flow of thought and the flow of language." in T. Givon (ed.) *Syntax and Semantics*, Vol. 12 of *Discourse and Syntax*, Academic Press, 1979.

(Chen 76). Chen, P. P. S., "The entity-relationship model - towards a unified view of data." *ACM Transactions on Database Systems*, Vol. 1, No. 1. (1976).

(Chester 76). Chester, D., "The translation of formal proofs into English," *Artificial Intelligence 7*, 1976, pp. 261-75.

(Chomsky 71). Chomsky, N. "Deep structure, surface structure and semantic interpretation." in Steinberg and Jakobovitz (eds.) *Semantics: An Interdisciplinary Reader in Philosophy, Linguistics and Psychology*, Cambridge University Press, London, 1971.

(Codd 78). Codd, E. F., et al., Rendezvous Version 1: An Experimental English-Language Query Formulation System for Casual Users of

Relational Databases, IBM Research Laboratory, San Jose, Ca., Technical Report RJ2144(29407), 1978.

(Cohen 78). Cohen, P., On Knowing What to Say: Planning Speech Acts, Technical Report No. 118, University of Toronto, Toronto, 1978.

(Cohen 81a). Cohen, P., "The need for identification as a planned action." *Proceedings of the 7th Annual Joint Conference on Artificial Intelligence*, 1981.

(Cohen 81b). Cohen, R., "Investigation of processing strategies for the structural analysis of arguments." in *Proceedings of the 19th Annual Meeting of the Association for Computational Linguistics*, Stanford, Ca., June 1981, pp. 71-6.

(Collins, Warnock and Passafiume 74). Collins, A., Warnock, and Passafiume, J., Analysis and synthesis of tutorial dialogues. BBN Report # 2789, March 1974.

(Davey 79). Davey, A., *Discourse Production*, Edinburgh University Press, Edinburgh, 1979.

(Encyclopedia 76). *Encyclopedia Americana*, Americana Corporation, New York, N. Y., 1976.

(Firbas 66). Firbas, J., "On defining the theme in functional sentence analysis." *Travaux Linguistiques de Prague* 1, Univ. of Alabama Press, 1966.

(Firbas 74). Firbas, J.," Some aspects of the Czechoslovak approach to problems of functional sentence perspective," *Papers on Functional Sentence Perspective*, Academia, Prague, 1974.

(Forbus 81). Forbus, K. and A. Stevens, Using Qualitative Simulation to Generate Explanations, Bolt Beranek and Newman, Inc., Technical Report 4490, March 1981. Also appeared in *Cognitive Science #3*, 1981.

(Goguen, Linde and Weiner 82). Goguen, J. A., Linde, C. and J. L. Weiner, Reasoning and natural explanation, unpublished proceedings of ISI Workshop on Explanation, 1982.

(Goldman 75). Goldman,N. M., "Conceptual generation," in R. C. Schank (ed.), *Conceptual Information Processing*, North-Holland, Amsterdam, 1975.

(Grice 75). Grice, H. P., "Logic and conversation," in P. Cole and J. L. Morgan (eds.) *Syntax and Semantics: Speech Acts*, Vol. 3, Academic Press, N.Y., 1975.

(Grimes 75). Grimes, J. E. *The Thread of Discourse*. Mouton, The Hague, Paris, 1975.

(Grishman 79). Grishman, R., "Response generation in question-answering systems," *Proceedings of the 17th Annual Meeting of the ACL*, La Jolla, Ca., August 1979, pp. 99-102.

(Grosz 77). Grosz, B. J., The representation and use of focus in dialogue understanding. Technical note 151, Stanford Research Institute, Menlo Park, Ca., 1977.

(Hall 73). Hall, R.L., "Toxicants occurring naturally in spices and flavors."

in *Toxicants Occurring Naturally in Foods*, National Academy of Sciences, Washington D. C., 1973.

(Halliday 67). Halliday, M. A. K., "Notes on transitivity and theme in English." *Journal of Linguistics* 3, 1967.

(Halliday 76). Halliday, M. A. K., *System and Function in Language*, Oxford University Press, London, 1976.

(Hendrix 79). Hendrix, G., "Encoding knowledge in partitioned networks." in N. V. Findler (ed.), *Associative Networks: Representation and Use of Knowledge by Computer*, Academic Press, N. Y., 1979.

(Hirst 81). Hirst, G., "Discourse-oriented anaphora resolution in natural language understanding: a review," *American Journal of Computational Linguistics*, Vol. 7, No. 2, April-June 1981, pp. 85-98.

(Hobbs 78). Hobbs, J., Coherence and Coreference. SRI Technical Note 168, SRI International, Menlo Park, Ca., 1978.

(Hudson 71). Hudson, R. A., *North-Holland Linguistic Series*. Volume 4: *English Complex Sentences*, North-Holland, London and Amsterdam, 1971.

(Jensen et al. 81). Jensen, K., R. Ambrosio, R. Granville, M. Kluger, and A. Zwarico, "Computer Generation of Topic Paragraphs: Structure and Style," in *Proceedings of the ACL*, New York, N.Y., December 1981.

(Joshi and Weinstein 81). Joshi, A. and S. Weinstein, "Control of inference: role of some aspects of discourse structure - centering," in *Proceedings of the 7th International Joint Conference on Artificial Intelligence*, Vancouver, Canada, August 1982.

(Lee and Gerritsen 78). Lee, R. M. and R. Gerritsen, "Extended semantics for generalization hierarchies," in *Proceedings of the 1978 ACM-SIGMOD International Conference on Management of Data*, Austin, Tex., 1978.

(Lockman 78). Lockman, A. D., Contextual reference resolution, PhD dissertation, Faculty of Pure Science, Columbia University, May 1978.

(Kaplan 79). Kaplan, S. J., Cooperative responses from a portable natural language database query system. Ph. D. dissertation, Univ. of Pennsylvania,Philadelphia, Pa., 1979.

(Kay 79). Kay, M. "Functional grammar." in *Proceedings of the 5th Annual Meeting of the Berkeley Linguistic Society*. (1979).

(Keenan 71). Keenan, E. L., "Two kinds of presupposition in natural language." in Fillmore and Langendoen (eds.), *Studies in Linguistic Semantics*, Holt, Rinehart, and Winston, New York, N. Y., 1971.

(Lee and Gerritsen 78). Lee, R. M. and R. Gerritsen, "Extended semantics for generalization hierarchies", in *Proceedings of the 1978 ACM-SIGMOD International Conference on Management of Data*, Austin, Tex., 1978.

(Luttwak 79). Luttwak, E. N., "The American Style of Warfare and the Military Balance," *Survival*, Vol. XXI, 2, March-April 1979, pp. 57-60.

(Lyons 68). Lyons, J. *Introduction to Theoretical Linguistics*, Cambridge University Press, London, 1968.

(Malhotra 75). Malhotra, A., Design criteria for a knowledge-based English language system for management: an experimental analysis. MAC TR-146, MIT, Cambridge, Mass. (1975).

(Mann 83). Mann, W. C., "An overview of the Penman text generation system," *Proceedings of the National Conference on Artificial Intelligence*, Washington D.C., August 1983, pp. 261-5.

(Mann and Moore 81). Mann, W. C., and J. A. Moore, "Computer generation of multiparagraph English text," *American Journal of Computational Linguistics*, Vol. 7, No. 1, January-March 1981.

(Martin 73). Martin, L., "Tactical nuclear weapons." in *Arms and Strategy: the World Power Structure Today*, David McKay Company Inc., 1973.

(Mathiesson 81). Mathiesson, C.M.I.M., "A grammar and a lexicon for a text-production system," in *Proceedings of the 19th Annual Meeting of the Association for Computational Linguistics*, Stanford, Ca., 1981, pp. 49-56.

(Mays 80). Mays, E., "Correcting Misconceptions about data base structure." *Proceedings 3rd CSCSI Biennial Meeting*, Victoria, B.C., May 1980.

(Mays 82). Mays, E., "Monitors as responses to questions: determining competence," *Proceedings of the National Conference on Artificial Intelligence*, Pittsburgh, Pa., August 1982, pp. 412-3.

(McCoy 82). McCoy, K. F., Automatic enhancement of a data base knowledge representation used for natural language generation. M. S. thesis, University of Pennsylvania, Philadelphia, Pa., 1982.

(McDonald 80). McDonald, D. D., Natural language production as a process of decision making under constraint. Ph.D dissertation, draft version, MIT, Cambridge, Mass. (1980).

(McDonald and Conklin 82). McDonald, D. D. and E. J. Conklin, "Salience as a simplifying metaphor for natural language generation," *Proceedings of the National Conference on Artificial Intelligence*, Pittsburgh, Pa., August 1982, pp. 75-8.

(McKeon 41). McKeon, R., *The Basic Works of Aristotle*, Random House, New York, 1941.

(McKeown 79). McKeown, K. R., "Paraphrasing using given and new information in a question-answer system," *Proceedings of the 17th Annual Meeting of the Association for Computational Linguistics*, August 1979, pp. 67-72.

(McKeown 80a). McKeown, K. R., Generating descriptions and explanations: applications to questions about database structure. Dissertation proposal, Technical Report _ MS-CIS-80-9, Univ. of Pennsylvania, Philadelphia, Pa. (1980).

(McKeown 80b). McKeown, K. R., "Generating relevant explanations: natural language responses to questions about database structure." in *Proceedings of AAAI*, Stanford Univ., Stanford, Ca. (1980). pp. 306-9.

(Meehan 77). Meehan, J.R., "TALE-SPIN, an interactive program that writes stories," in *Proceedings of the 5th International Joint Conference on Artificial Intelligence*, August 1977, pp. 91-8.

(Moore 80). Moore, R. C., Reasoning about knowledge and action, SRI International AI Center Technical Report No. 191, 1980.

(Moore 81). Moore, R. C., "Problems in logical form." in *Proceedings of the 19th Annual Meeting of the Association for Computational Linguistics*, June 1981, pp. 117-24.

(Nelson 77). Nelson, J., *The Poorperson's Guide to Great Cheap Wines*, McGraw-Hill Book Co., New York, N. Y., 1977.

(Palmer 81). Palmer, M., "A case for rule-driven semantic processing." *Proceedings of the 19th Annual Meeting of the Association for Computational Linguistics*, June 1981, pp. 125-32.

(Paterson 80). Paterson, J., *The Hamlyn Pocket Dictionary of Wines*, Hamlyn, New York, N. Y., 1980.

(Prince 79). Prince, E., "On the given/new distinction." *CLS* 15, 1979.

(Quick 73). Quick, J., *Dictionary of Weapons and Military Terms*, McGraw-Hill, New York, N. Y., 1973.

(Quirk and Greenbaum 73). Quirk, R. and S. Greenbaum, *A Concise Grammar of Contemporary English*, Harcourt, Brace and Jovanovich Inc., New York, N.Y., 1973.

(Reichman 81). Reichman, R., Plain Speaking: A Theory and Grammar of Spontaneous Discourse. Ph.D. Thesis, Harvard University, Cambridge, Ma., 1981.

(Reinhart 81). Reinhart, T., "Pragmatics and linguistics: an analysis of sentence topics." in *Philosophica*, special issue on Pragmatic Theory, 1981.

(Rich 79). Rich, E., "User modeling via stereotypes," *Cognitive Science 3*, 1979, pp. 329-54.

(Robinson 71). Robinson, J. A., "Computational logic: the unification algorithm," *Machine Intelligence*, Vol. 6, American Elsevier, New York, pp. 123-33.

(Rosen 76). Rosen, S., *Future Facts*, A Touchstone Book, Simon and Schuster, New York, N. Y., 1976.

(Rumelhart 75). Rumelhart, D. E., "Notes on a schema for stories," in D. G. Bobrow and A. Collins (eds.), *Representation and Understanding: Studies in Cognitive Science*, Academic Press, N.Y., 1975, pp. 211-36.

(Sacerdoti 77). Sacerdoti, E., *A Structure for Plans and Behavior*, Elsevier North-Holland, Inc., Amsterdam, 1977.

(Schubert, Goebel and Cercone 79). Schubert, L. K., Goebel, R. G., and Cercone, N. J., "The structure and organization of a semantic network for comprehension and inference." in N. V. Findler (ed.), *Associative Networks: Representation and Use of Knowledge by Computer*, Academic Press, N. Y., 1979.

(Searle 75). Searle, J. R., "Indirect speech acts," in P. Cole and J. L. Morgan (eds.) *Syntax and Semantics: Speech Acts*, Vol. 3, Academic Press, N.Y., 1975.

(Sgall, Hajicova and Benesova 73). Sgall, P., E. Hajicova, and E. Benesova,

Topic, Focus and Generative Semantics, Scriptor Verlag, Democratic Republic of Germany, 1973.

(Shipherd 26). Shepherd, H. R., *The Fine Art of Writing*, The Macmillan Co., New York, N.Y., 1926.

(Shipley 80). Transcripts of mother-child dialogues. Unpublished manuscript, Univ. of Pennsylvania, Philadelphia, Pa., 1980.

(Sidner 79). Sidner, C. L., Towards a computational theory of definite anaphora comprehension in English discourse. Ph.D. dissertation, MIT, Cambridge, Mass., 1979.

(Simmons and Slocum 72). Simmons, R., and J. Slocum, "Generating English discourse from semantic networks," *Communications of the ACM*, Vol. 15, No. 10, October 1972, pp. 891-905.

(Smith and Smith 77). Smith, J. M. and Smith, D. C. P., "Database abstractions: aggregation and generalization." University of Utah, *ACM Transactions on Database Systems*, Vol. 2, 2, June 1977, pp. 105-33.

(Stevens and Steinberg 81). Stevens, A., and C. Steinberg, A Typology of Explanations and its Application to Intelligent Computer Aided Instruction, Bolt Beranek and Newman, Inc., Technical Report 4626, March 1981.

(Swartout 81). Swartout, W. R., Producing Explanations and Justifications of Expert Consulting Programs, Massachusetts Institute of Technology, Technical Report MIT/LCS/TR-251, January 1981.

(Tennant 79). Tennant, H., Experience with the evaluation of natural language question answerers. Working paper 18, Univ. of Illinois, Urbana-Champaign, Ill., 1979.

(Terkel 72). Terkel, S., *Working*, Avon Books, New York, N. Y., 1972.

(Thompson 77). Thompson, H., "Strategy and tactics: a model for language production." *Papers from the 13th Regional Meeting, Chicago Linguistic Society*, 1977.

(Waltz 78). Waltz, D. L., "An English language question answering system for a large relational database," *Communications of the ACM*, Vol. 21, No. 7, July 1978.

(Weiner 80). Weiner, J. L., "BLAH, A system which explains its reasoning," *Artificial Intelligence 15*, 1980, pp. 19-48.

(Weischedel 75). Weischedel, R. M., Computation of a Unique Class of Inferences: Presupposition and Entailment, Ph.D. dissertation, University of Pennsylvania, Philadelphia, Pa., 1975.

(Wilensky 81). Wilensky, R. "A knowledge-based approach to language processing: a progress report," *Proceedings of the Seventh International Joint Conference on Artificial Intelligence*, Vancouver, B.C., Canada, August 1981, pp. 25-30.

(Williams 1893). Williams, W., *Composition and Rhetoric*, D.C. Heath and Co., Boston, 1893.

(Winograd 83). Winograd, T., *Language as a Cognitive Process: Syntax*, Vol. I, Addison-Wesley, Reading, Mass., 1983.

(Winston 79).   Winston, P. H., "Learning by Understanding Analogies,"
   Memo 520, MIT Artificial Intelligence Laboratory, 1979.
(Woods 70). Woods, W. A., "Transition network grammars for natural
   language analysis." *Communications of the ACM*, Vol. 13, No. 10,
   October, 1970, pp. 591-606.

Index

Active   2, 9, 78, 133, 138, 147
Alternatives   25, 37, 46, 49, 53,
        60, 122
Analogy   20, 33, 178
Anaphora   21, 38, 55
Arc actions   123
Arc tests   123
Arc-types   122
Argument   20, 38
ATN   74, 122, 186
ATN graphs   124
ATN registers   123
ATN traversal   124
Attribute value pair   134
Attributive   20, 25, 30, 38, 40,
        42, 45, 124
Automatic generation of sub-types
        90, 98

Backtracking   5, 190
Based database attributes   88

Canned text   185
Closing a topic   66
Co-present foci   73
Coherence relations   21, 38
Coherency   1, 3, 8, 9, 17, 56, 67,
        196
Communicative goal   34
Compare and contrast   33, 39, 40,
        41, 44, 130
Comparisons   114
Computer assisted instruction   15
Conceptual closeness   114
Conceptual dependency   186
Conceptual similarity   44
Conduit metaphor   190
Conjunction   149, 189
Consecutive focus shifts   64
Constant database attributes   111
Constituency   9, 11, 20, 26, 38, 40,
        42, 46, 74, 79, 124
Context   178
Contrastive   26
Coreferentiality   8

Data types   87
Database   11, 13, 14, 15, 168, 188,
        196
Database attributes   87, 88, 92, 97,
        158
Database entity classes   95
Database entity generalizations   103
Database entity subsets   96, 102, 106
Database models   16, 87, 91
Deep structure   84, 133
Default focus   69
Definitions   3, 178
Dictionary creation   164
Dictionary entries   156
Dictionary input   155
Dictionary interface   84
Dictionary output   155
Dictionary processing   155
Dictionary task   155
Dictionary translation example   160
Difference questions   172
Direct translation   6
Discourse goals   1, 3, 4,
        5, 6, 9, 10, 24
        37, 53, 74, 192
Discourse history record   171
Discourse purpose   40, 42
Discourse structure   1, 3, 8, 9, 16
        17, 19, 195, 197
Distinguishing descriptive attribute
        88, 102, 103, 109, 156,
        162, 165
Domain dependent modules   90

Entity   87, 157
Entity-relationship model   16, 92
Evaluation of the text   197
Expert system   190
Explanation grammar   192
Explanation structure   191
Explicit focus   56

Flow of control   84
Focus and syntactic structure   138,
        153

Focus assignment   69, 70
Focus constraints   8, 9, 10, 17, 46,
        49, 52, 58, 84, 193, 198
Focus space   57
Focusing constraints   16
Functional description   133, 134
Functional description alternatives
        134
Functional description paths   135,
        142
Functional description patterns
        134
Functional grammar   11, 133, 188
Functional grammar alternatives
        144, 153
Functional grammar debugging   153
Functional grammar processing speed
        152
Functional information   138
Functional notation   83

Gapping   141
General dictionary entries   157
Generation method   9
Generic relation   102
Given argument   46, 48
Given/new   75
Global focus   113
Global focus definition   56
Global focus shift   59, 203
Grammar of text   37, 53

Hand-encoding   159, 164, 167, 185
Hierarchical plans   32, 53
Hierarchy   16, 87, 93, 116, 178
Hierarchy creation   90, 98

Identification   21, 26, 33, 37
        38, 40, 47, 124, 129
Immediate focus algorithm   71
Immediate focus choices   60, 62
        65
Immediate focus ordering   66,
        69, 196
Immediate focus preference   63,
        66
Immediate focus representation   57
Immediate focus shift   62, 73
Immediate focus structures   203

Implicit focus   56, 59, 203
Inferencing   16, 87, 91, 113,
        121, 199
Instance   92
Interactive dictionary creation
        165, 167
Interpretation   1, 2, 9, 16, 38,
        53, 122
Interpretation and focus   55, 56

KAMP   189
Knowledge base implementation
        88
Knowledge delivery system   191
Knowledge pool   34
Knowledge representation   16,
        190

Level of detail   34, 52, 169,
        199
Lexical choice   3, 5, 155, 167,
        186
Linearization   151
Linguistic background   20
Linguistic component   187
Lookahead   122

Message formalism   46
Meta-level questions   168
Modified schemata   38
Morphology   151
Multi-sentential text   168, 191
Multiple goals   189
MUMBLE   187
Mutual exclusion   97

Naturally occurring texts   8
Non-deterministic production
        187
Noun phrase grammar   137,
        141, 148
Noun phrase translation   157
Number agreement   135

ONR   14, 46, 83

Parallel discourse structure   173,
        176
Parallel sentence structure   79

Parallelism   67
Paraphrase   186, 188
Parentheticals   149
Partition-attributes   102
Passive   2, 78, 133, 138, 147
Patterns   37, 53
Planning   4, 5, 8, 189, 191
Possessives   151
Potential focus links   68
Preceding discourse   4
Predicate arguments   45, 46
Predicate semantics   227
Presumption failures   15
Presupposition   75
Previous discourse   17, 168
Principles of discourse   1
Pronominalization   55, 76, 77, 133
Pronominalization tests   152
Proposition   22, 45
Punctuation   151

Qualitative simulation   193
Quantification   189
Question coverage   168, 169
Question-types   40, 42, 83, 183

Re-editing   191
Recursion   21, 30, 52, 59, 130,
    200
Recursive schema invocations   34
Relations   83, 87, 92, 100
Relevance   1, 5, 121, 203
Relevant knowledge pool   10, 11,
    34, 44, 46, 74,
    84, 113, 195, 197
Repetition   173, 176, 180
Requests for information   180
Returning to a topic   63
Rhetorical predicates   20, 21, 22,
    38, 45, 74, 160, 166, 192,
    195

Salience   203
Sample system output   205
Schema   10, 11, 19, 24,
    25, 33, 37, 74, 113
Schema filler   11
Schema filling   47, 84
Schema implementation   122

Schema selection   42, 84
Schema selector   11
Segmentation of discourse   200
Semantic connectivity   67
Semantic networks   93, 186
Semantics   45, 46
Side-tracking   65
Single sentences   4, 5, 6
Speech   1, 4, 187
Speech acts   45, 189
Story generation   191
Story grammars   38
Structural units   8
Subordinate sentence structure   80
Supporting database attributes   88, 1
Syntactic constructions   8, 11, 79
Syntactic structure   55, 76, 133
System components   84
System resources   225
Systematic grammar   186, 188

Templates   185, 188
Text defects   198
Textual connectives   80, 133, 148,
    167, 186
Theme/rheme   75, 76
There-insertion   79, 133, 147
Topic clusters   63
Topic hierarchy   97, 104
Topic/comment   75, 138
Transcripts   14, 21

Unattached attributes   141
Unification   133, 140
Unification example   144
Unification of patterns   135, 144
Updated relevant knowledge pool
    49
User model   16, 34, 37, 46, 52,
    113, 121, 167, 169,
    178, 199, 200, 204
User needs   168
User's beliefs   52

Variability   37
Verb conjugation   152
Verb constructions   147
Verb theme   70